IMAGES
of America

ENDICOTT-JOHNSON

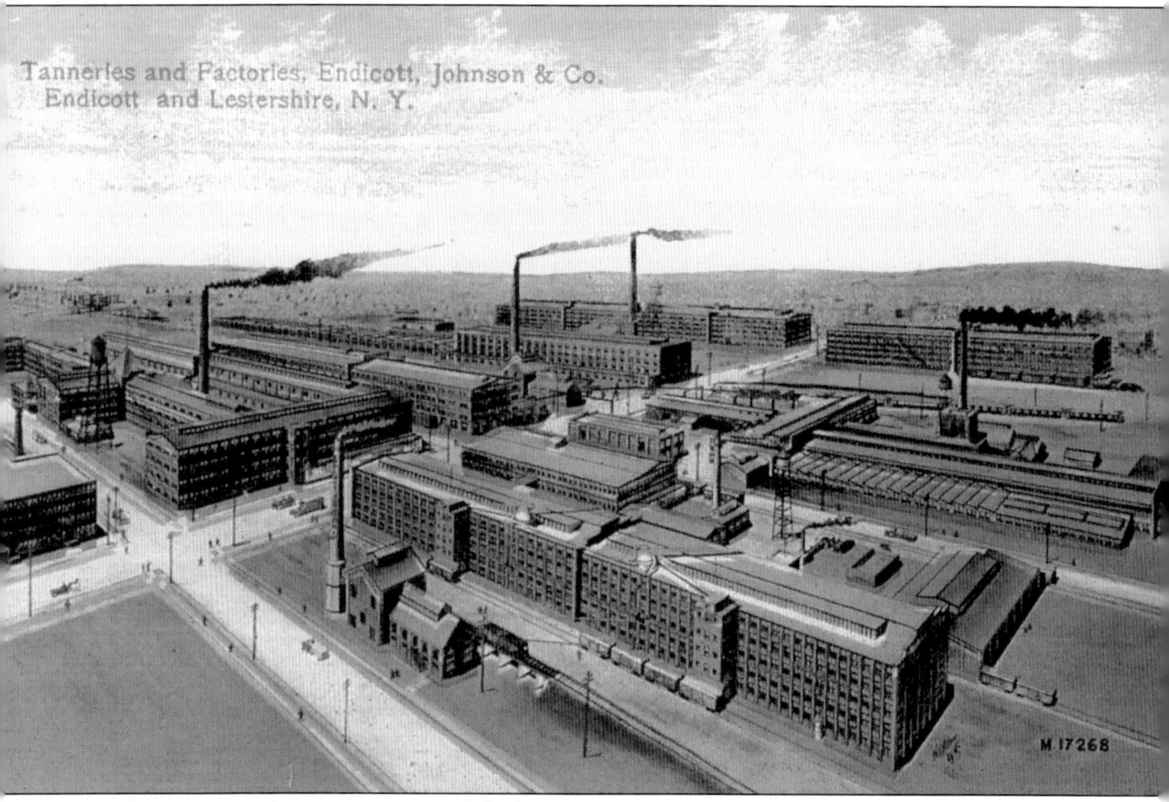

This photograph is a composite of the buildings comprising the Endicott Johnson Corporation factories *c.* 1913. The corporation became one of the largest and most interesting shoe manufacturers in America.

IMAGES
of America

ENDICOTT-JOHNSON

Ed Aswad and Suzanne M. Meredith

ARCADIA
PUBLISHING

ISBN 978-0-7385-1306-5

Published by Arcadia Publishing
Charleston, South Carolina

Printed in the United States of America

Library of Congress Catalog Card Number: 2003107445

For all general information contact Arcadia Publishing at:
Telephone 843-853-2070
Fax 843-853-0044
E-mail sales@arcadiapublishing.com
For customer service and orders:
Toll-Free 1-888-313-2665

Visit us on the Internet at www.arcadiapublishing.com

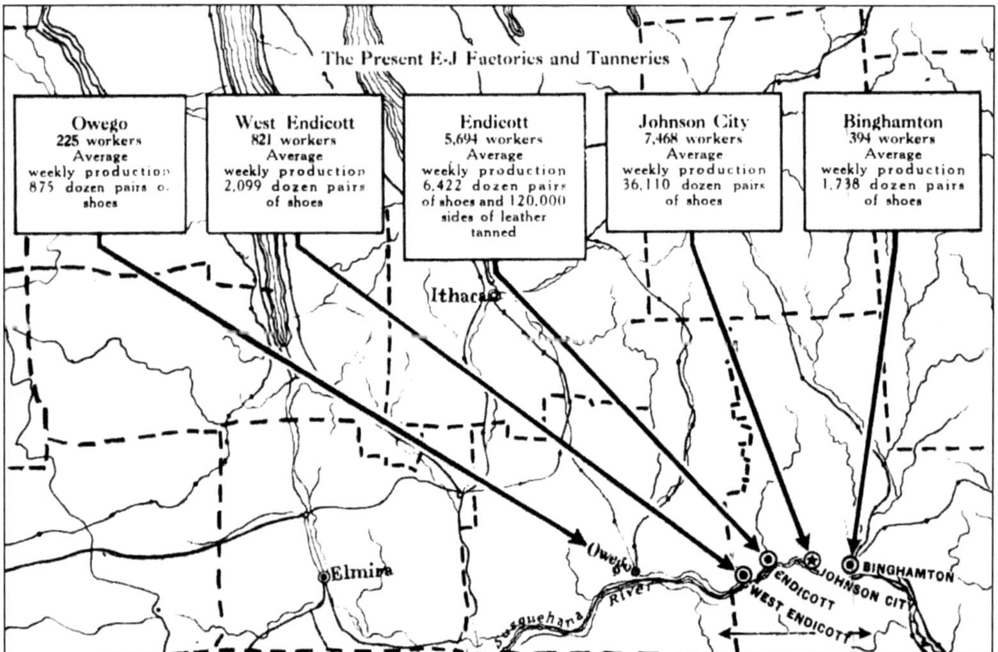

This map of the Susquehanna River Valley shows the locations of all the main factories for the Endicott Johnson Corporation. Within this 12-mile radius, a shoe manufacturing empire was created that changed industrial history.

CONTENTS

FOREWORD

Although my life began long after Henry B. Endicott and George F. Johnson were gone and their shoe company had ceased to exist, it was touched in many ways by the legacy Endicott-Johnson left behind. Renowned through the country for fair and paternalistic policies, the company was the premier employer in Broome County for the first half of the 1900s. This was the home of the "Square Deal," and arches bearing that phrase were prominent landmarks draping over the area's main street.

Growing up in Endwell, a hamlet in the town of Union rumored to have been named after a type of EJ shoe, the local dialect was replete with references to the shoe manufacturing giant. It was not uncommon to hear locals quip, "Which way EJ?"—a question commonly understood to have been uttered by scores of immigrants who spoke only a few words of English. New Americans flocked to this area in the early 1900s with hopes of working for EJ. Childhood in the post-EJ era was blessed with weekends playing at community parks donated by EJ and enjoying endless rides on the half-dozen carousels EJ scattered throughout those parks. Remarkably, thanks to Johnson, merry-go-round rides have always remained free of charge. The only requisite at times was to save the park from a piece of litter.

There were afternoons spent listening to children's stories at a library bearing Johnson's name, evenings dining at one of the many Italian restaurants (thanks to the ethnically diverse population that EJ attracted), and friends living in neighborhoods full of quaint two-story homes originally constructed by EJ. More recently, there were summers operating one of the carousels and watching a new generation of children experiencing, probably unknowingly, a bit of the EJ legacy.

These memories are only a small part of the story of George F. Johnson, the company, and community he forever changed as a result of his innovative labor management attitudes. This book expands on that story through historic photographs and unique accounts of life in the EJ company towns.

—Amanda Meredith, Esq.

Introduction

In the first quarter of the 20th century in the Binghamton area of New York State, the Endicott Johnson Corporation was in its heyday. The "Triple Cities" of Endicott-Johnson included Endicott, Johnson City, and Binghamton. In the hub of the Triple Cities, the "EJ phenomenon" took place.

During that era, EJ was the area's largest employer and one of the world's largest shoe manufacturers, with 19,000 employees turning out 120,000 pairs of shoes daily. It was innovative in the shoe manufacturing trade, as well, claiming "hoof to foot" and later "hide to wearer" shoes. It dealt with no middlemen, making every component of the product from tanning the raw hides to manufacturing shoeboxes—a process not duplicated before or since.

EJ was also unique in the industry in selling products under its own name as well as custom manufacturing for the military and for private labels, distributing products to independent retailers in an EJ chain of stores and through catalog sales.

Perhaps most distinctive was the corporate relationship with workers, known as "the EJ life."EJ and George F. Johnson are entwined in the EJ story. Johnson demanded hard work and company loyalty from employees, but in return virtually adopted them as personal wards. He saw that the corporation provided for their every need.

The EJ life offered low-cost homes, parks, recreation, libraries, practical education, free medical care, support for widows, and guidance in all the daily affairs of life and citizenship; these services were rendered by Johnson himself, who was never a stranger to his workers. His strong opinions were conveyed to employees in pay envelope inserts, in monthly magazines the company published, and in the weekly full-page "To the Workers" advertisements in the local newspapers.

Immigrant families from many nations often sent more than one generation to the EJ factories, creating a fascinating demographics study . . . all part of the EJ phenomenon.

While abandoned factories and crumbling smokestacks may abound, the true memory is perpetuated in the larger-than-life monuments, arches, and memories of a still loyal community. In this book, authors Ed Aswad and Suzanne Meredith preserve the pictures and details of this corporation's important history, creating yet another monument to the EJ era.

—Paul Klein

ACKNOWLEDGMENTS

For sharing their knowledge, their photographs, and their memories, we are very grateful to the following friends: Amos Patterson Museum, Broome County Historical Society, Nick Dranchak, Amanda Meredith, Paul Klein, Palmira Hicks, Charlotte Harrington, Grace and Len Ireland, the New York State Archives in Albany, Jan Mangan, Janet Otman, Dave Potchnak, Sal Poliziano, Joan Sacco, Sandy and Bill Scanlon, Deputy Broome County Historian Charles Brown, Broome County Historian Gerald Smith, Joanne (Grassi) Florini, Vestal Town Historian Betty Bartlow, and Laddie Vanna.

One

Dream of Fair Play

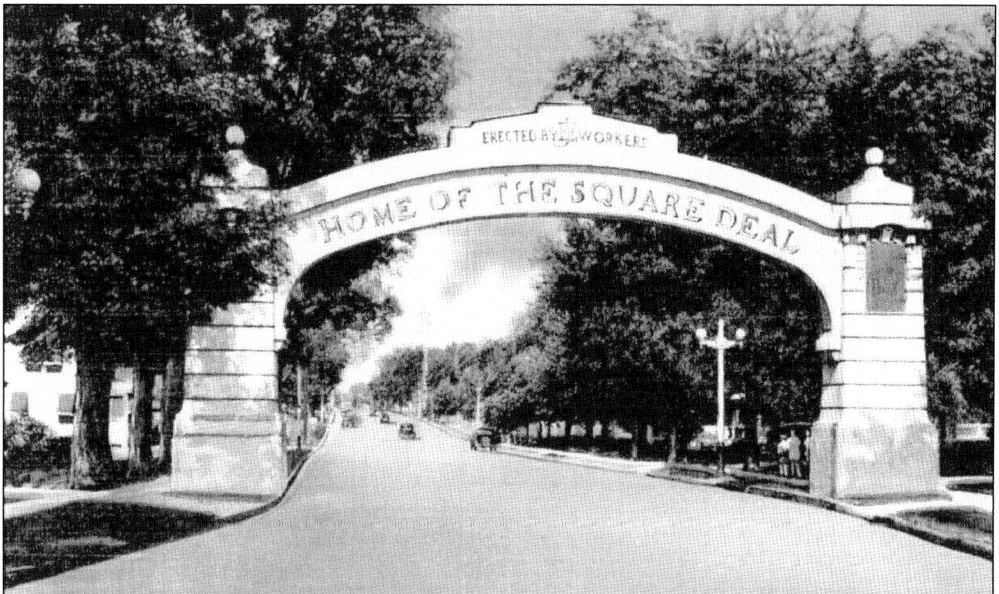

The EJ arches remain a visible symbol of the era of industrial democracy. In 1919, Endicott-Johnson supervisors encouraged workers to donate $3 each for construction of two stone arches, one spanning Main Street in Johnson City at the Binghamton border and the other between the villages of Union and Endicott. Wages at the time were approximately $20 per week. The prodigious monuments were a tribute to the square deal policies and the workers' "big friend" George F. Johnson. To Johnson, the square deal meant equal opportunity, no special privileges, and no favors . . . just the rewards of hard work.

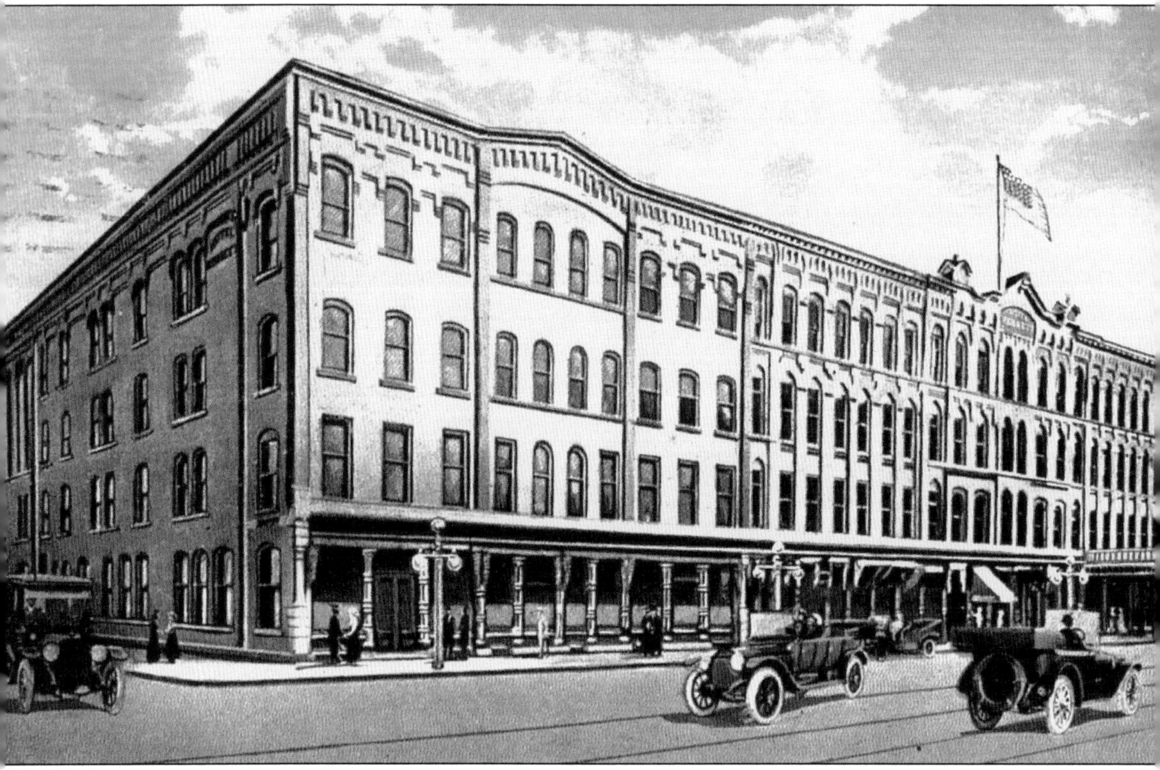

In 1850, Horace N. Lester settled in Binghamton and began a shoe business. By 1854, his brother George joined him, and the Lester Brothers and Company, manufacturer of boots and shoes, was established, thus conceiving a business destined for world recognition as Endicott-Johnson. In 1882, when Horace's son organized a stock consortium with "capital unparalleled in the history of southern New York," the largest shoe factory in the world under a single roof was built on acreage west of Binghamton in the town of Union. For many years, the factory was known as the "mother of them all" or the Pioneer Factory. This area became Lestershire. The Lester company sold lots for homes and donated land for public buildings, churches, schools, and a fire department, thus setting an example for the Endicott-Johnson of the future. An economic depression forced the Lesters to lose control of the company in the 1890s to Henry B. Endicott of Massachusetts. At the far left is the original location in Binghamton of Lester Brothers, near the Hotel Bennett.

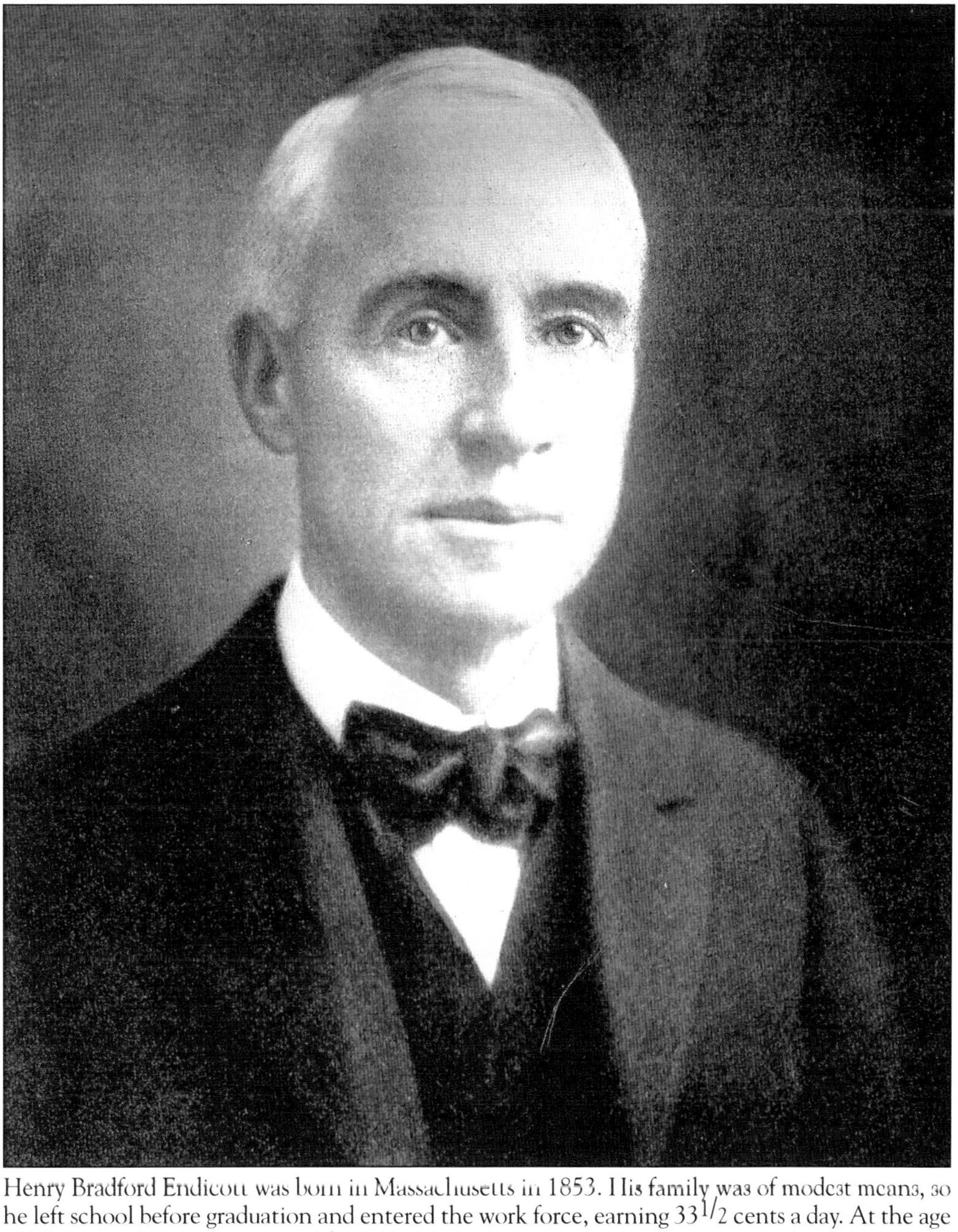

Henry Bradford Endicott was born in Massachusetts in 1853. His family was of modest means, so he left school before graduation and entered the work force, earning 33 1/2 cents a day. At the age of 20, he used an inheritance of $1,900 plus small savings to purchase his own leather business. He sold his product to shoe companies across the country, including Lester Brothers and Company. Endicott purchased stock in the concern, eventually becoming treasurer and then sole owner. Admiring the spirit of employee George F. Johnson, he made Johnson manager and never regretted the choice. Endicott controlled EJ finances but maintained a home in Massachusetts. The company prospered with daily operations left in the hands of Johnson. During World War I, Endicott gave overwhelming support to the war effort. Due to a weakened state of health, he succumbed to death in 1920 at the age of 67. Left behind was a legacy of service to his country, to his fellow man, and to a shoe corporation that would make history.

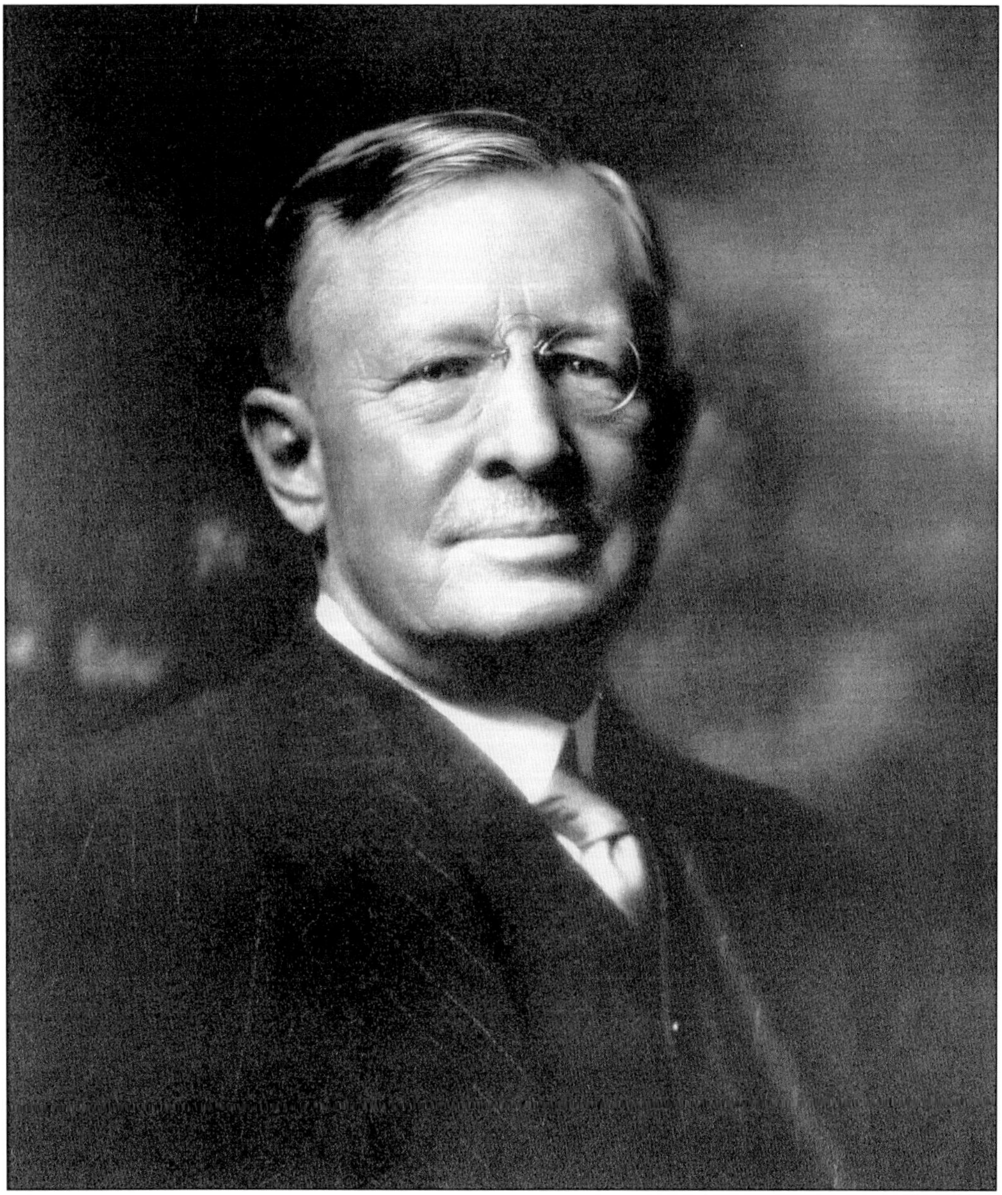

The story of the Endicott Johnson company is also the story of the life of George Francis Johnson, known to all as "George F." More than any man involved in shoe production before or since, Johnson was a man of destiny. His vision brought the "Magic City" of Endicott into being and turned the tiny village of Lestershire into a world-renowned shoe manufacturing center. Born in 1857, he left school at the age of 13 to work and escape poverty. He learned to use his hands as tools—and fists—and to pitch a decent game of baseball. By 1882, he had talked his way into a job at the Lester Shoe Company in Binghamton in the treeing room. When business began to falter in 1887, he offered to manage the business without a pay increase if Lester would give him the opportunity. Johnson got that chance and convinced Lester to build a new factory west of Binghamton. A few years later, he suggested to the new owner, Henry Endicott, that it would be a good investment to make him a full partner and loan him $150,000 to complete the deal.

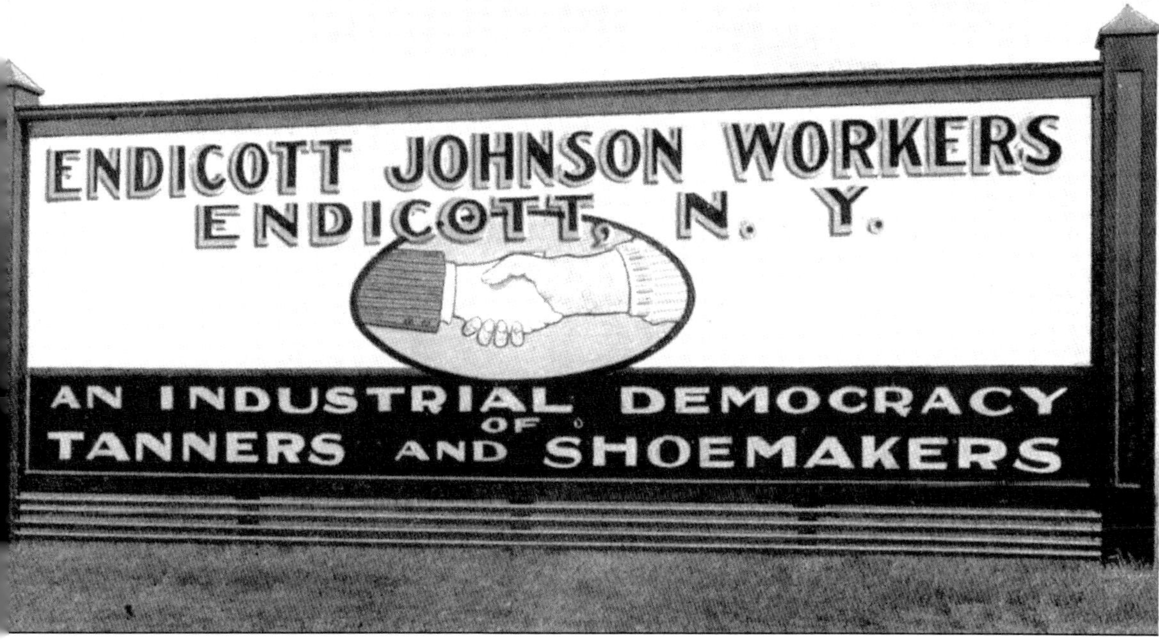

When George F. Johnson gave his promissory note to Henry Endicott, his socialist leanings gave way to a "desire to make a lot of money and make it quick." However, he never forgot that he was a "common" man, and he worked to ease the burden of life for employees of Endicott-Johnson. Just as he was familiar with every step of the shoe industry, so he guided cradle-to-grave policies for workers' care. "Live and Help Live," benevolent socialism, industrial paternalism, and the square deal policy are all associated with EJ. From modest beginnings, Johnson built one of the greatest shoe industries in the world. He implemented revolutionary labor and management relations, reduced the workweek, and instituted free medical coverage for employees, along with housing, playgrounds, markets, restaurants, and sports facilities, thereby gaining the loyalty and gratitude of an entire community. In 1913, he was urged to move to Binghamton and run for mayor on the Progressive ticket. He declined, stating that he was already working where he could do the most good. And he did—for decades EJ dominated the Southern Tier as employer and benefactor.

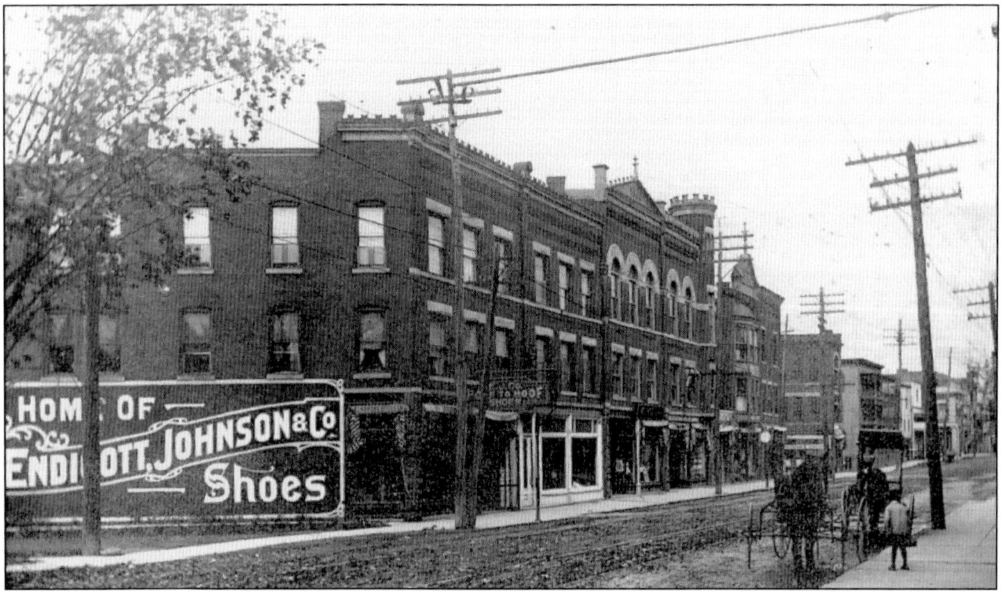

One of the reasons George F. Johnson suggested to his employer, Lester, in 1897 that the new factory should be built west of Binghamton was to escape the city taxes. Several years after the construction of the building, an effort was made by Binghamton to annex Lestershire. Johnson became president of the anti-annexation committee and traveled to Albany to lobby the New York State legislature against supporting consolidation. The picture above is of an early Main Street in Lestershire, and the one below is just a few years later. The sign on the building still advertises EJ shoes, but progress can be seen from horse to horsepower and trolley cars, and from mud to brick-paved streets. The name of Lestershire was changed to Johnson City in 1916.

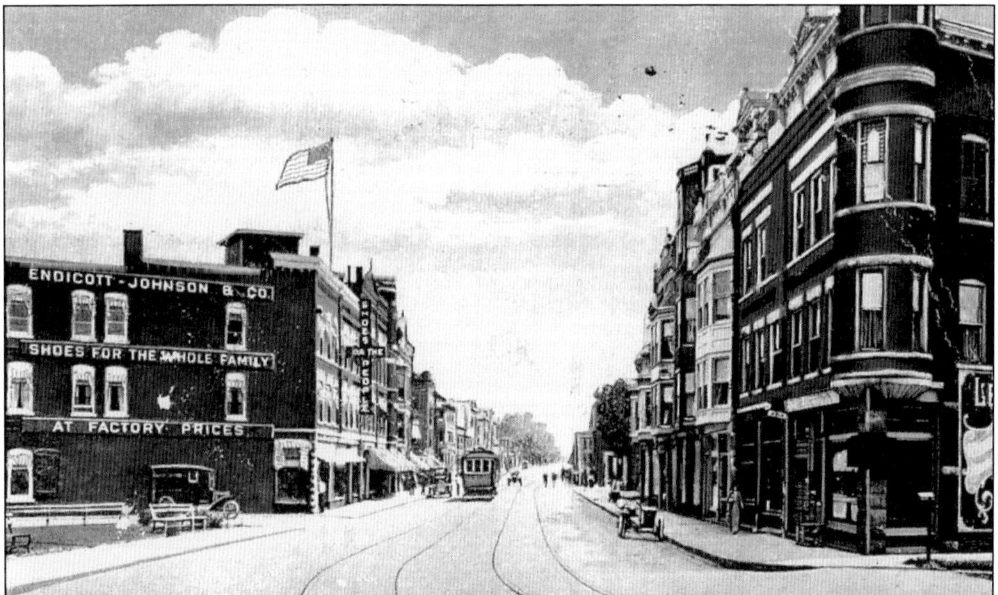

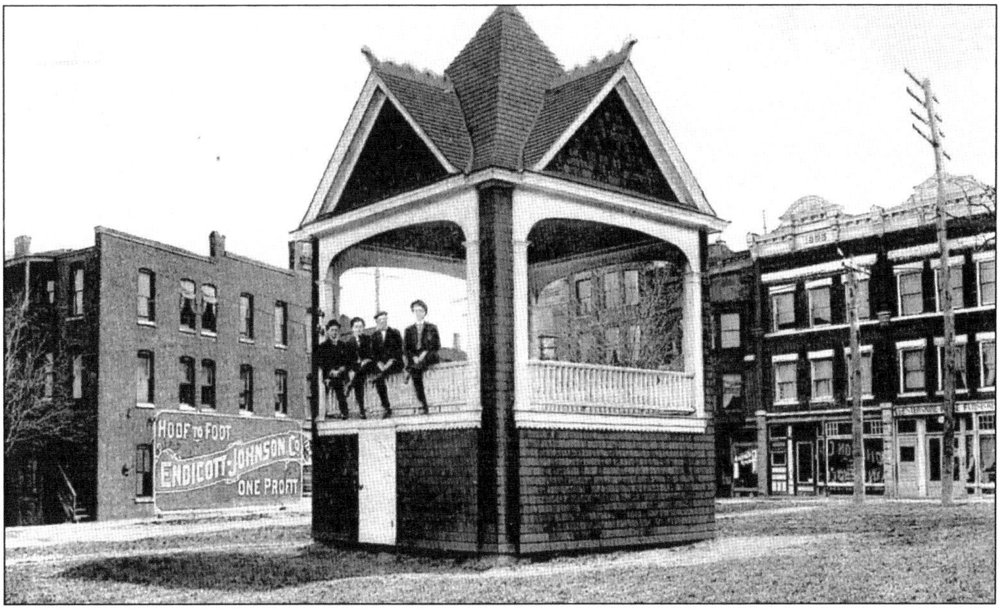

The evolution of Main Street in Johnson City was one of growth. Once again pictured is an EJ retail store sign painted on the side of the same building with a new company slogan, "From hoof to foot." In the foreground is the ornate Johnson City bandstand.

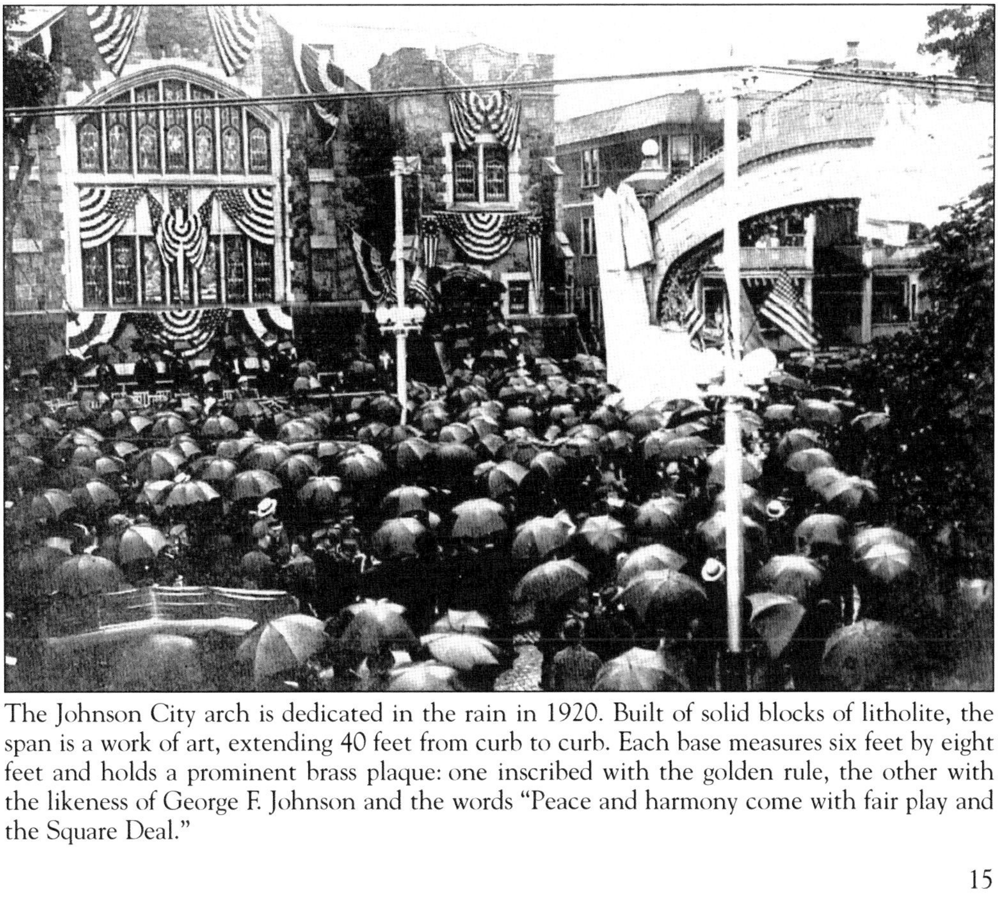

The Johnson City arch is dedicated in the rain in 1920. Built of solid blocks of litholite, the span is a work of art, extending 40 feet from curb to curb. Each base measures six feet by eight feet and holds a prominent brass plaque: one inscribed with the golden rule, the other with the likeness of George F. Johnson and the words "Peace and harmony come with fair play and the Square Deal."

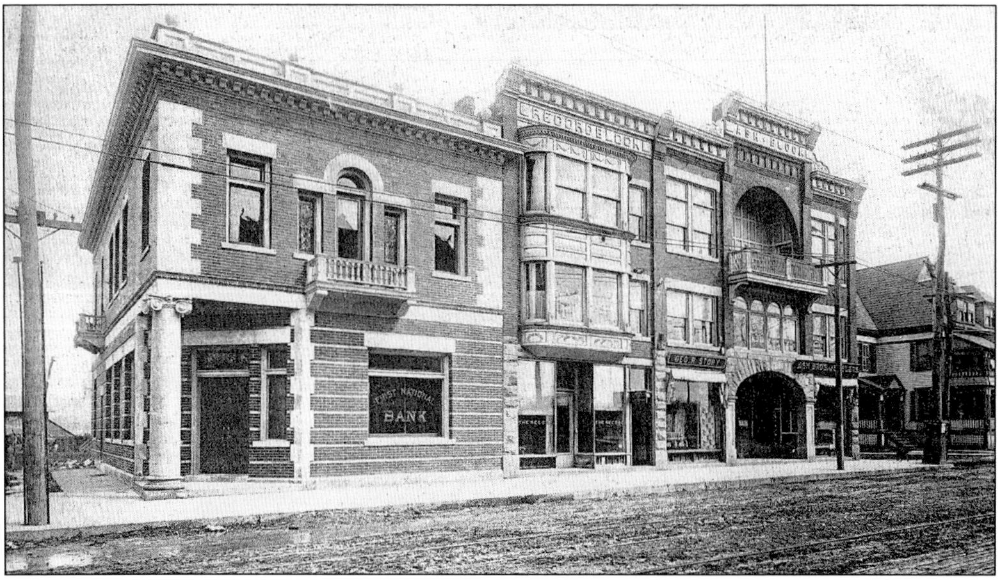

The First National Bank of Lestershire began operations on July 5, 1905. In 1916, George F. Johnson recommended that the name be changed to the Workers Trust Company to honor workers whose business contributed to the success of the bank. Eliot Spaulding, treasurer of the Endicott Johnson Corporation, became president of the bank when the change was completed.

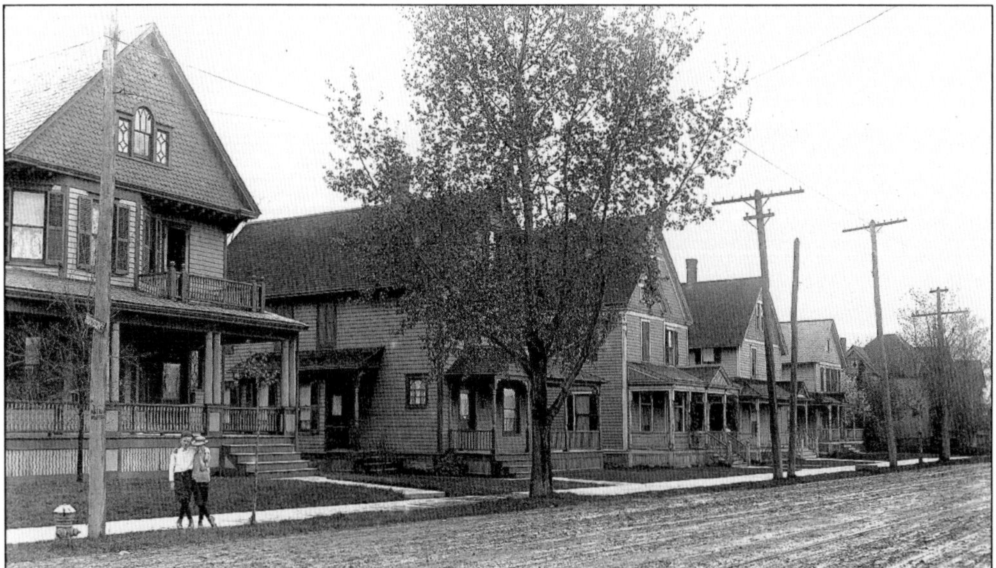

As the Lester Boot and Shoe Company prospered, so did the community. These houses are on Main Street in 1913, when the trolley tracks still ran along the dirt thoroughfares.

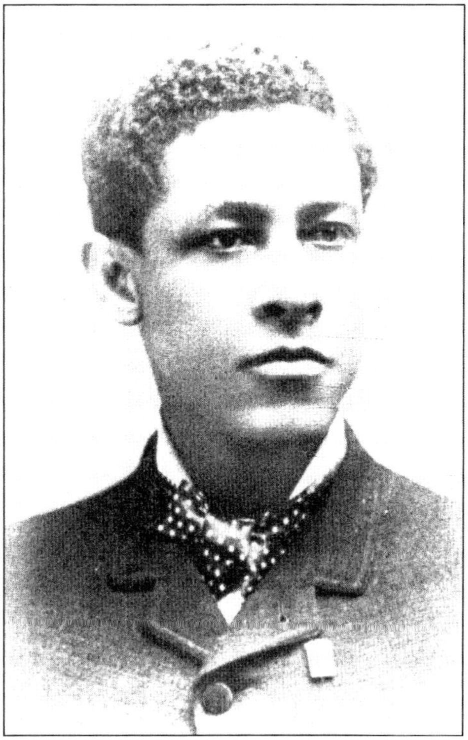

Many inventions led to the industrialization of the shoe industry: the rolling machine, used to beat leather to increase wear; Elias Howe's sewing machine; the McKay machine for sewing soles; and, one of the most important, the lasting machine patented by J.E. Matzeliger in 1883. The machine revolutionized shoe manufacturing. An immigrant from Dutch Guiana, Matzeliger worked for 10 years to perfect a machine capable of performing all of the steps required to hold a shoe on a last, grip and pull the leather down and around the heel, and guide and drive the nails into place. The laster helped to cut the price of shoes and improve working conditions. Endicott-Johnson relied heavily on this machine, which helped the company become one of the largest manufacturers of shoes in the world.

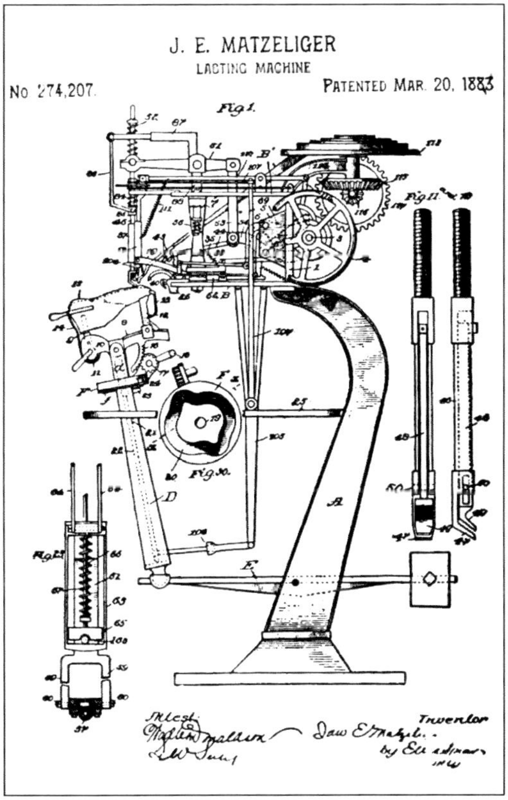

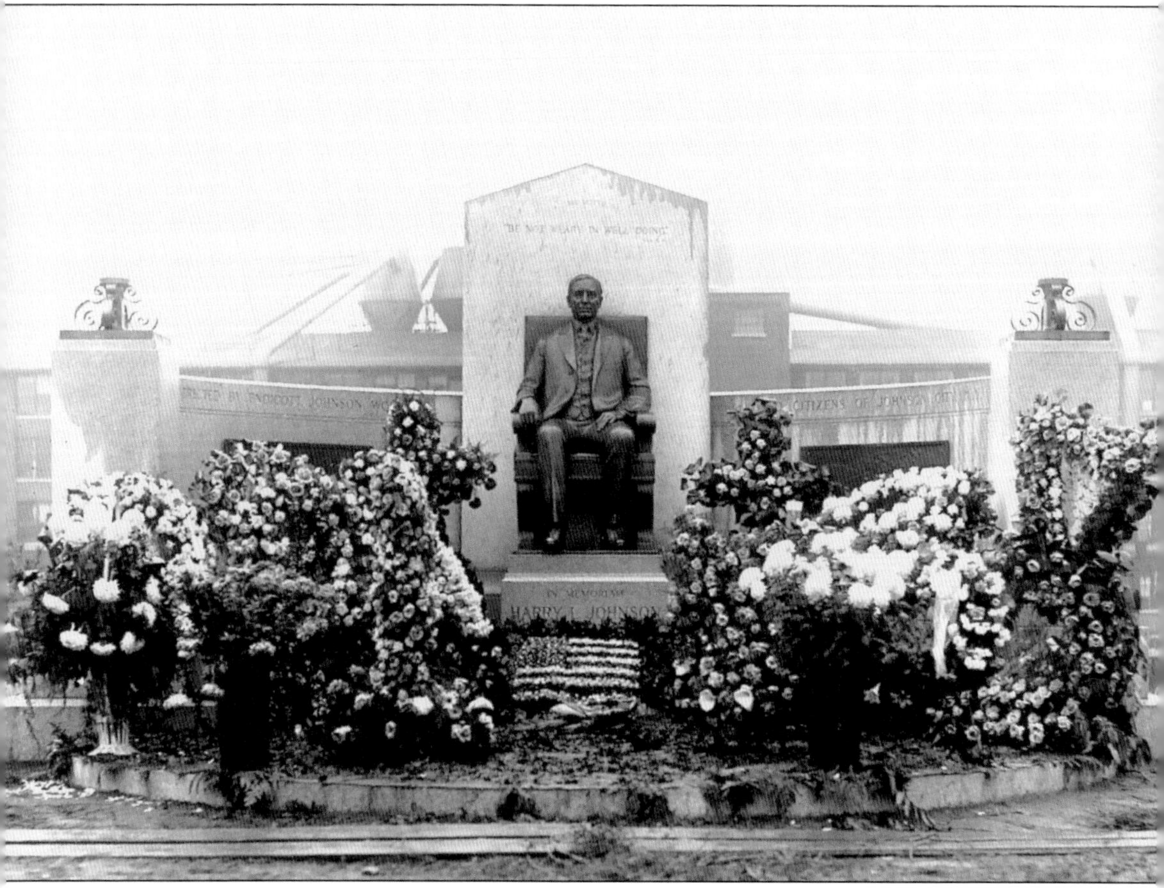

The local community regarded Harry L. Johnson as a truly good man. Born in 1873, the youngest brother of George F. Johnson came from Massachusetts to work for Endicott-Johnson at the age of 22. He worked his way up in the shoe business from the lowest position, all the while showing depth of character, a great willingness to work, and an intense loyalty to his brother George. He always exhibited a love for church, his country, and the average laborer at EJ. In his eulogy it was stated, "the Johnson brothers do not believe in absentee lordism, and it was necessary for Harry L. to have a home in Johnson city to live and work near the EJ employees . . . entering into the life of the people of the village." He became general manager of EJ factories in Johnson City, maintaining that position until his death. Patriotism led him to work tirelessly for the World War I effort. The eulogy went on to say, "It weakened his strength and in 1921 he suffered a complete nervous breakdown. Later that year he died due to apoplexy, worry and over work of the brain."

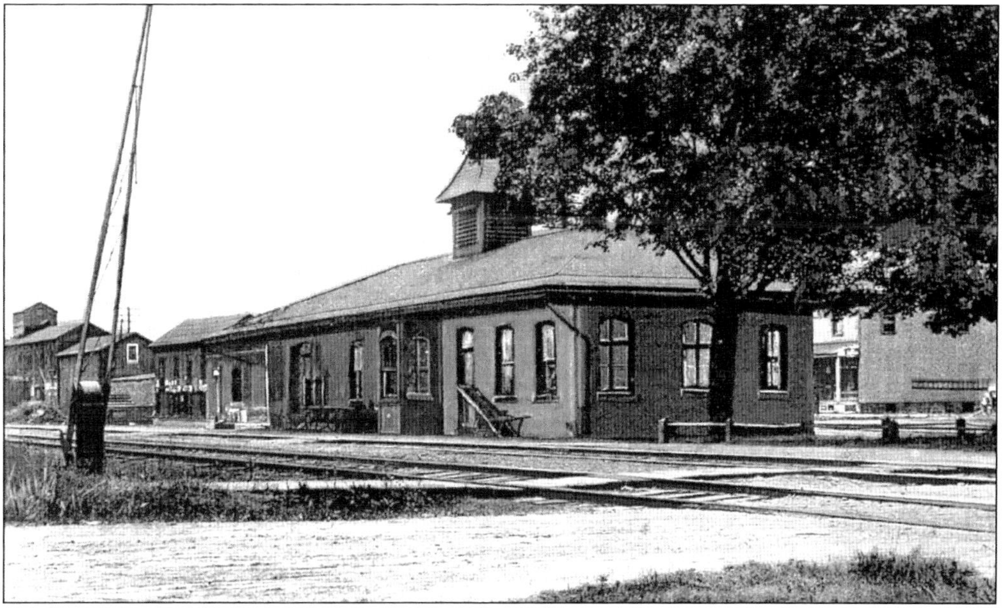

The railroad era put the Southern Tier on the track to industrial superiority. In 1849, the New York and Erie Railroad was the first to come to the small village of Union. In 1904, a large new station house was constructed to encourage freight, mail, and passenger service and to serve the needs of industry. Endicott-Johnson built factories close to rail connections. Sidings made it convenient to ship shoes and boots to all points in the United States. Pictured are the railroad station in Union and the Lestershire spurs near the EJ factories.

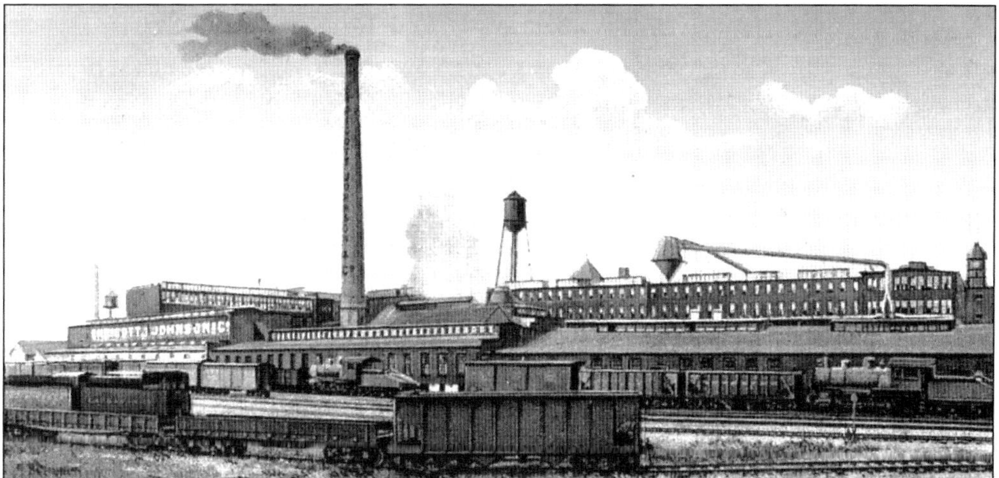

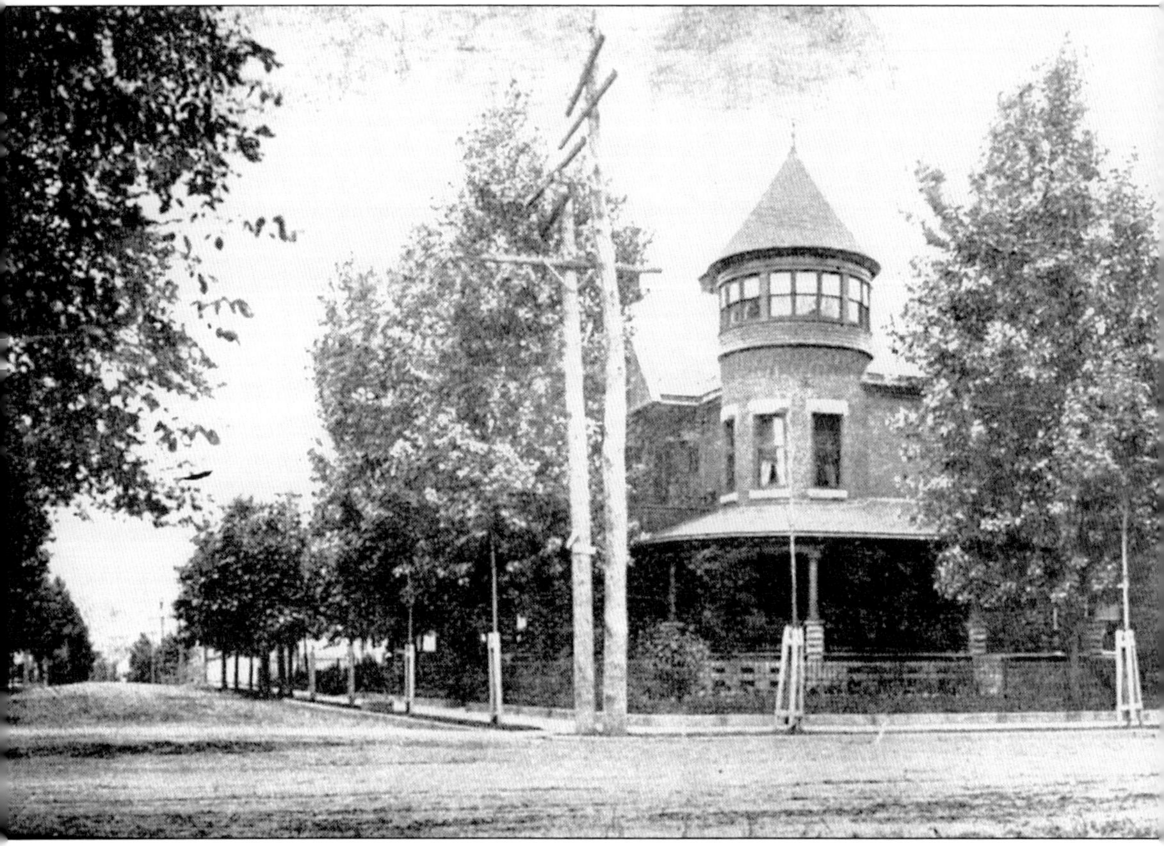

C. Fred Johnson, born in 1856, was an elder brother of George F. Johnson. He moved to Lestershire in 1890 and built one of the first houses in the village. He designed and planned the layout of Endicott streets, but his lifelong passion was firefighting. In 1916, he organized the EJ fire company, with firehouses constructed in the center of Endicott and in Johnson City. In 1907, he made history by being unanimously nominated by both the Republican and the Democrat caucuses to serve as mayor of Lestershire. One of his first improvements in the village government was to reduce the tax rate from $13.50 to $10. This move greatly helped EJ as well as other residents. Pictured is the C. Fred Johnson home on Main Street in Lestershire. The house was eventually used as a YMCA and then torn down for a parking lot.

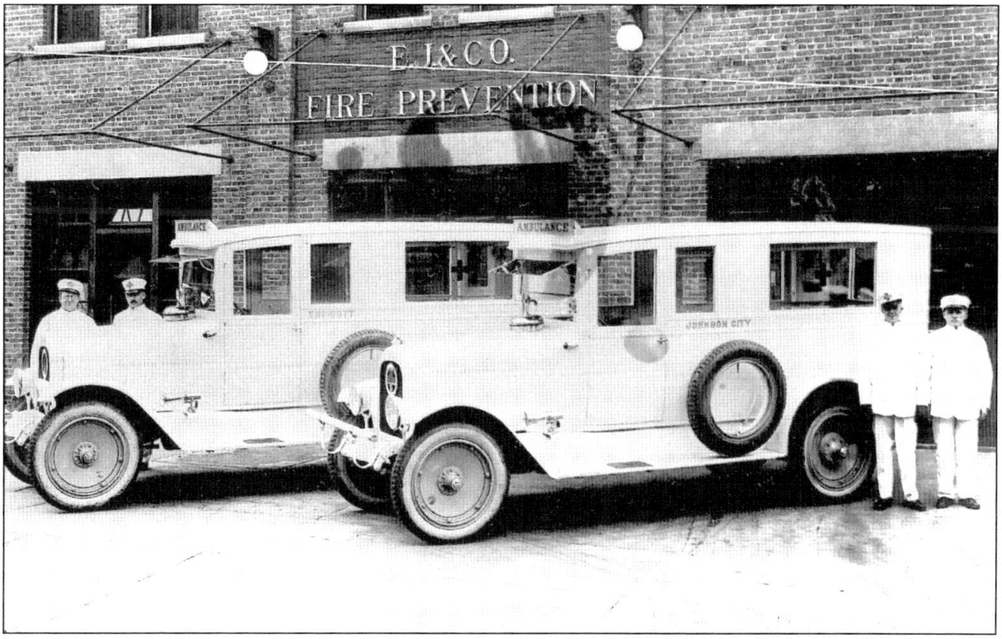

Pictured are some of the early, modern, and up-to-date EJ fire prevention vehicles. By 1948, Endicott-Johnson had 28 shoe factories, six tanneries, and three rubber mills producing 45,000,000 pairs of shoes per year. As well as being ready to fight fires, the fire prevention crews patrolled the properties night and day, making sure that the safety and health of the workers were protected. Clean, well-lighted, and well-ventilated buildings were the goals.

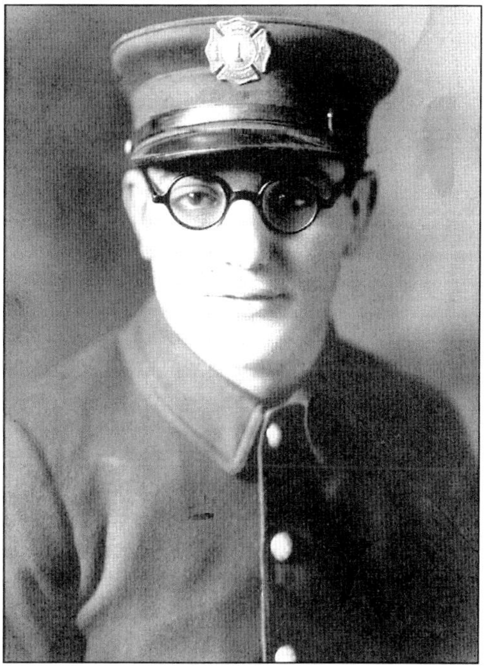

Pictured is John Gimmey, Endicott firefighter.

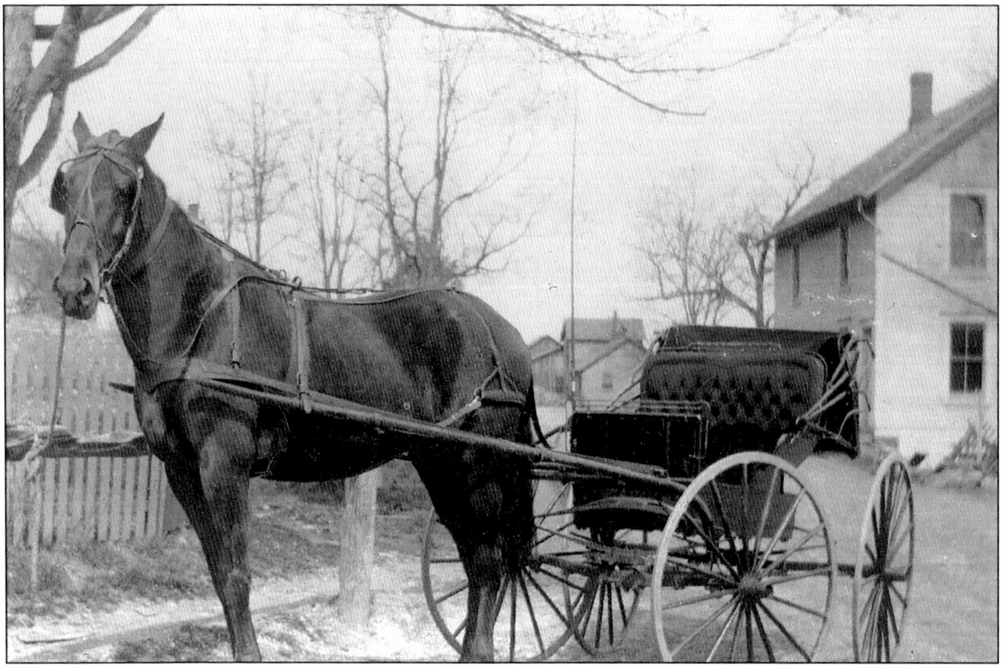

Shortly after George F. Johnson was made superintendent of the Pioneer Factory, he lived in a home several miles away. Embarrassment about spending $80 on a horse and buggy while his fellow workers walked led him to drive only part of the way to the factory. His wife drove the buggy home, and he walked the last few blocks to the factory. A few years later, when Johnson and his wife agreed to divorce, the lady was awarded the horse and buggy as part of the settlement.

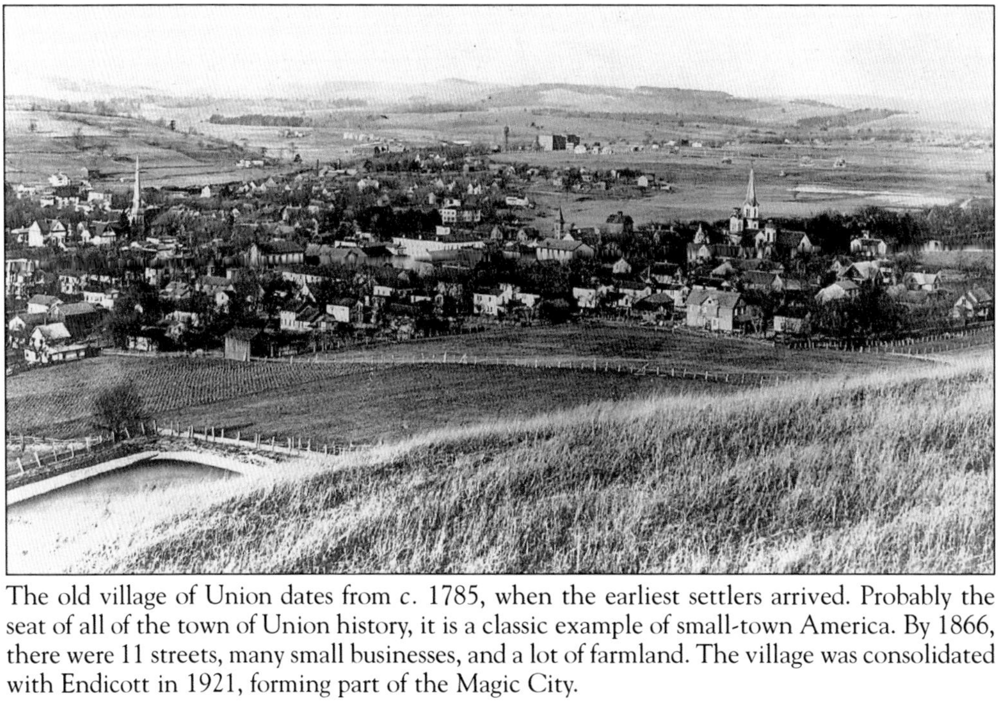

The old village of Union dates from c. 1785, when the earliest settlers arrived. Probably the seat of all of the town of Union history, it is a classic example of small-town America. By 1866, there were 11 streets, many small businesses, and a lot of farmland. The village was consolidated with Endicott in 1921, forming part of the Magic City.

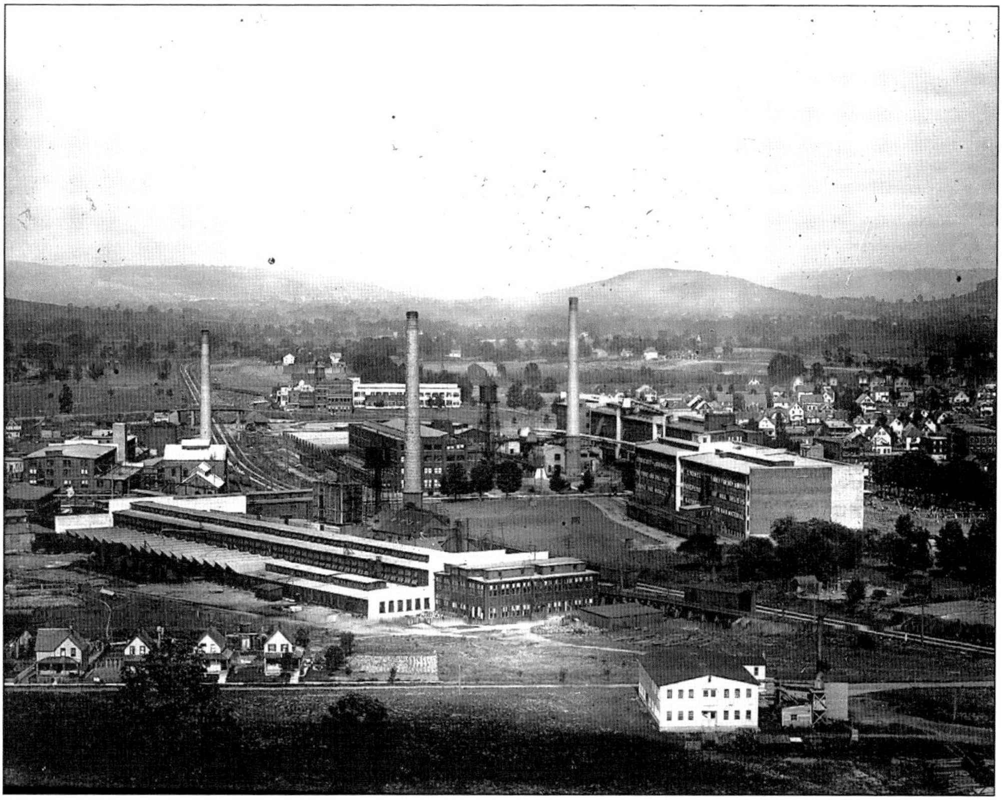

Endicott, the Magic City, is shown as it looked when being developed from farmland between the embracing hills c. 1906. Above is the Endicott-Johnson factory area; below are the early housing projects built by EJ in the same era. George F. Johnson was a tenacious visionary who planned every detail of his "shoe town."

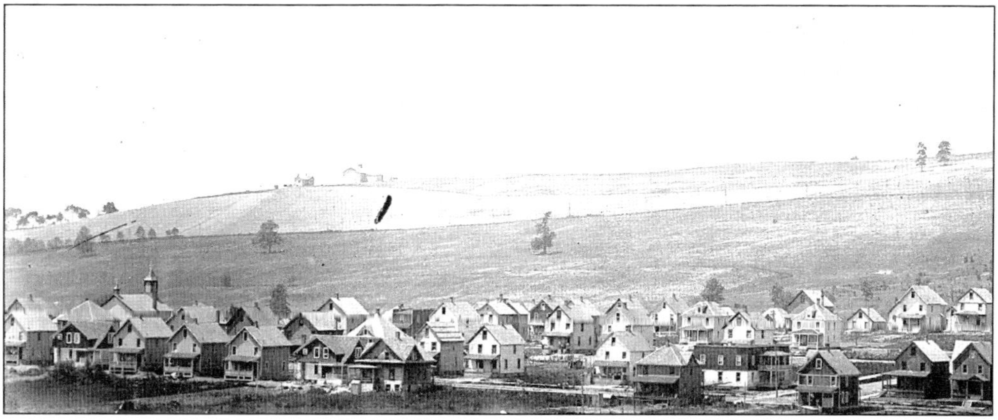

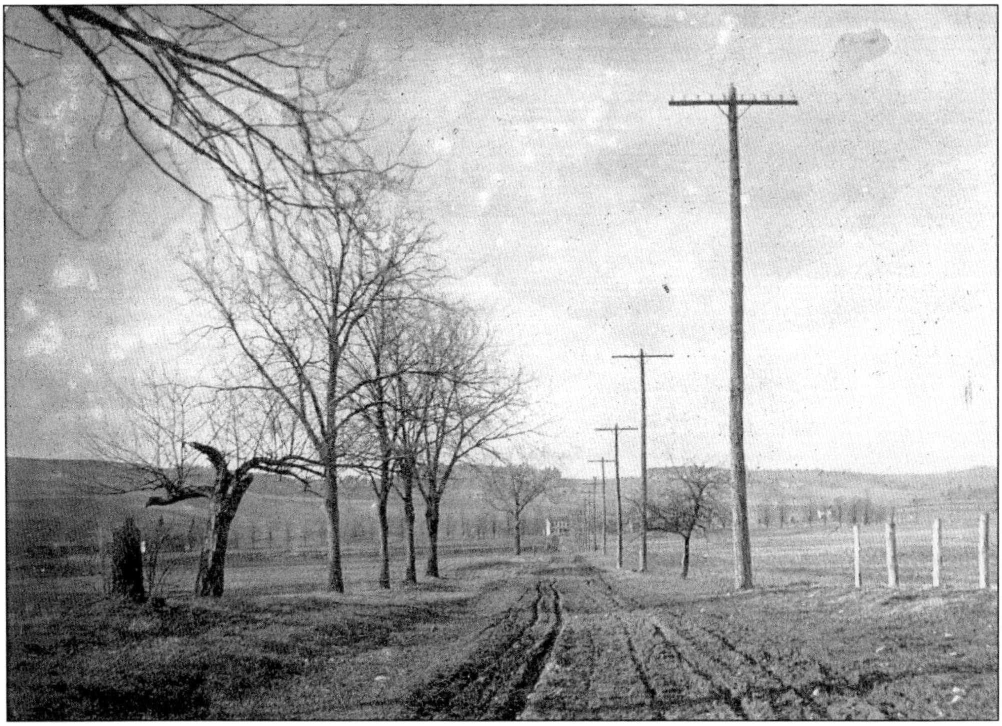

Washington Avenue in Endicott is pictured before the beginning of Magic City *c*. 1895.

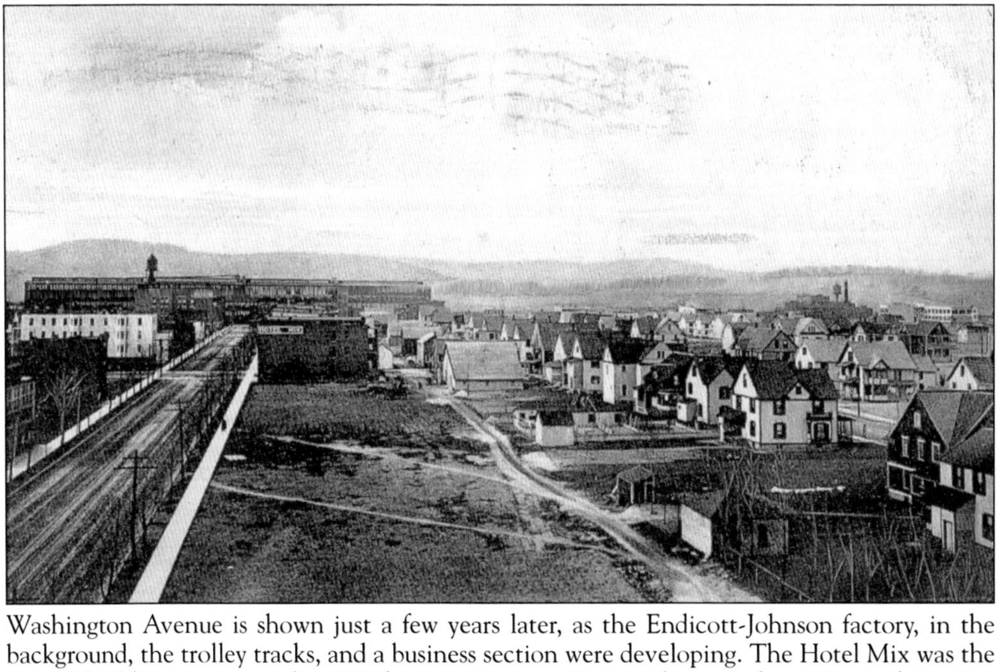

Washington Avenue is shown just a few years later, as the Endicott-Johnson factory, in the background, the trolley tracks, and a business section were developing. The Hotel Mix was the second building constructed on Washington Avenue. Later, it became the eating and meeting place Avenue Confectionery; today, it is the Cheevers Hand & Angeline Office building.

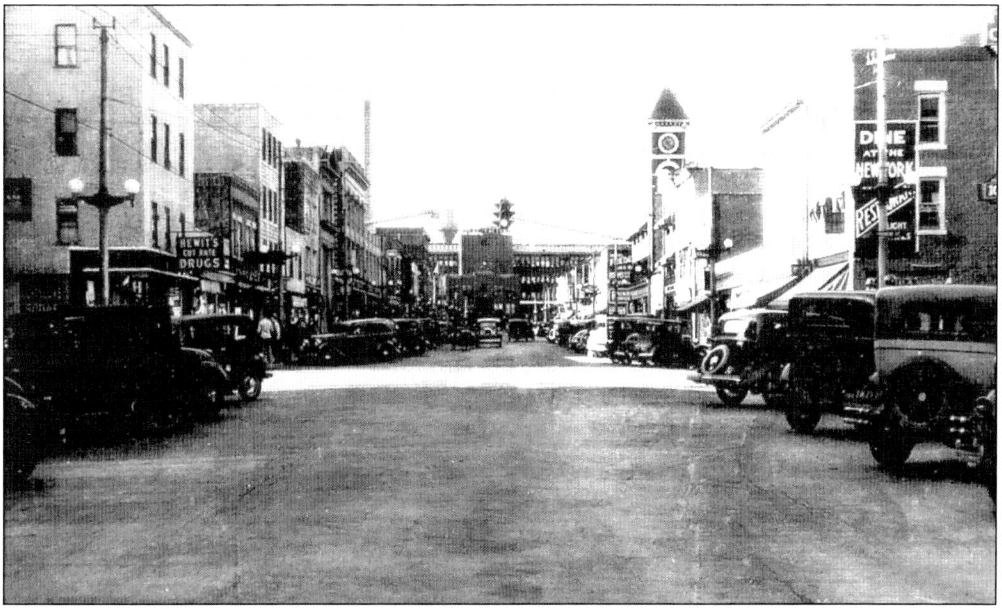

The 1920s and 1930s brought phenomenal progress on Washington Avenue, as the village bloomed with paved streets and dozens of small businesses. The Endicott-Johnson factory maintained a position of prominence as the largest employer in the area.

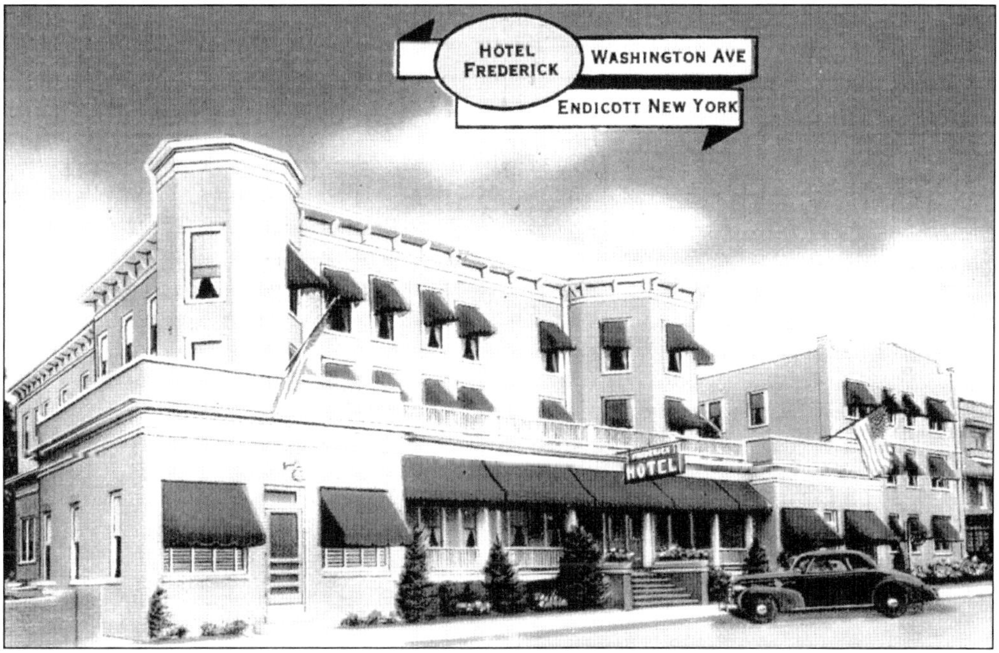

Hotel Frederick was built by Endicott-Johnson in 1906 to accommodate anticipated visitors to the Magic City. Initially, there were a total of 12 rooms available. By 1926, the number of rooms had increased to 50, and 20 of those were furnished with their own baths; for the rest, it was a walk down the hall to facilities. The cost for a night's stay ranged from $1 to $2.

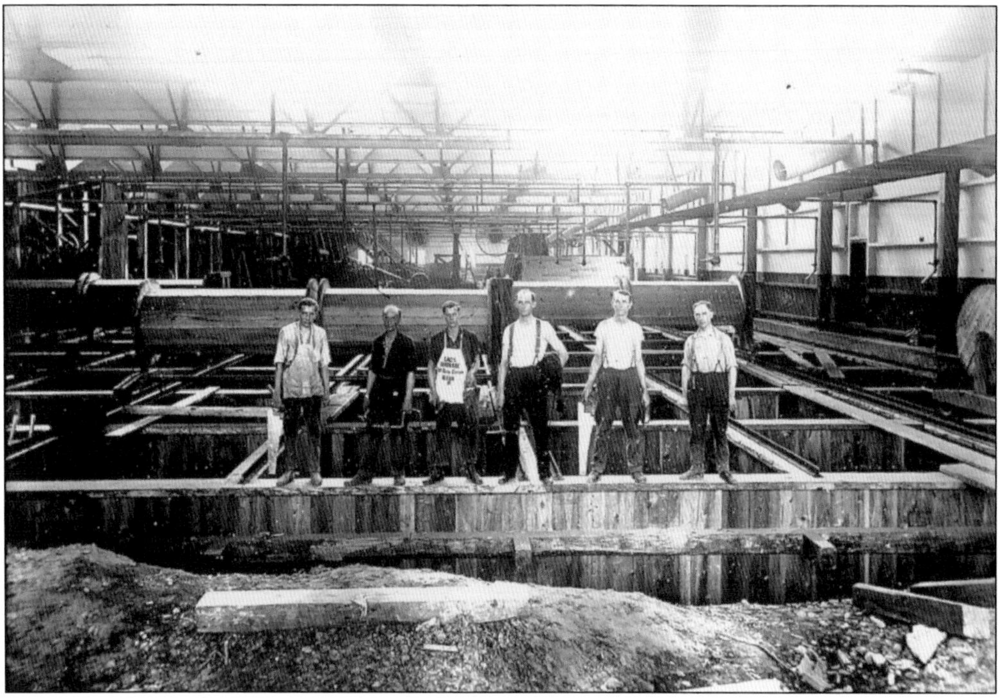

Phenomenal growth necessitated the building of more tanneries in Endicott. Pictured is a tannery under construction in 1916. Endicott-Johnson began to control the whole shoe-manufacturing process, eliminating the middlemen in every level of production.

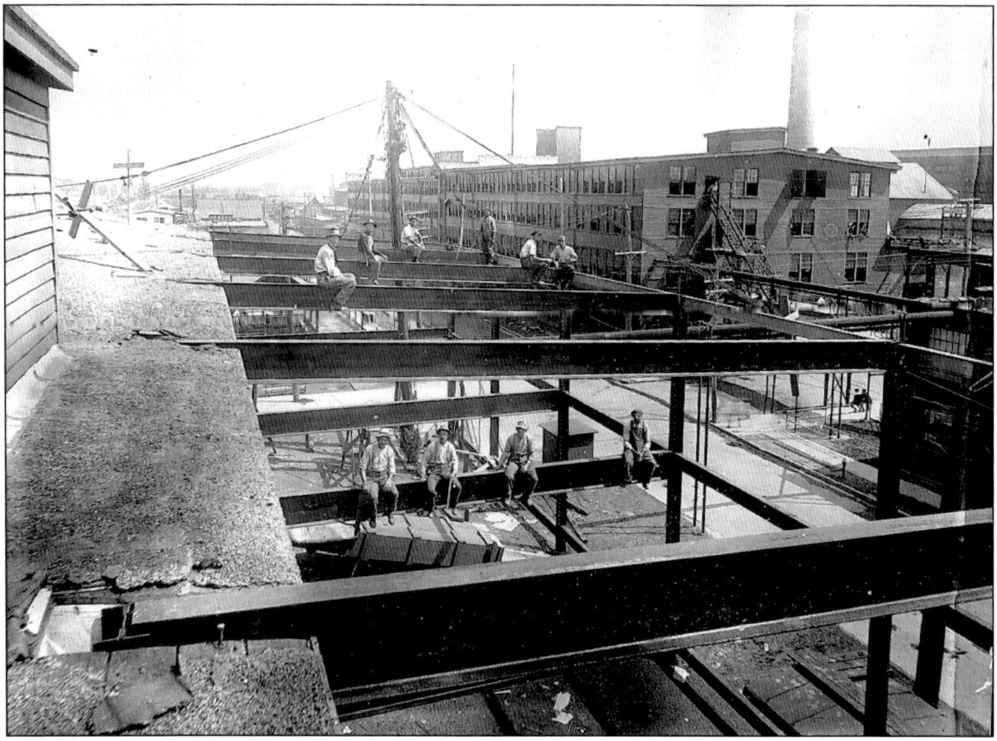

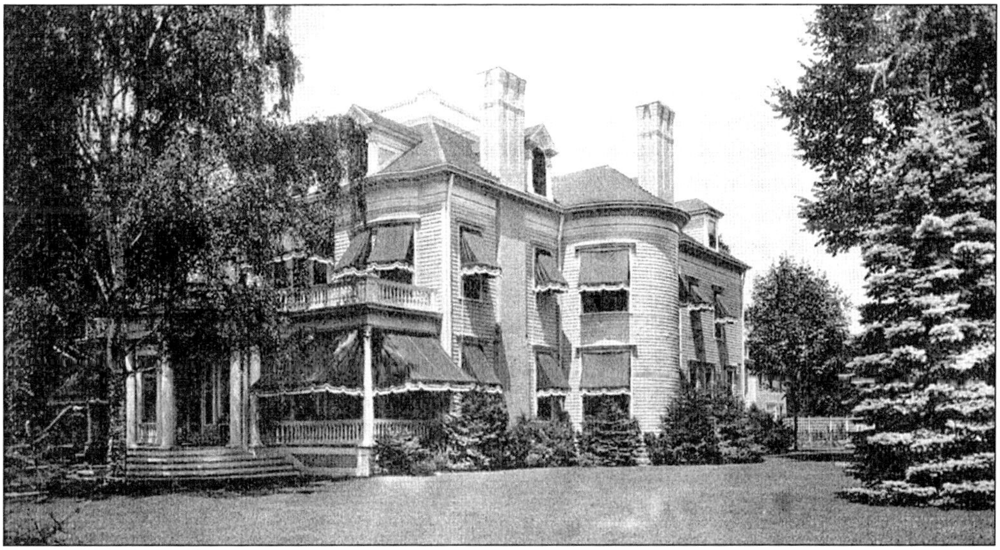

The George F. Johnson home was constructed *c.* 1902 on Park Street in Endicott. It was donated to the village as a memorial to Johnson. The gracious mansion became the village library until the "perpetual" memorial was demolished to build a modern brick building to house the library.

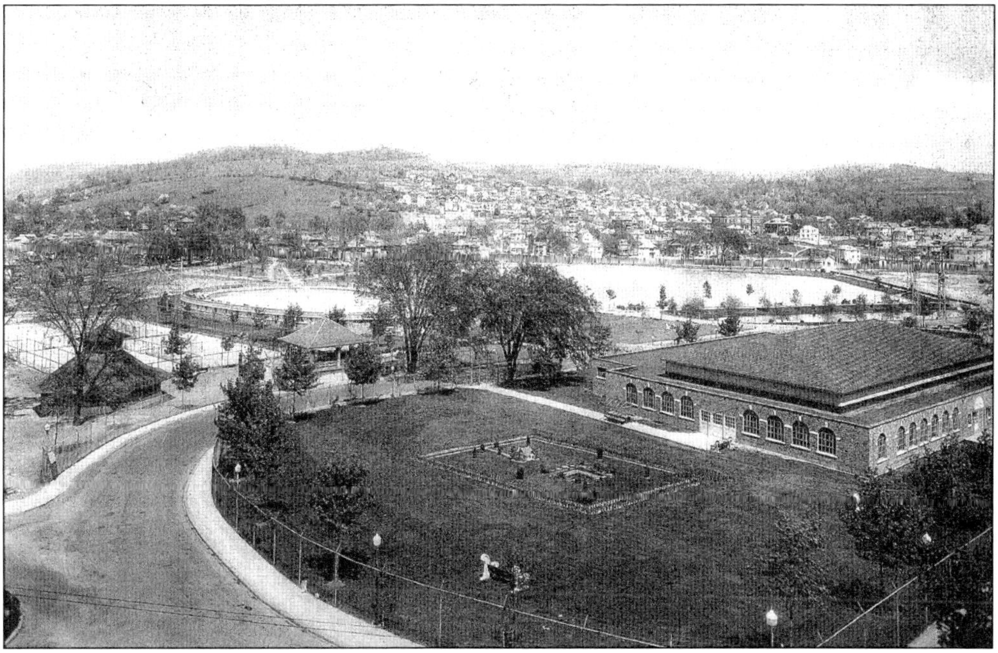

The George F. Johnson Pavilion was built in Johnson City in 1924 to provide a wholesome place for evenings out for adults. It became an entertainment landmark in Broome County. Local music groups, sporting events, and the most well-known bands of the era played at the pavilion. In later years, it became a roller-skating rink and, then, the Fountains Pavilion banquet facility.

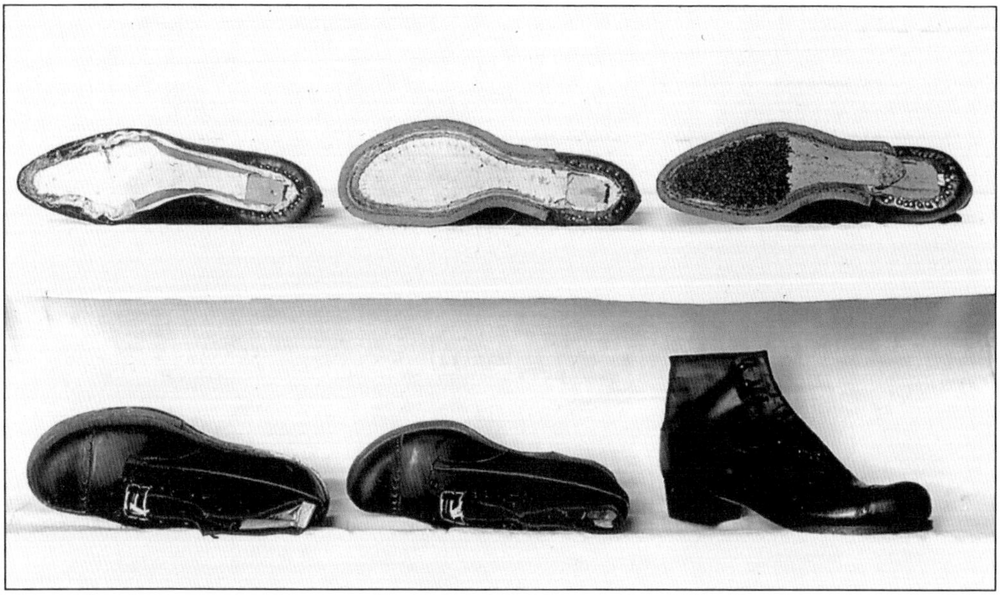

Pictured is the lasting operation. In 1920, Endicott-Johnson used thousands of miles of thread each day, as well as 14 tons of tacks and nails. In one of George F. Johnson's letters to employees, he stated, "Any EJ worker or anyone who derives support from the EJ workers industry" who does "NOT patronize EJ stores" is "NOT LOYAL."

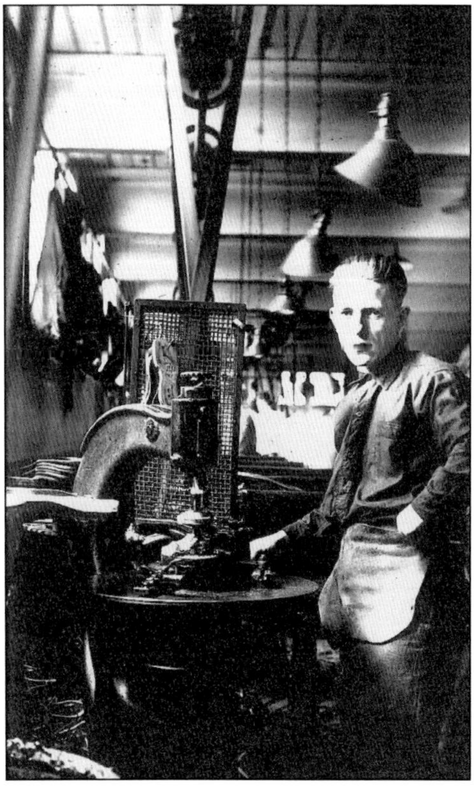

A worker in the Endicott-Johnson factory performs one of the 285 separate operations that were necessary to make make a single shoe. Gone from shoe town valley are terms that were once part of every day life: jigger, skivers, beamers, welt beaters, vamping, clicking, and cack.

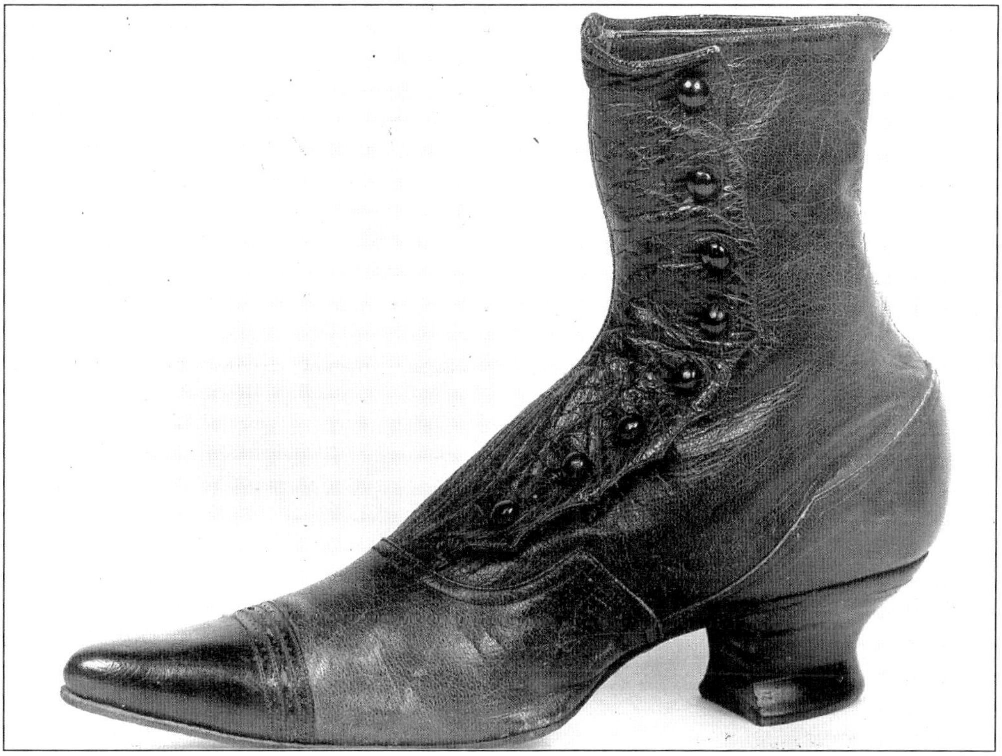

The style changes of EJ shoes over the years are reflected in these photographs. The first pair was made in 1901 and the second pair c. 1960. To cover the cost of all the employee benefits, $2^1/2$¢ were added to the cost of every pair of shoes made. Recreation, medical care, restaurants, markets, and sick relief were all paid by this tax.

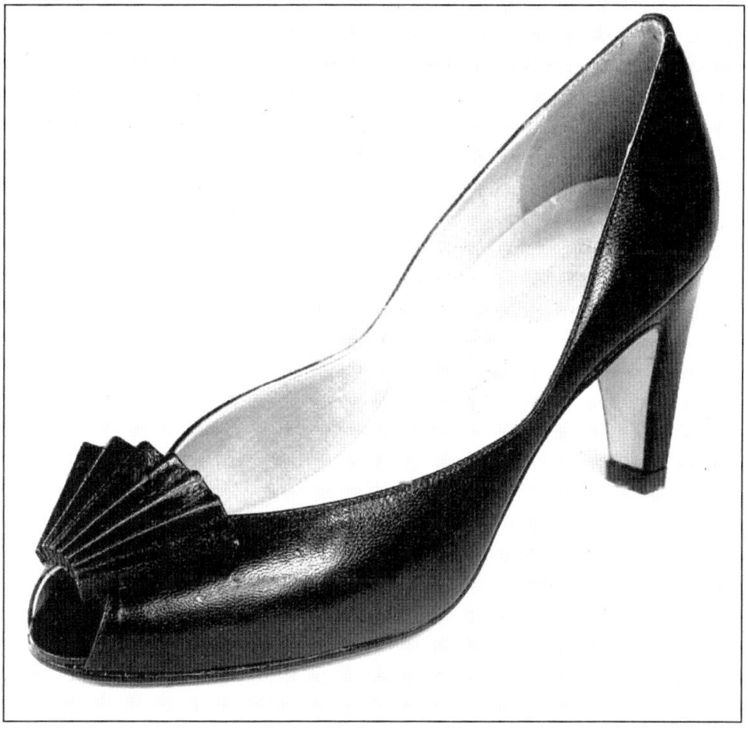

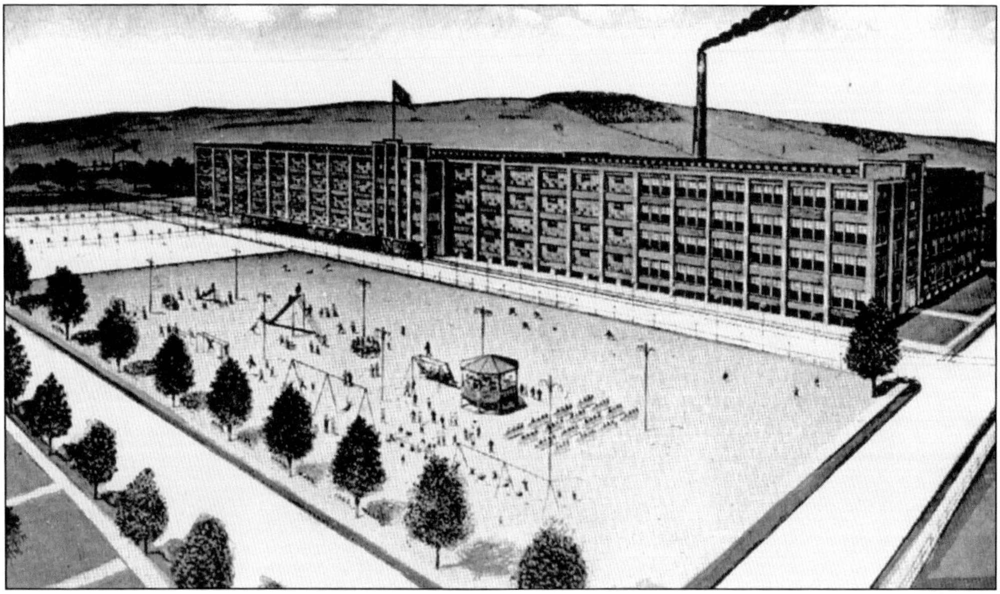

Pictured is the Endicott-Johnson sales building in Endicott. From this location the distribution of shoes to stores all across the country was coordinated.

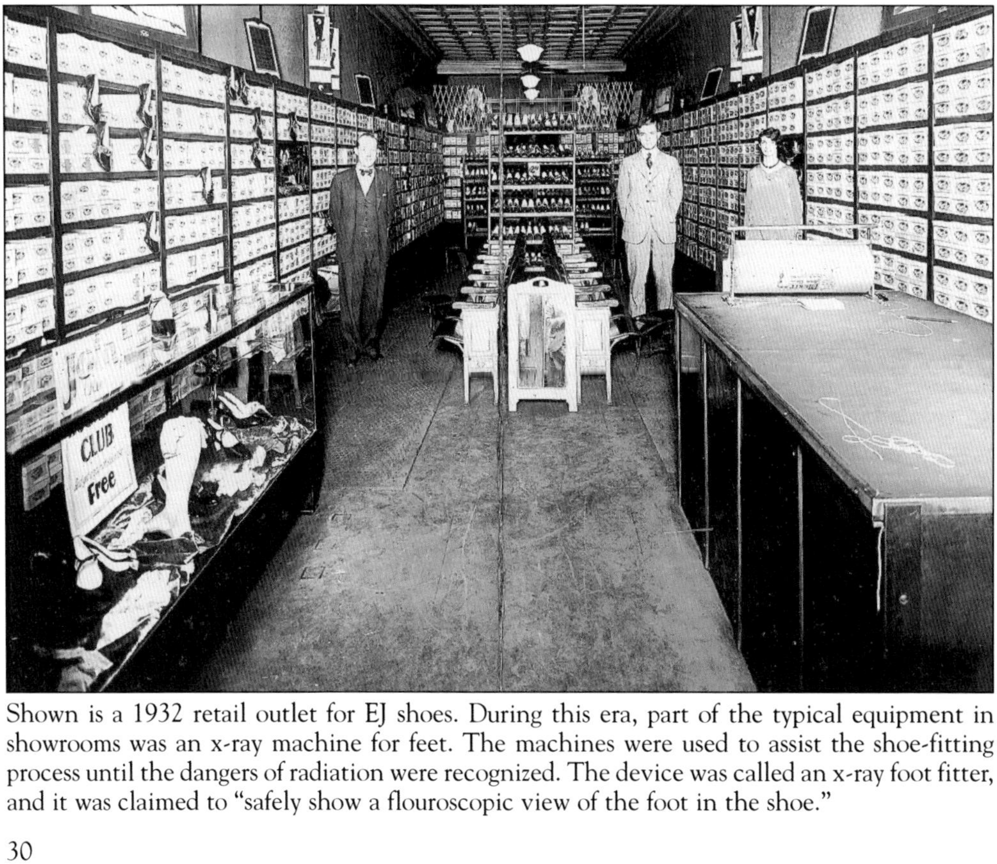

Shown is a 1932 retail outlet for EJ shoes. During this era, part of the typical equipment in showrooms was an x-ray machine for feet. The machines were used to assist the shoe-fitting process until the dangers of radiation were recognized. The device was called an x-ray foot fitter, and it was claimed to "safely show a flouroscopic view of the foot in the shoe."

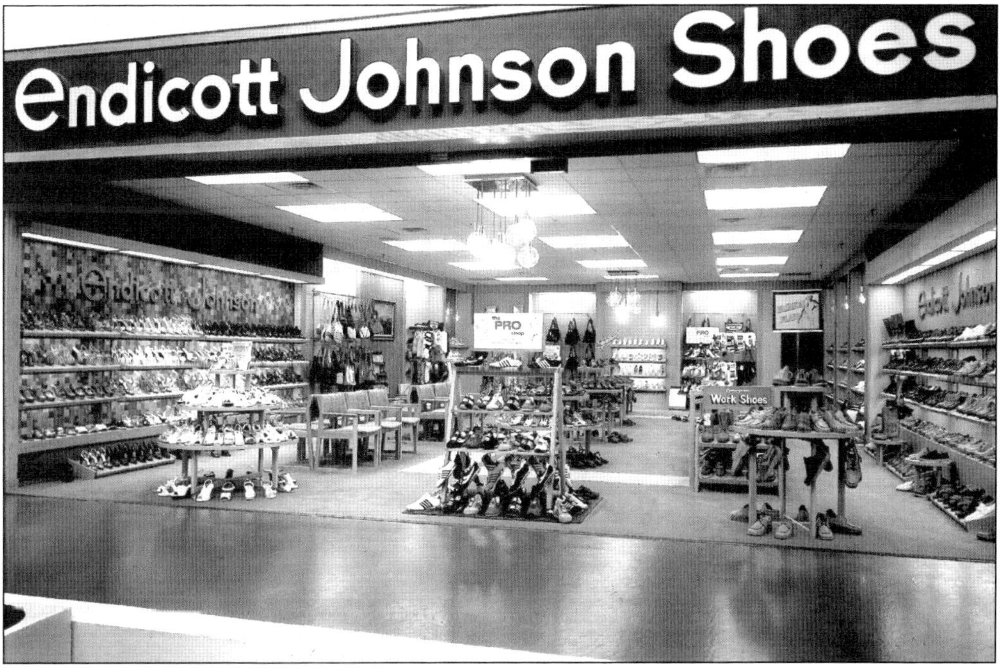

"From hoof to foot" was more than just an Endicott-Johnson slogan. The company cut out all middlemen by making the footwear and selling it in their own outlets. This is a typical shoe store *c.* 1970.

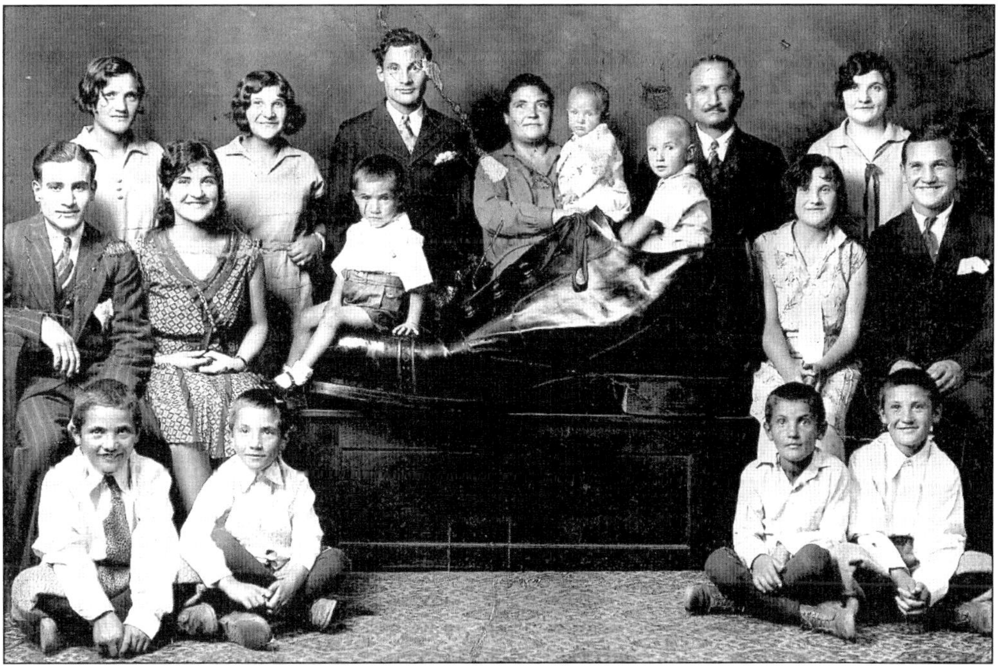

The shoemakers at Endicott-Johnson enjoyed making unusual display shoes. In 1930, they created this huge shoe to be pictured with the largest family of EJ workers in the area, the Grassi family. The parents and all adult children worked in the factories. For this special portrait, George F. Johnson paid to purchase new clothes and shoes for the entire family.

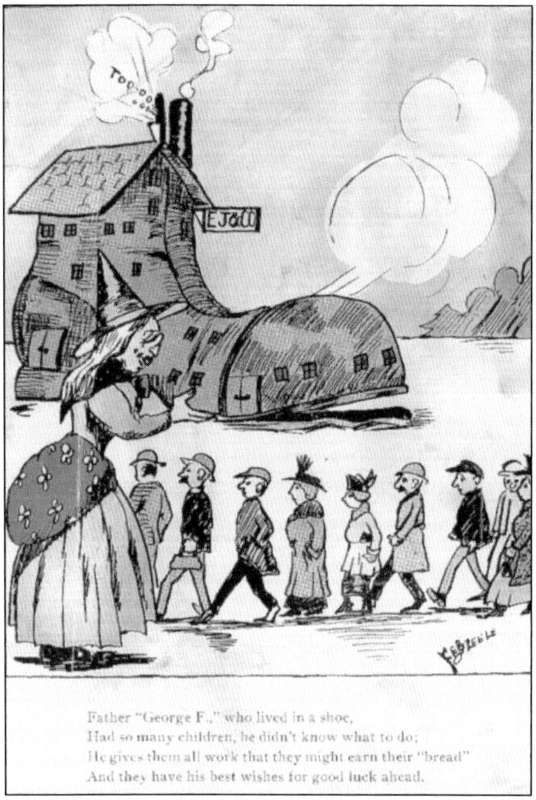

George F. Johnson encouraged the image of himself as the "father" figure of Endicott-Johnson, often referring to the employees as "boys and girls" and assuring them that "the Johnson administration does indeed know what is best for the company and its people." This cartoon was published in the *EJ Workers Magazine*, clearly indicating the paternal attitude.

NIFTY SHOES

For the Chap Who Is Aiming to Be Somebody

Neatness counts a lot these days. It's the fellow with neatly combed hair, carefully tied scarf, smart suit and stylish shoes who gets the attention . . . whether he's in school, at a social affair, holding down a job, or out with his pals. It's a pretty sure sign he's going to amount to something.

But this isn't a sermon. It's an advertisement telling you about the nattiest, snappiest, best wearing shoes you ever set your eyes on, or foot into.

SEE DISPLAY IN YOUR LOCAL STORE WINDOW

ENDICOTT JOHNSON

"BETTER SHOES FOR LESS MONEY"

Using language of the era, this advertisement offers "nifty" shoes. It was printed in the year 1934.

Today, this advertisement would not be considered politically correct, but in the year it was published, *c.* 1921, it was thought very funny. The caption read, "I just discovered the shoes the last missionary wore were made by George F. Johnson.

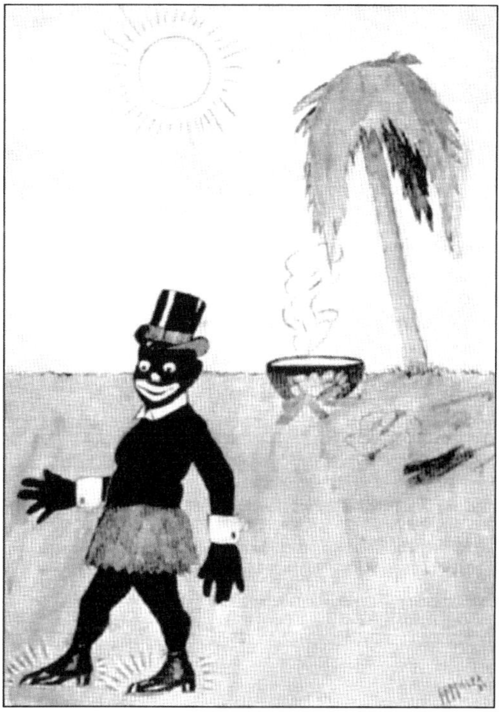

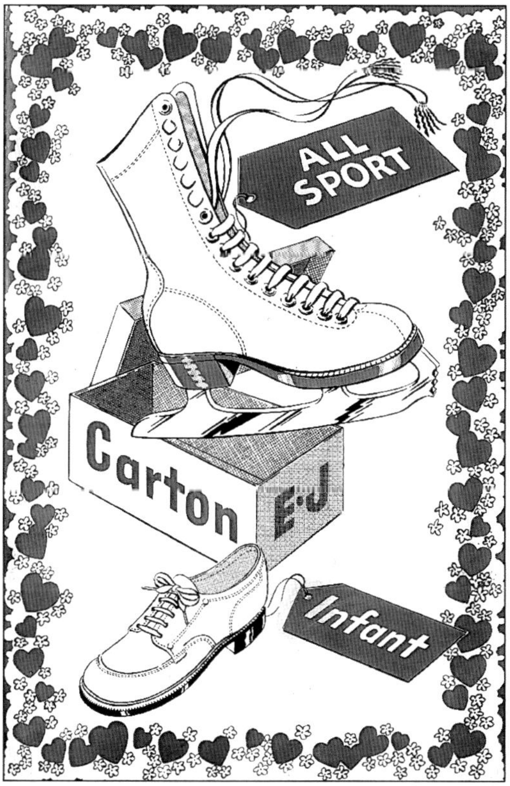

One of the lesser-known Endicott-Johnson factories was the All Sport. Among other products, it manufactured ice skates under the EJ brand. The picture is from the cover of a 1950s retirement banquet.

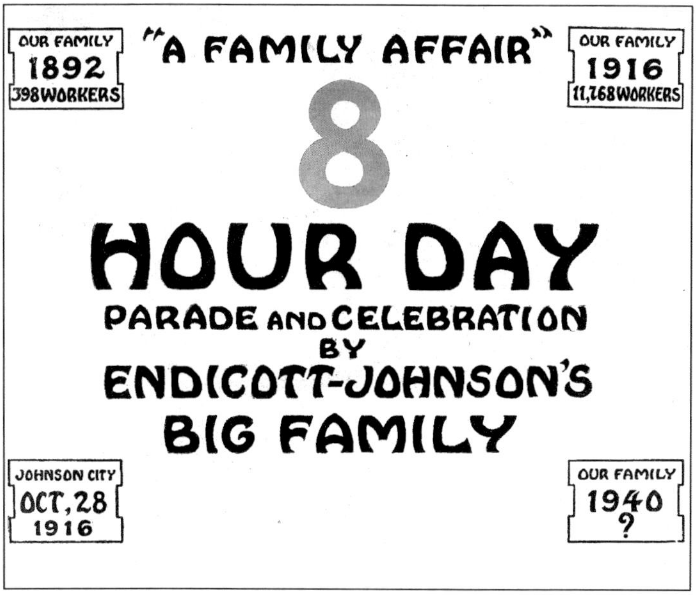

The year 1916 brought about one of the greatest changes in working America. An eight-hour day was established by Endicott-Johnson. Partly because of the EJ policy of concern for workers, an eight-hour day was established to replace the traditional ten-hour day. EJ was the first manufacturer of shoes and leather tanning to adopt the 48-hour workweek. Thousands of people marched in the streets to celebrate the new freedom—extra time at home.

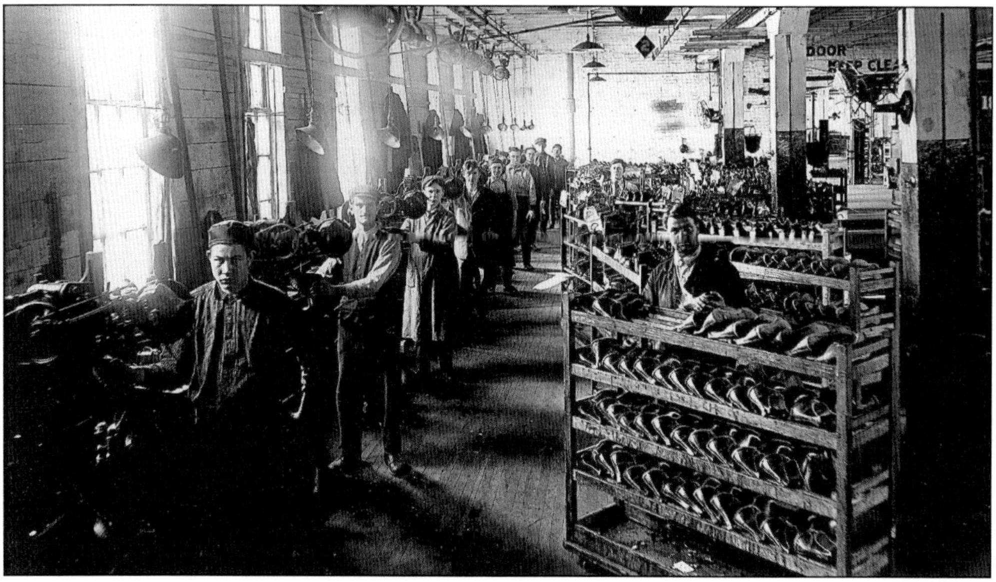

Workers line up to have their picture taken in 1919. In a book written in 1900, author William S. Lawyer describes Endicott-Johnson as an unusual and successful business relationship because "the interests of master and servant are identical."

The term "Magic City" was so appealing that several area companies used it in their corporate name. The Magic City Ice and Milk Company was organized in 1922, when delivery was made by horse and wagon. The company stayed in business until purchased by the Crowley Milk Company of Binghamton. The advertisement, on the right, was used in 1938; the letter, below, was left by delivery man Dan in a customer's milk box in 1946.

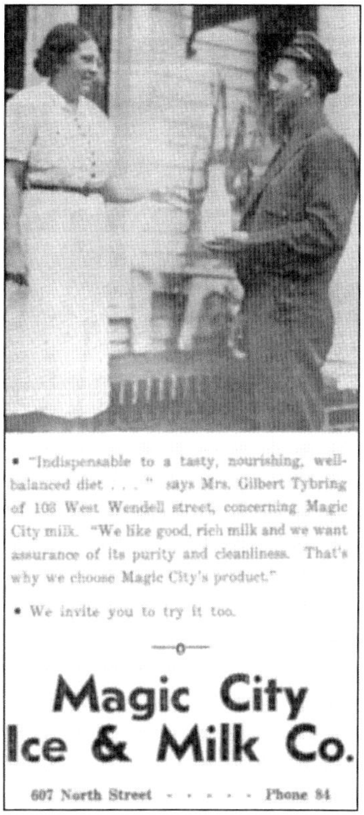

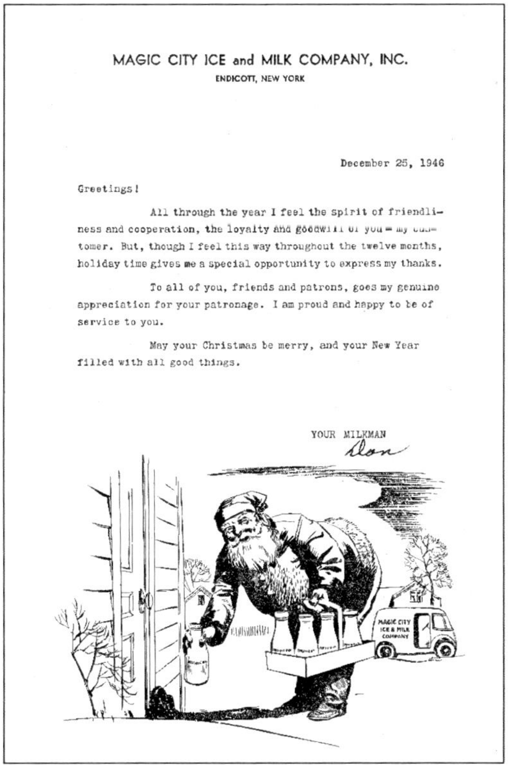

MAGIC CITY ICE and MILK COMPANY, INC.
ENDICOTT, NEW YORK

December 25, 1946

Greetings!

All through the year I feel the spirit of friendliness and cooperation, the loyalty and goodwill of you — my customer. But, though I feel this way throughout the twelve months, holiday time gives me a special opportunity to express my thanks.

To all of you, friends and patrons, goes my genuine appreciation for your patronage. I am proud and happy to be of service to you.

May your Christmas be merry, and your New Year filled with all good things.

YOUR MILKMAN
Dan

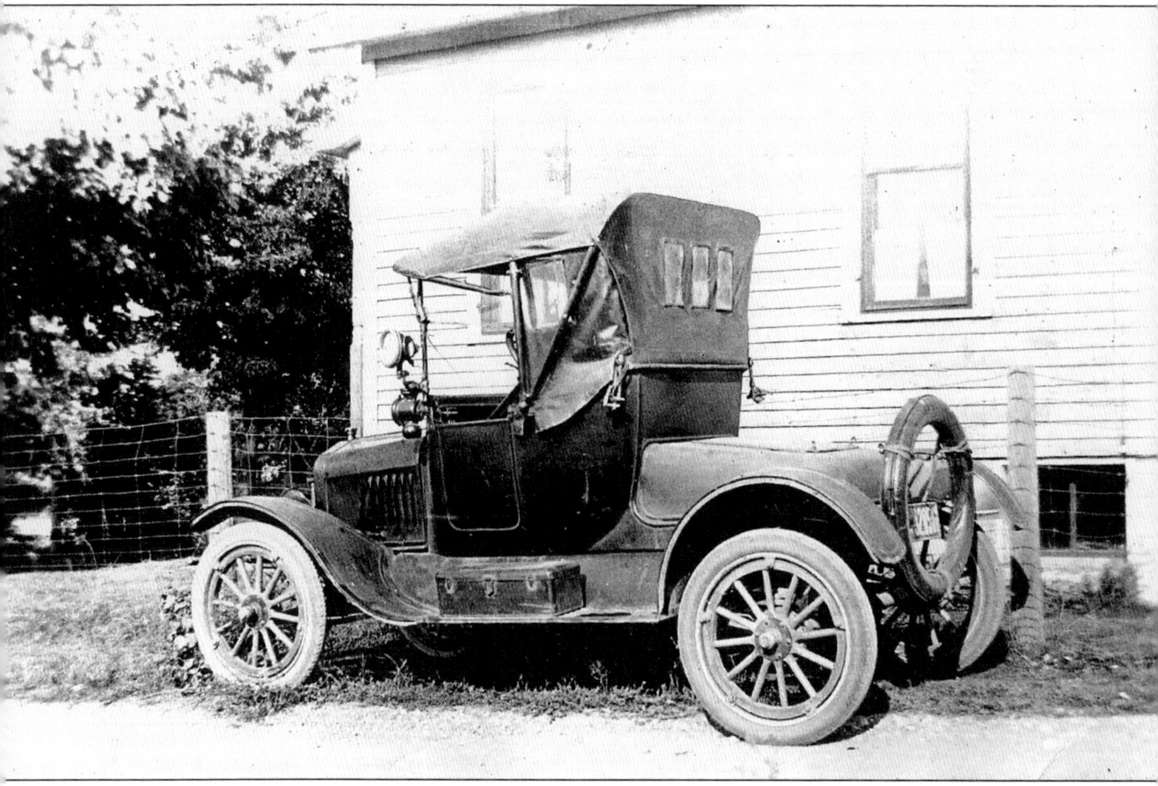

During World War I, Harry L. Johnson and George W. Johnson visited the Ford automobile plants. They were impressed with the efficiency but reported to George F. Johnson that a personal touch between labor and management was missing: "the people do not live around the factories and Mr. Ford does not live with the people and goes into the factories but seldom." In 1934, Ford gave an interview stating that love was not necessary in efficient labor relations. He claimed that all the employer and employee needed was to "just try to do each other justice." George F. Johnson rebutted with, "If that is his policy he will die one of the greatest failures the world has ever known." Henry Ford also wrote and published articles that offended Johnson's sense of ethnic tolerance.

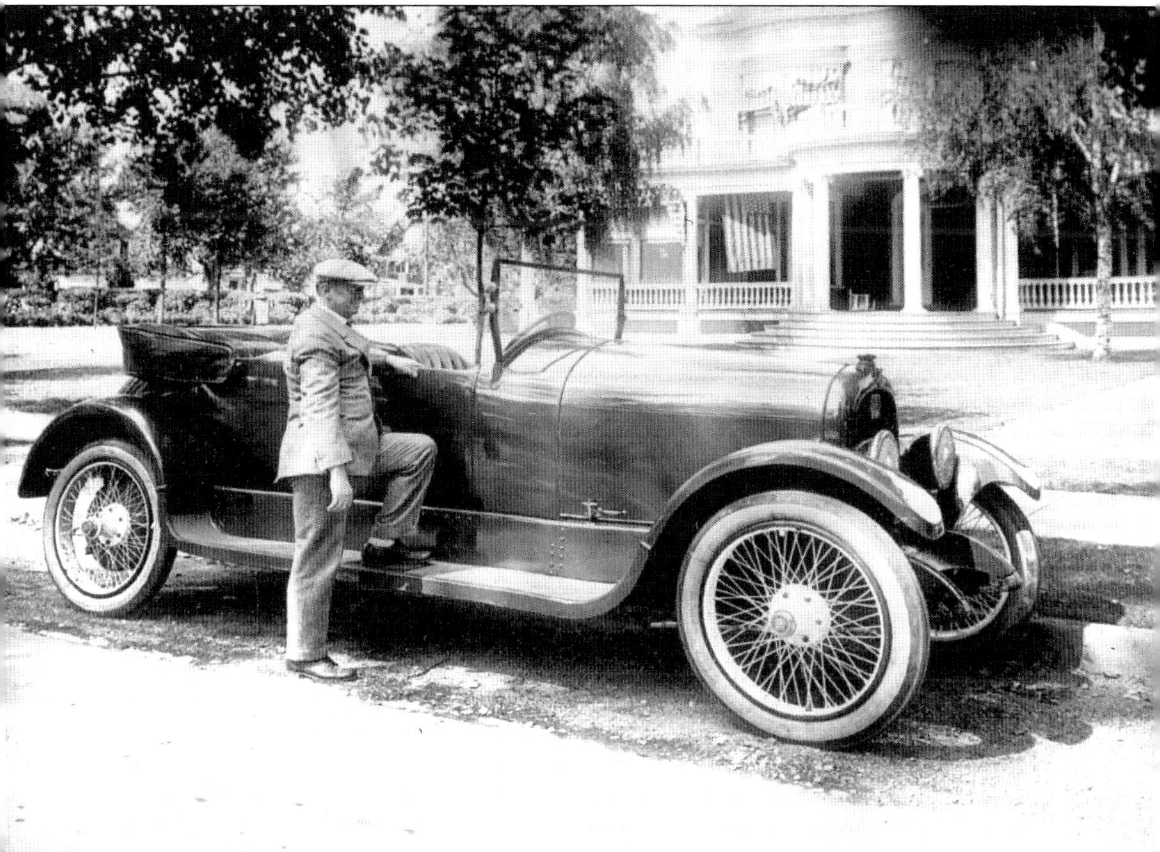

George F. Johnson rode through the villages in an open automobile waving to the natives. However, he did not approve of workers owning such devices. He wrote to employees in the company magazine asking: "Why have a garage? People go without things they need to pay the cost of keeping up a tin 'Lizzie.' We [EJ] will not build garages behind the homes we build. We WILL build an attractive chicken coop free of charge. I wish I could see a cow in garages instead of a tumble-down car. You will get the benefit of milk products and the healthful benefit of walking." In 1913, a gangster organization known as the Black Hand sought to extort cash from Johnson by throwing a letter into his car threatening violent destruction of his property if $2,000 was not paid. The letter was ignored, and when the grace period for the demand had expired, the Endicott livery stable—in which Johnson had a financial interest and where he housed his auto—was destroyed by fire, along with numerous horses.

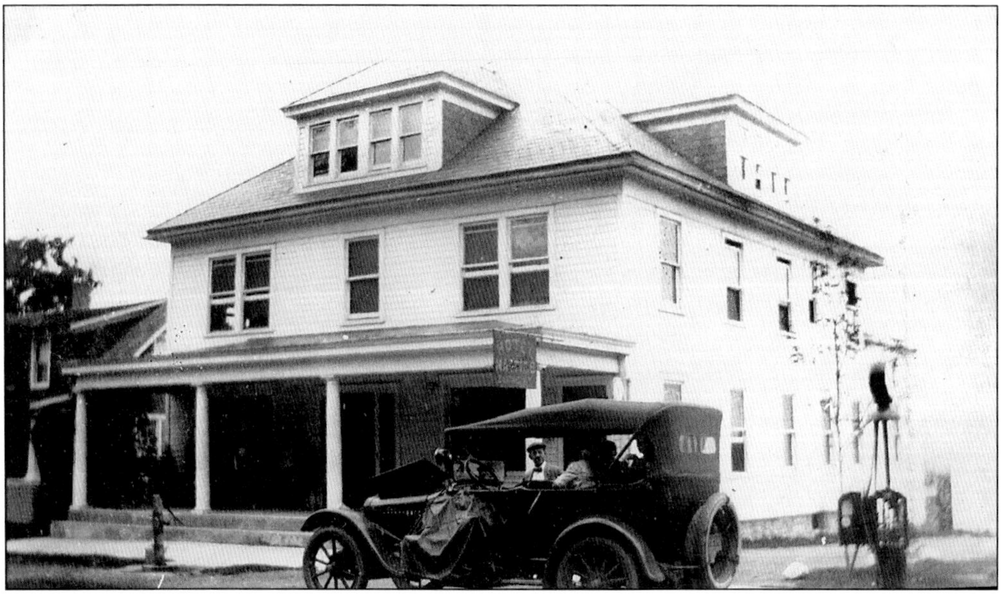

In spite of George F. Johnson's warnings, automobiles proliferated—and less shoe leather was used in walking. As Endicott-Johnson workers and their counterparts in neighboring industries purchased automobiles, service stations like the two pictured were common along the roadsides. Advertising "fuel for folks & flivver," the stopping places became part of the changing landscape of progress in and around the Magic City.

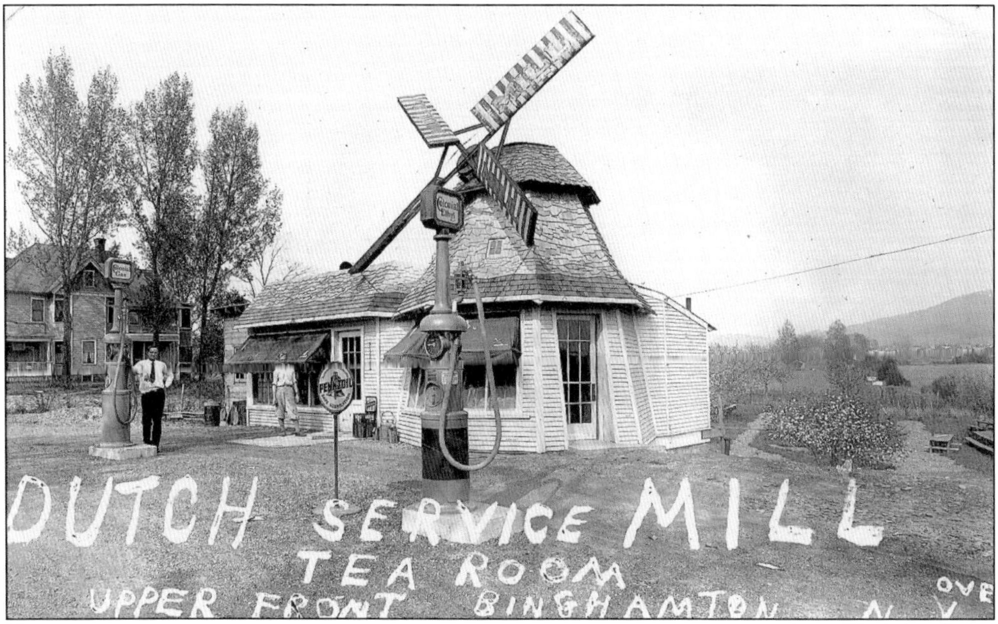

Two

EJ ON ITS WAY

TO THE WORKERS:

With the thought that few of our workers understand the volume of our business and just where the money goes, please note the following figures, that have been prepared by our Administration Dept., and study them at your leisure, so as to be better posted regarding these important matters pertaining to your business.

Sales of Endicott Johnson for the Year Ending November 30, 1948, Were $148,650,282.15

Total Payments and Charges Were as Follows:

Item		% to Wages		% to Sales
Wages, salaries and commissions			$52,066,064.96	35.03%
Other benefits:				
Vacations and holidays	$2,748,510.89			
Discretionary bonuses	3,843,037.81			
Retirement Plan-Current Service	1,308,807.28			
-Past Service	1,993,126.00			
Medical Services, Death Benefits, Health Insurance, etc.	2,365,544.16			
All other expenses for the benefit of the workers	733,772.21			
Set aside for recreation buildings and other welfare facilities	1,500,000.00			
Benefits (represent % to wages)		27.84%	14,492,798.35	9.75%
Total Wages and Benefits			$66,558,863.31	44.78%
Hides, leather and all other materials			55,455,126.27	37.30%
Rents, royalties, power and other operating expenses			12,235,285.93	8.23%
Taxes - federal, state and local			5,291,998.35	3.56%
Upkeep and repairs			4,198,914.16	2.82%
Dividends to stockholders			1,992,032.00	1.34%
Replacement cost for use of machinery (depreciation)			1,287,092.76	.87%
Increase in reserves due to inflated values			1,179,376.85	.79%
Appropriation for replacement costs of plant and equipment			500,000.00	.34%
			148,698,689.63	100.03%
Payments and charges exceed sales by			48,407.48	.03%
			$148,650,282.15	100.00%

February 15, 1949

Geo. W. Johnson
Chas. F. Johnson, Jr.

Each year, the Endicott Johnson Corporation published a report of payments and expenses. George F. Johnson wanted the workers to know how much was spent for the many "free" services and benefits they received. This accounting was printed in 1948. EJ claimed to offer "fair, disinterested friendship and loyalty between partners in industry . . . labor and capital. We believe we must maintain principles that promote peace and harmony—this is just as important in government as in industry—Fair Play, Square Dealing, and the Golden Rule."

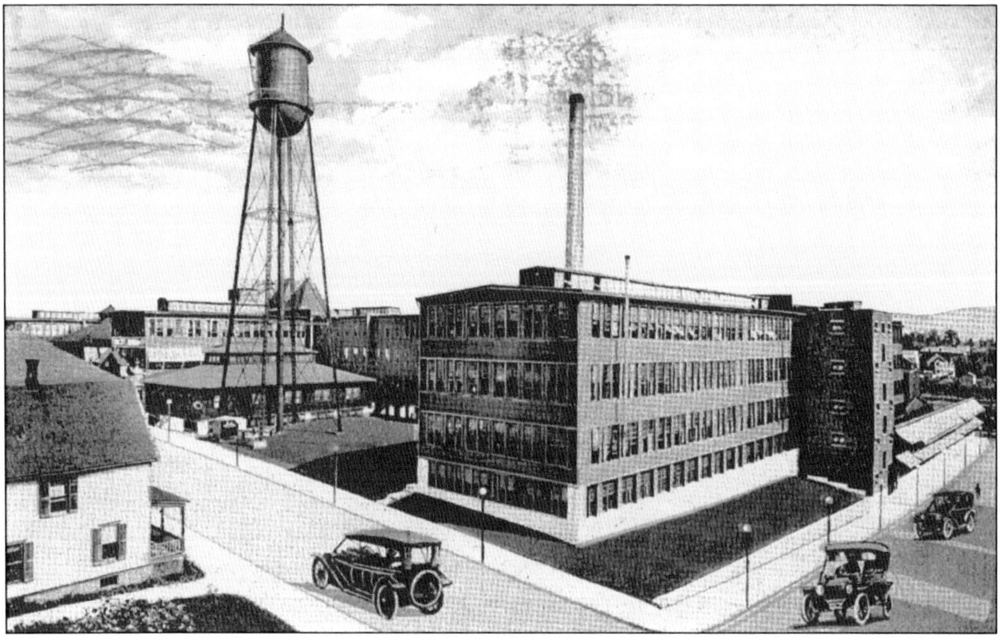

Endicott-Johnson owned company diners in six locations. Workers and other community members could purchase nourishing meals at breakfast and supper seven days a week. The cost ranged from 15 to 25 cents per meal. At the height of the Great Depression of the 1930s, Endicott-Johnson gave more than 250,000 meals absolutely free to anyone who walked through the doors. Families and children of workers were among those saved from bread lines and hunger.

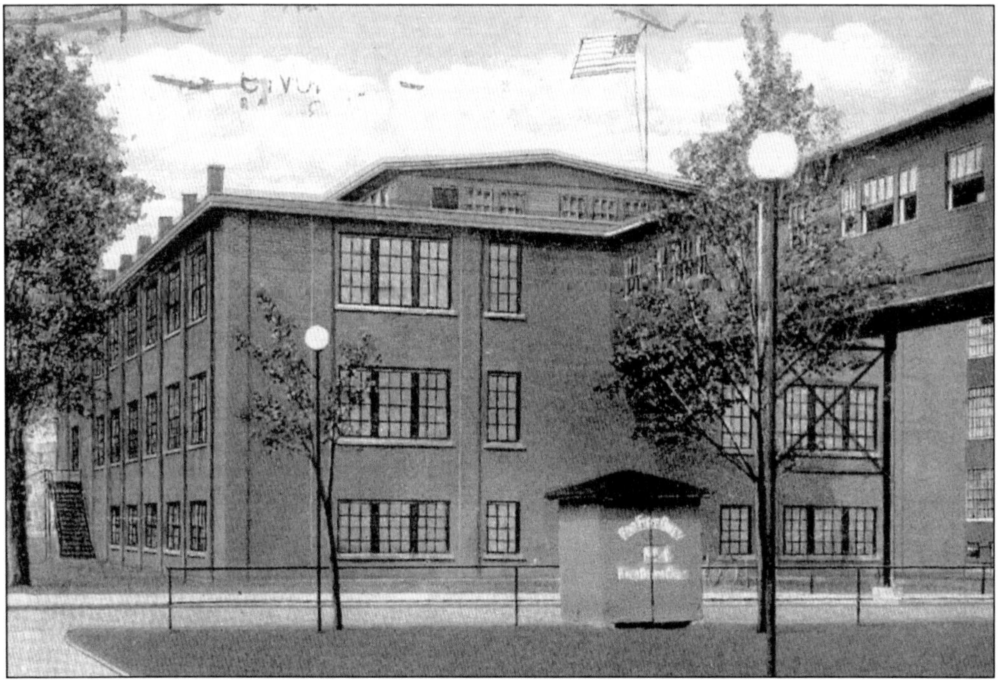

The Endicott-Johnson workers' stores and public markets made meat, fresh vegetables, and staple groceries available at reduced prices. Farmers were paid $2 by EJ each time they brought produce to the market. "The farmers get most of the money that would go to the middleman and customers save approximately 25% on all they buy," read a quote from the *Public Market News* published in 1922. The photograph of the farmers with a load of pumpkins is from the same era.

JOHNSON CITY-ENDICOTT

Public Market News

Vol. 3 | Johnson City-Endicott, January 7, 1922 | No. 27

Edited by the Market Master

Devoted to the Producers and Consumers of Johnson City and Endicott

Published Every week
Advertising Rates—Free

Market Places—Johnson City, Corliss avenue; Endicott, North street.

Market Days—Tuesday, Thursday, Saturday.

Market Hours—9:30.

Market Stalls—Free to Producers.

Market Bags—6c.

Market News—Free. Published every week.

Market Prices—Regulated by Market Master.

Assistant Market Master.
Endicott—Chester Goodenow, Phone 6508.

COUNTRY-WIDE MARKET PRICES

Most of the large markets throughout the country are for the first time in many months selling all kinds of produce at about the same price.

Taking the prices at the first of the year they are as follows:
Apples—Supplies limited; demand good; average $7.00 to $10 barrel.
Cabbage—Supplies; demand limited; market weak; $40 to $55 per ton.
Celery—Supplies liberal; demand good; $2.50 to $3 per 2-3 crate.
Carrots—Supplies liberal; demand good; $2.00 to $2.35 per 100 bag.
Onions—Supplies limited; demand good; $5.00 to $5.50 per 100 bag.
Potatoes—Supplies liberal; demand light; $3.50 to $3.75 per 150 lbs.
Parsnips—Supplies liberal; demand good; $2.50 to $3.00 per barrel.
Squash—Supplies limited; demand good; $2.00 to $2.50 per barrel.

LIVE POULTRY

Fowls—Average run, 22c to 25c per lb.
Ducks—Average run, 30c to 32c per lb.
Geese—Average run, 24c to 26c per lb.

DRESSED POULTRY

Fowls—Average run, 28c to 33c per lb.
Ducks—Average run, 32c to 36c per lb.
Geese—Average run, 25c to 34c per lb.
Butter—Creamery, highest score, 40c to 42c per lb.
Dairy—State, fine to fancy, 40c to 41c per lb.
Cheese—Market steady; state, whole milk, 22c to 24c per lb.
Eggs—Market weak; nearby gathered whites, fine to fancy, 60c to 65c.
Nearby gathered browns, fine to fancy, 63c to 56c.
Nearby gathered pullets, fine to fancy, 50c to 58c.

(Johnson City and Endicott Prices on Page Two)

Last Week's Statement

JOHNSON CITY MARKET
Dec. 27 Sales ....$ 423.60; loads 30
Dec. 29 Sales ....$ 573.04; loads 38
Dec. 31 Sales ....$2,771.85; loads 86
Total Sales ....$3,768.49; loads 154

ENDICOTT MARKET
Dec. 27 Sales ....$ 352.82; loads 26
Dec. 29 Sales ....$ 482.40; loads 36
Dec. 31 Sales ....$1,757.80; loads 68
Total Sales ....$2,593.02; loads 130

Totals, Both Markets:
Sales ....$6,361.51; loads 284

December Gains

ENDICOTT MARKET
1921 Sales ....$14,792.19; loads 688
1920 Sales ....$14,231.91; loads 644
Gain ....$ 560.28; loads 44

JOHNSON CITY MARKET
1921 Sales ....$21,954.91; loads 811
1920 Sales ....$21,231.87; loads 705
Gain ....$ 723.04; loads 106

Keep Busy the Year Around

Plan your work this Winter—Work your plan next Summer.

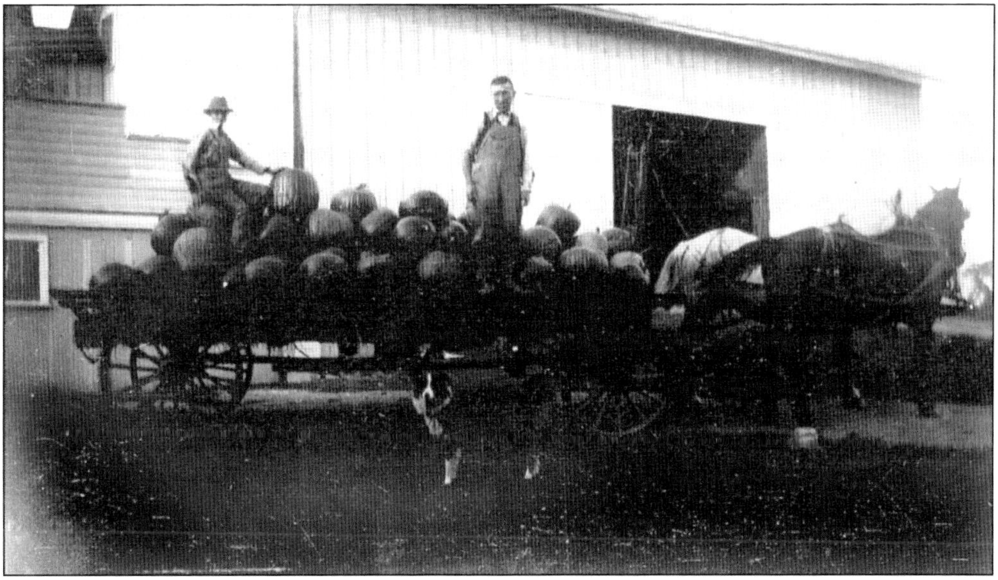

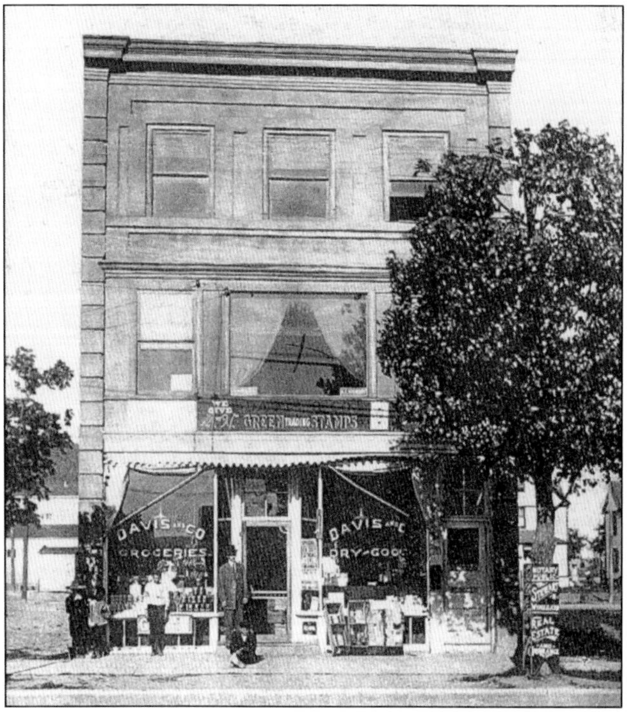

Endicott-Johnson was originally hesitant about sponsoring community markets. George F. Johnson was afraid local grocers' business would be hurt by discount produce. However, the urge to make the workers' dollar stretch further overcame his doubts. When the EJ markets opened, Broome County grocers were assured of a booth, and reasonable subsidies would be paid to businesses experiencing a loss due to the popularity of the markets. Pictured are the Davis and Company Grocery and Dry Goods store, in Endicott, and the Mann Brothers, who operated a grocery on Nanticoke Avenue.

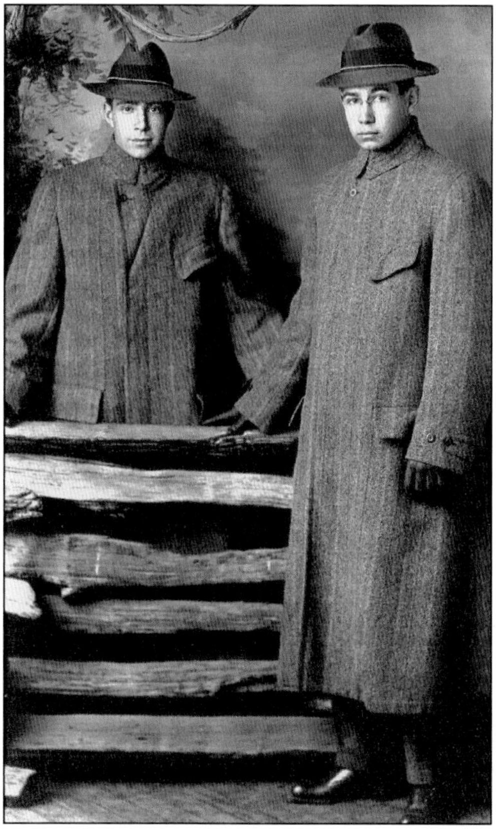

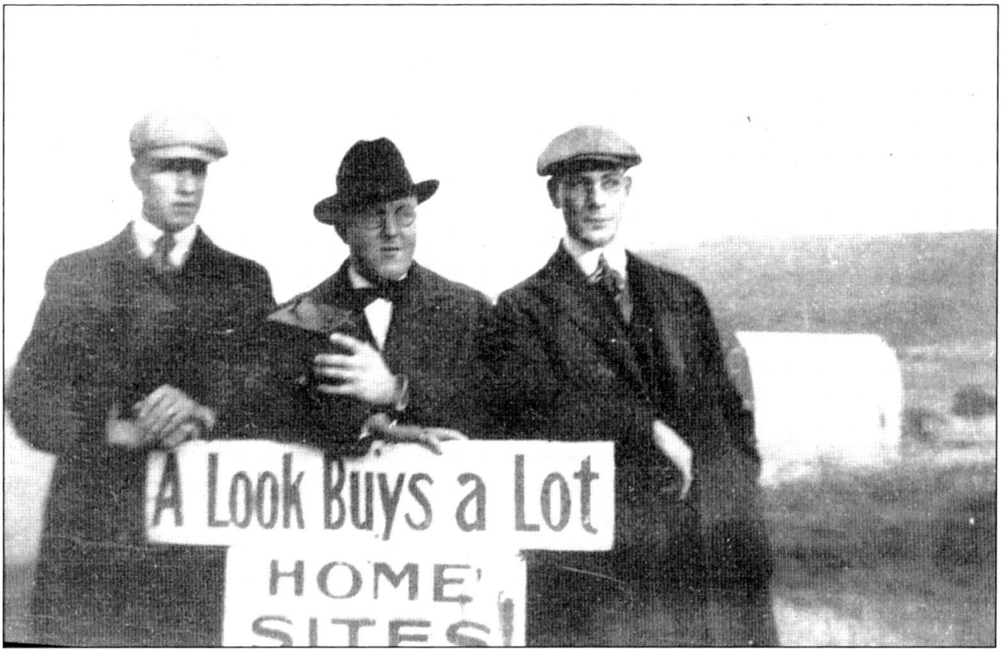

A sign on the tree in front of the Davis store, pictured on the previous page, advertises real estate—property was in demand in the growing village. Here is another sign marking the lots ready to sell in the boomtown known as Magic City, this one surrounded by eager buyers and sellers. Commenting on building lots, George F. Johnson said, "Another foolish thing for people to invest in—at least people who work with us—is building lots . . . this company owns 1,400 acres of land in West Endicott . . . we are not charging a penny for any of our housing lots. All we aim to do is get the cost of the house . . . so why buy lots from speculative promoters?"

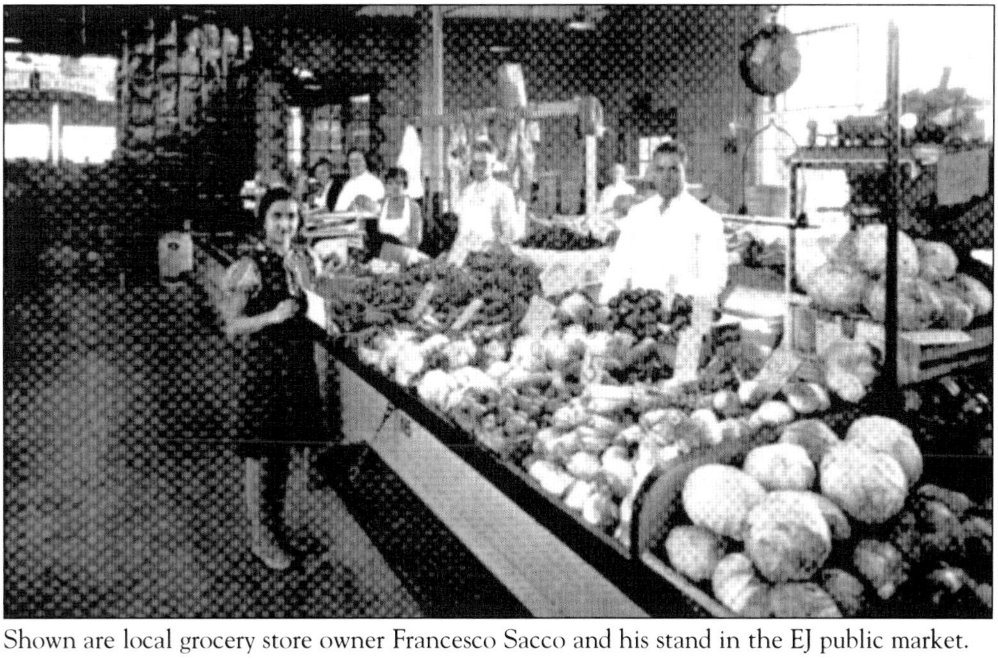

Shown are local grocery store owner Francesco Sacco and his stand in the EJ public market.

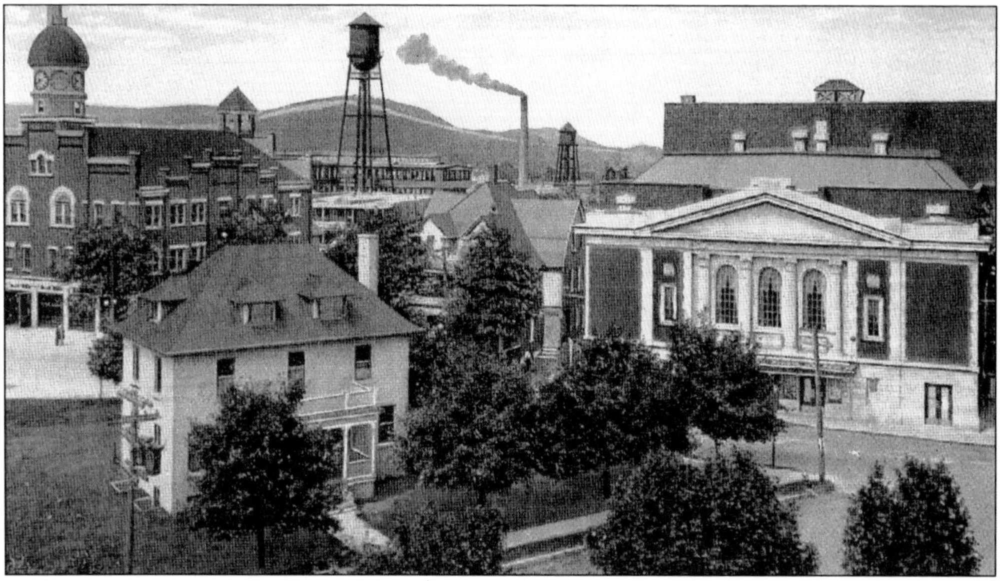

STORE AND RESTAURANT REVIEW

PARTIAL GROCERY PRICE LIST

Shredded Wheat	@ .11c	Codfish, 1 lb	@ .16c
Kellogg's Corn Flakes	@ .08c	White Tuna Fish	@ .19c
Post Toasties	@ .08c	Pink Salmon	@ .10c
Puffed Rice	@ .15c	Del Monte Red Salmon	@ .24c
Cream of Wheat	@ .22c	Horse Radish	@ .13c
Mothers' Oats	@ .09c	Paul's Apricot Jam	@ .25c
Warner's Macaroni	@ .09c	Bread, 1-lb loaf	@ .05c
Corn Starch	@ .07c	Salt, 4-lb bag	@ .06c
Nabiscos, large	@ .16c	Salt, 10-lb bag	@ .13c
Saltines	@ .15c	Purity Salt, 2-lb	@ .09c
S. S. Butters	@ .15c	Eagle Brand Milk	@ .18c
American Beauty Ginger Snaps	@ .28c	Sugar	@ .05c
Grated Pineapple	@ .18c	Sugar, XXXX	@ .08c
Egg Plums	@ .25c	Hershey's Cocoa, ½-lb	@ .15c
Sugar Corn	@ .11c	Hershey's Cocoa, 1-lb	@ .28c
Early June Peas	@ .13c	Walter Baker's Cocoa, ½-lb	@ .19c
Dill Pickles	@ .18c	Sunmaid Seeded Raisins	@ .18c
Golden Pumpkin	@ .13c	Sunmaid Seedless Raisins	@ .23c
Clark's Tomatoes, No. 3	@ .19c	Franco American Spaghetti	@ .09c
Tomato Catsup, 16 oz	@ .19c	Corn Meal, 10 lb	@ .24c
Catsup, 1 gal	@ .52c	Martha Washington Flour, 5-lb.	@ .27c
Cider Vinegar	@ .11c	George Washington Flour 24½-lb	@ $1.10
Blue Ribbon Mayonnaise	@ .26c	Good size, No. 7 Broom	@ .59c
Cream Dove Mustard, pint	@ .18c	Honey, 5-lb pail	@ .65c
Cream Dove Peanut Butter, pt.	@ .28c		

OTHER GROCERIES PROPORTIONATELY LOW

GOODWILL

Fri. **Fox Super Special** *Fri.*

"SHAME"

Romance rides on top of stirring adventure in a colorful story of unusual treatment.

"THE FOUR SEASONS"

Is a masterpiece of nature, made under the supervision of Dr. Raymond L. Ditmars, Curator of the New York Zoological Society.

Sat. **Somerville Players** *Sat.*

in "Fair and Warmer"

The Funniest Play Ever Written

MATINEE	EVENING
Any Seat 25c	Lower floor, 50c; Balcony, 35c
2:15—"Fair and Warmer"	"SHAME"—6:00
4:30—Photo Feature "SHAME"	"Fair and Warmer"—8:15

The Goodwill Theater, in Johnson City, was built by Endicott-Johnson in 1921. Only a small price was charged for the "best high grade, moral motion pictures and Vaudeville." Programs were augmented with the sounds of a professional quality, locally produced pipe organ. The theater was later renamed the En-Joie and for many years was left empty and deteriorating. Currently, there are plans to restore the building as a performing arts center. Pictured are the theater, from a distance, and an advertisement from the 1922 *EJ Workers Review*.

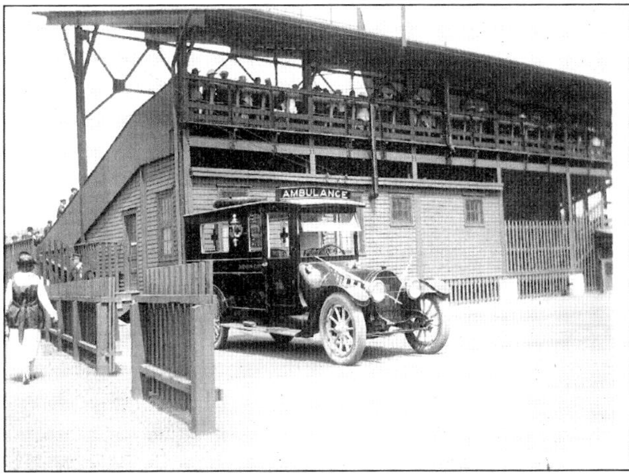

REPORT OF JOHNSON CITY
AMBULANCE SERVICE

From Oct. 1st to Oct. 25, inclusive

Number calls answered	426
Number miles traveled	1,593
Number hours spent	193

REPORT OF ENDICOTT
AMBULANCE SERVICE

From Oct. 1st to Oct. 25, inclusive

Number calls answered	270
Number miles traveled	1,232
Number hours spent	131
Total calls answered (End. and J. C.)	696
Total miles traveled (End. and J. C.)	2,825
Total number hours spent (End. and J. C.)	324

All the benefits given to Endicott-Johnson workers were paid with company profits. Explicit accounting of the costs were published monthly in the *EJ Workers' Review*. The corporation ambulance was made available to EJ workers and their families, and often to other members of the community. This ambulance was on duty and ready for emergencies at the Johnson City baseball field. The ambulance service report is from 1924.

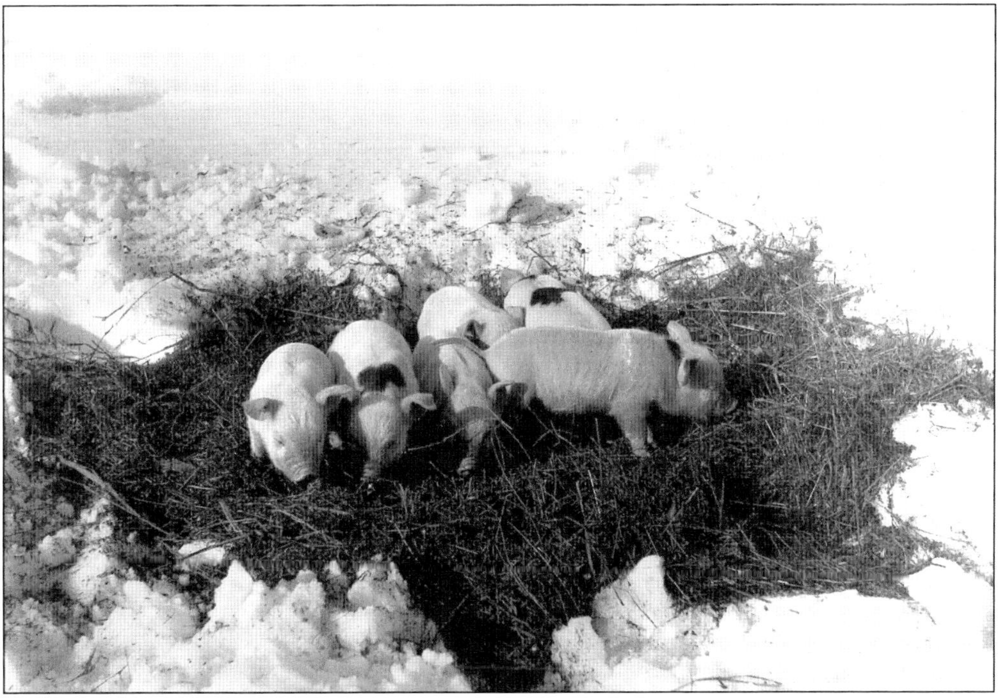

Ponderous porkers prevalent in Magic City could have read the headline. Henry Endicott seemed pleased with the EJ piggery in an article he wrote for *EJ Workers Magazine*, describing the location: "west of Oak Hill Avenue, a bit west of the mechanical department building, and north of the rail road tracks . . . we have 300 pigs currently. About 150 per year are used in the EJ restaurants . . . they are fed on leavings from the cafeterias. J.W. Chrysler is the current caretaker and butcher."

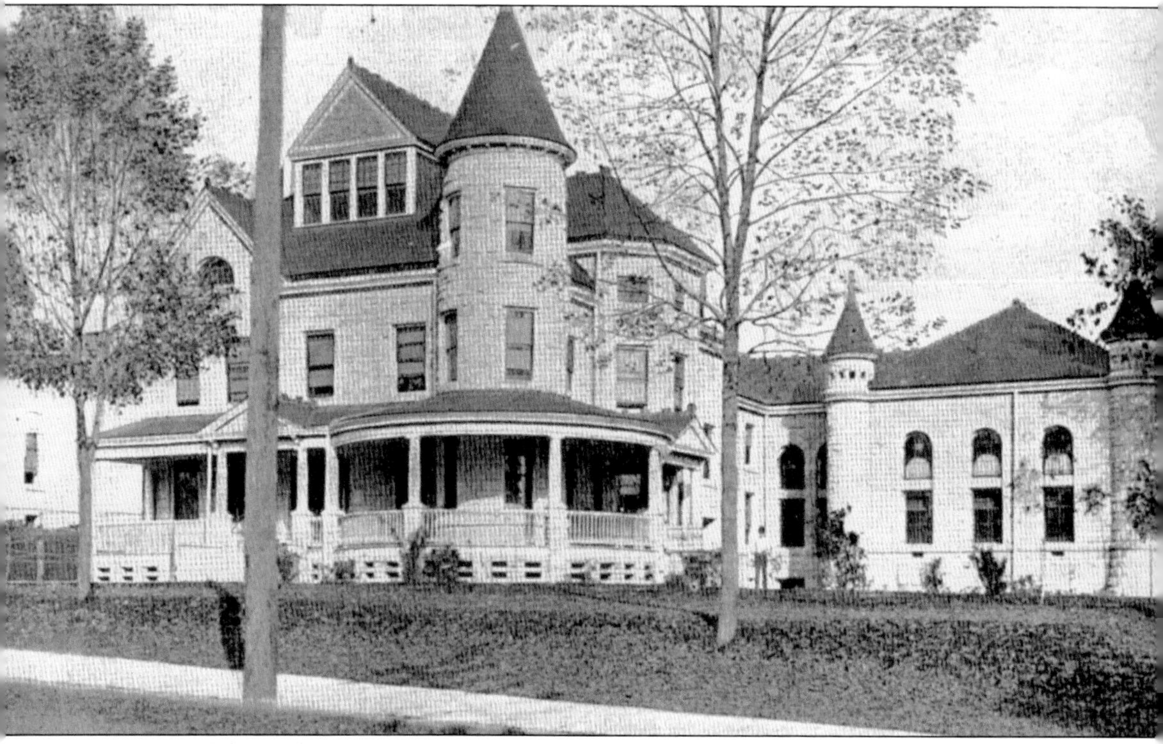

As part of the Endicott-Johnson goodwill policy, George F. Johnson would visit local jails and dispense 10-dollar gold pieces to the inmates. In June 1920, word of his charity had passed through the prison system, and an unusual request was received at EJ. A lifer who had served 28 years behind bars wrote, "I yearn and have a heart eating desire for a pair of tan shoes. I have never worn any but government brogues. It does not seem possible I shall ever get out. I would appreciate if you would stretch a point and make me a present of a pair of real shoes. If I live but ten more years I will still have those shoes. There has been 10,000 prisoners come & gone since I been here . . . in the last 18 years we has been numbered from one to 11,020. I am #22." Endicott-Johnson sent tan shoes to federal prisoner #22 the next day.

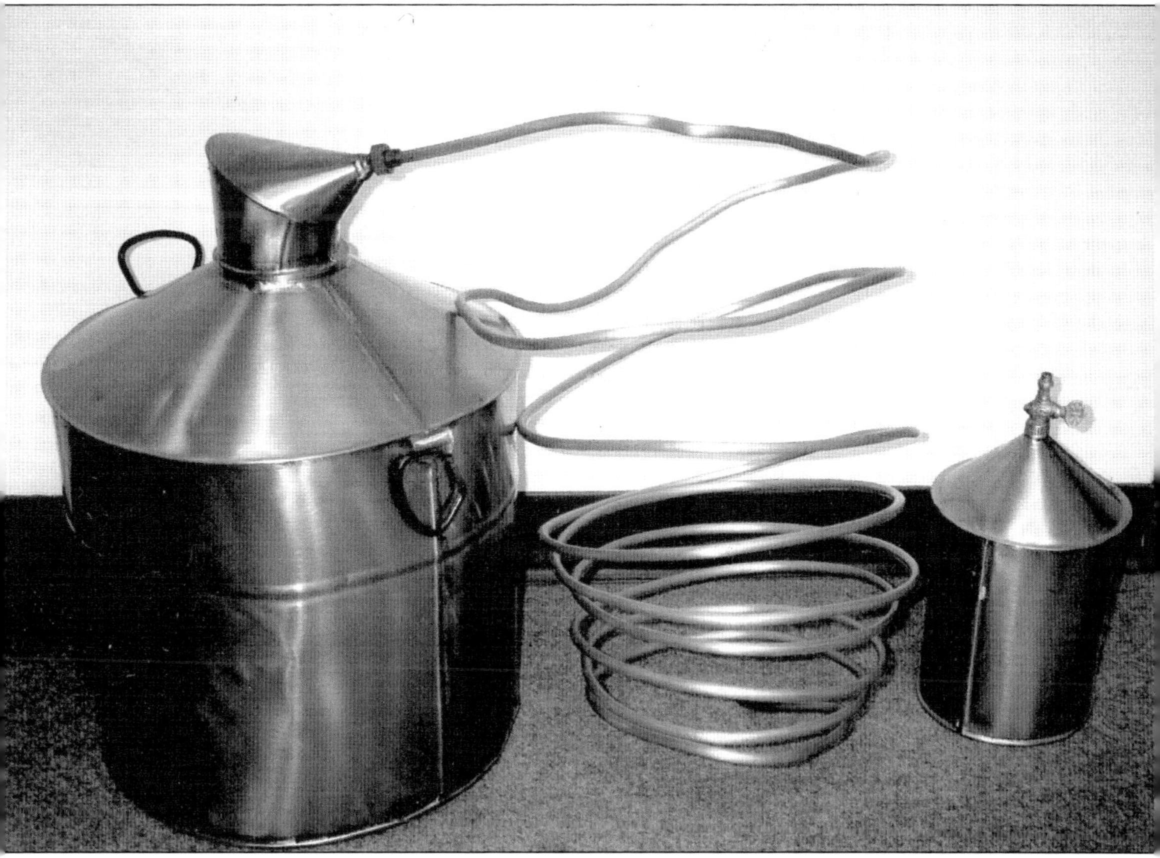

In 1919, George F. Johnson commented on Prohibition: "I told New York Senator Lusk I believed the present Prohibition law (which gives to the wealthy man the right to all the 'booze' he has been able to store, which denies the poor man even a glass of beer of $2^1/4$ percent alcohol), would create more trouble, more opposition, and make the working man more ugly and sore than any thing which has happened in twenty years in this country. It is a serious mistake to take away the poor man's beer. It is the rottenest legislation—bound to bring the worst possible results. We never had much drunkenness before, but now the stuff the people drink makes them crazy." In 1921, the local newspaper reported, "Bootleggers fight back! Angered by police search and destroy tactics against stills and contraband liquor . . . bootleggers started an uprising by giving their customers on the North Side of Endicott large quantities of intoxicants free—and sending into the streets dozens of drunken men looking to fight."

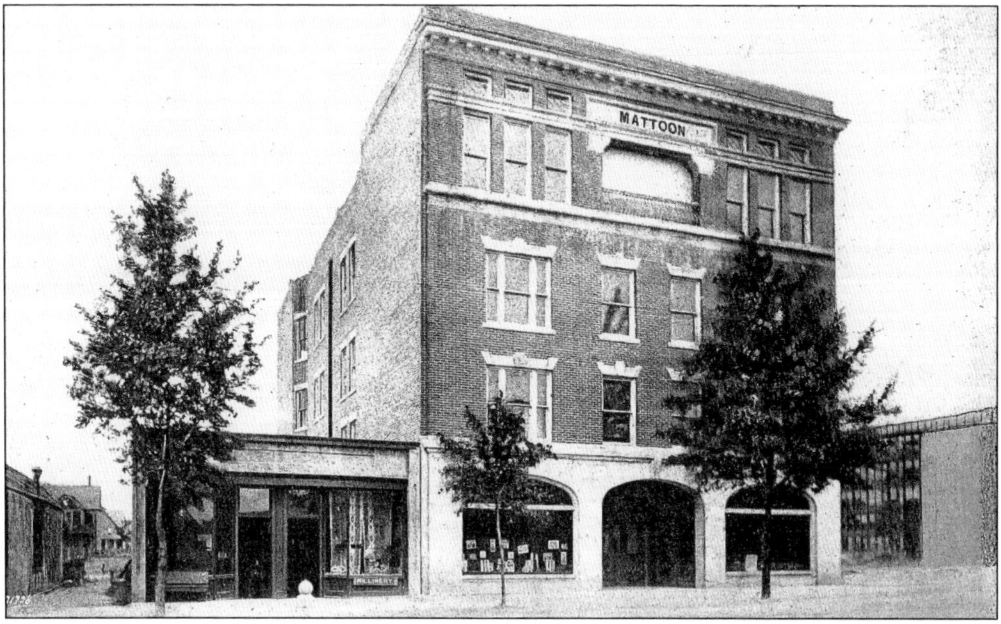

In 1915, a community library was established on Washington Avenue in Endicott in part of a building owned by Lou Mattoon, a personal friend of George F. Johnson. The facility was established at the urging of Chester B. Lord, treasurer of Endicott-Johnson. It was replaced in 1918. Johnson and his wife donated the home formerly owned by Harlow Bundy of IBM to serve as a library and community center; it was named the Ideal Home Library. During the war the library was a distribution center for the War Savings, Liberty Loan, and Red Cross campaigns. It also held food conservation lectures and collected 2,500 books for soldiers.

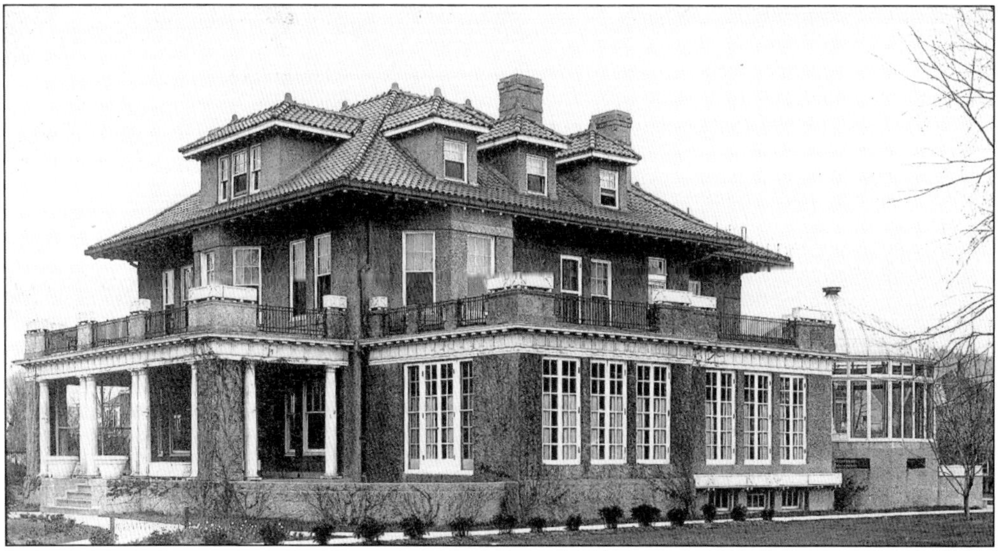

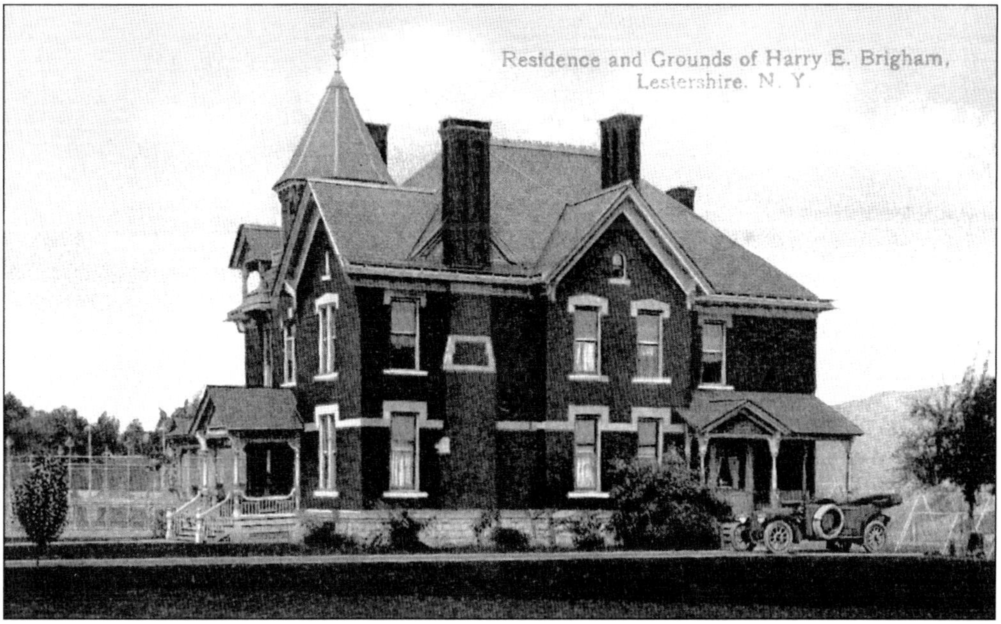

Another library, simply named Your Home Library, was opened on Main Street in Johnson City in the Brigham home. Some Endicott-Johnson executives were skeptical that libraries would be wanted by the common people, as they were not regarded as "a reading population." A compromise was reached by promoting the buildings as meeting places, in hopes that an individual would pick up a book inadvertently and be enticed to read. This photograph of a woman reading a magazine at the Endicott library was taken in 1916.

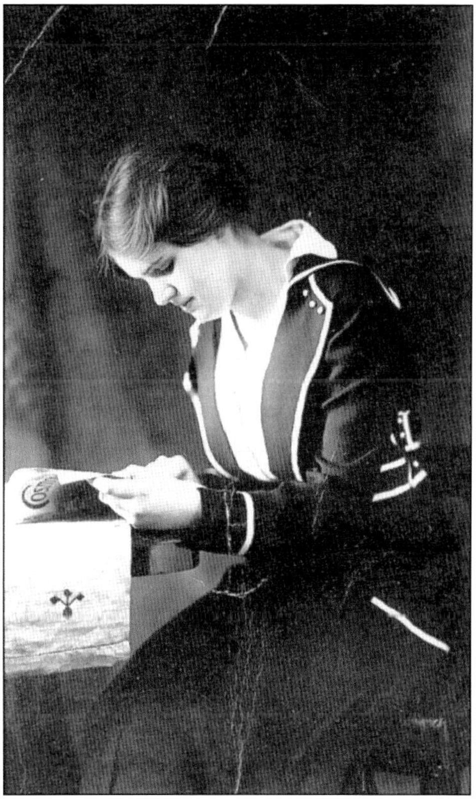

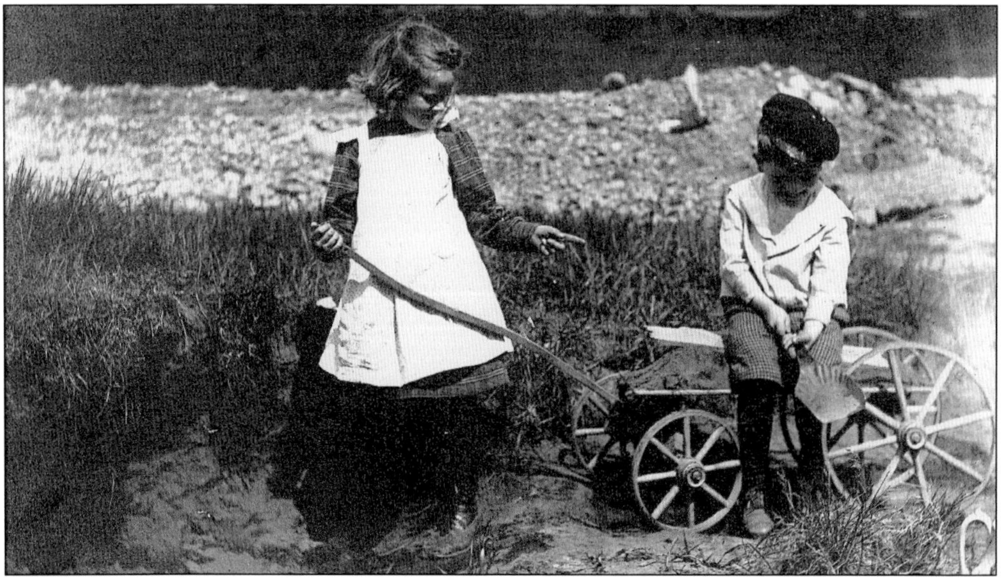

The Endicott-Johnson bond with children of workers began at birth, and the children soon became useful as ambassadors in the community. When EJ faced labor union problems, public schools cooperated to thwart the invading union by canceling classes for a day so that all children could make posters and pass petitions calling for support of the EJ management team. Children born to EJ employees were considered "future shoe town laborers." Every issue of the *EJ Workers Magazine* contained photographs of EJ children.

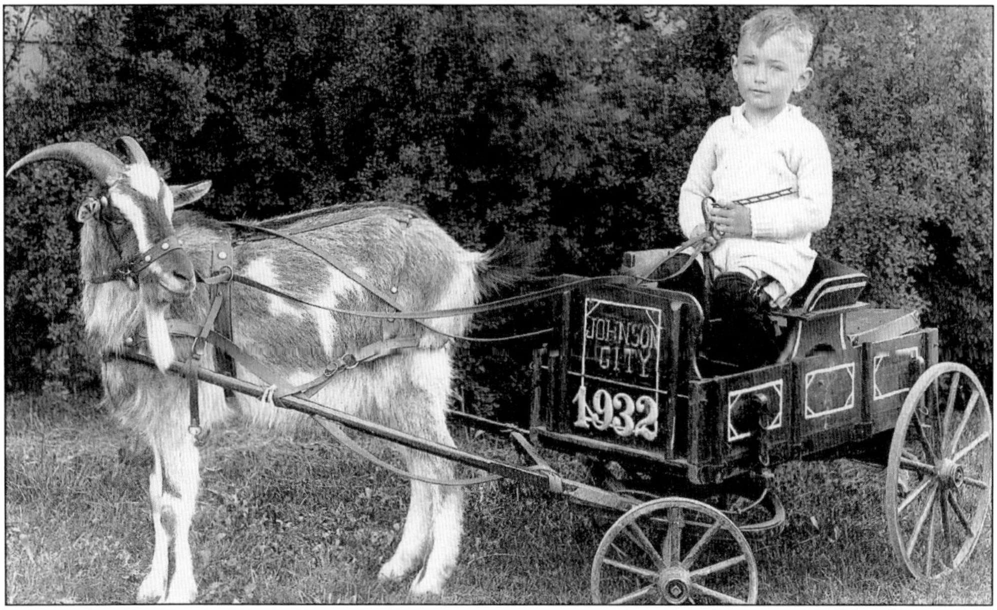

Workers in the Endicott-Johnson plants were not hit quite as hard as the rest of the country during the Great Depression of the 1930s. Though hours were cut and the company had to charge each employee five percent on salaries for medical care, everyone was kept employed, so occasionally there were a few cents extra for a photograph of a child. After the economy improved, all workers were reimbursed for the amount taken from their checks during the Depression.

A 1924 *EJ Workers' Review* article noted that "at EJ lovers and marriage are as popular as shoes," and lunch hour "spooning" was OK with EJ. George F. Johnson stated that "a man is not a man until he has a wife and children. We will give housing preference to married men with families to obtain houses built by EJ." The purpose of this policy was to encourage a stable work force. This family photograph is c. 1936. The average pay in 1938 was $24.44 per week.

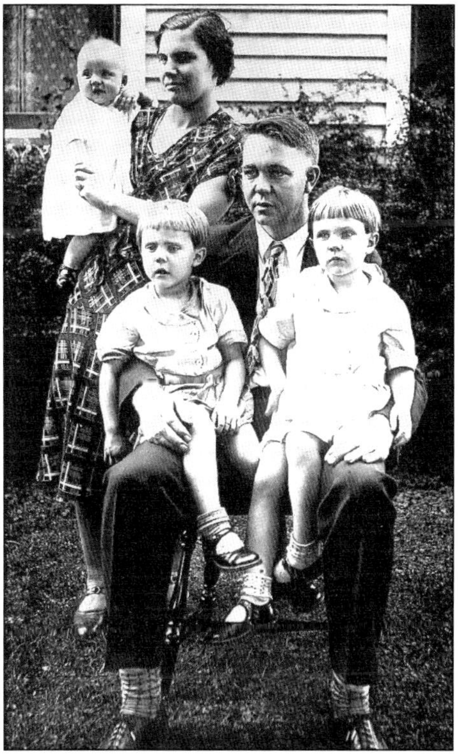

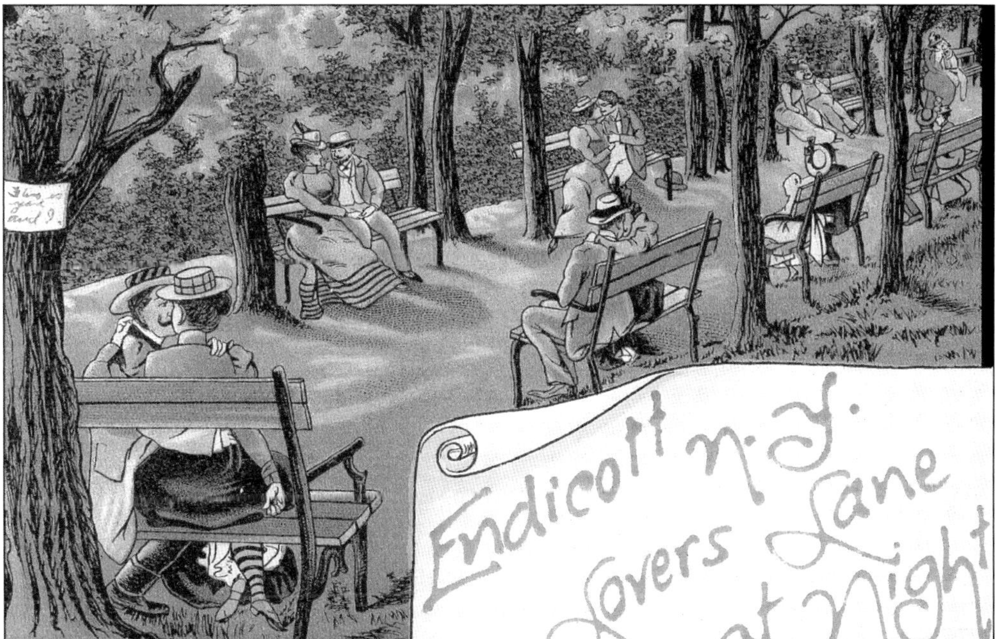

When George F. Johnson heard that the police force was chasing young people away from a popular lovers lane known as Round Top or Round Hill in Endicott, he purchased the site for a community park, stipulating that it would always be open for stargazing—without the presence of the law.

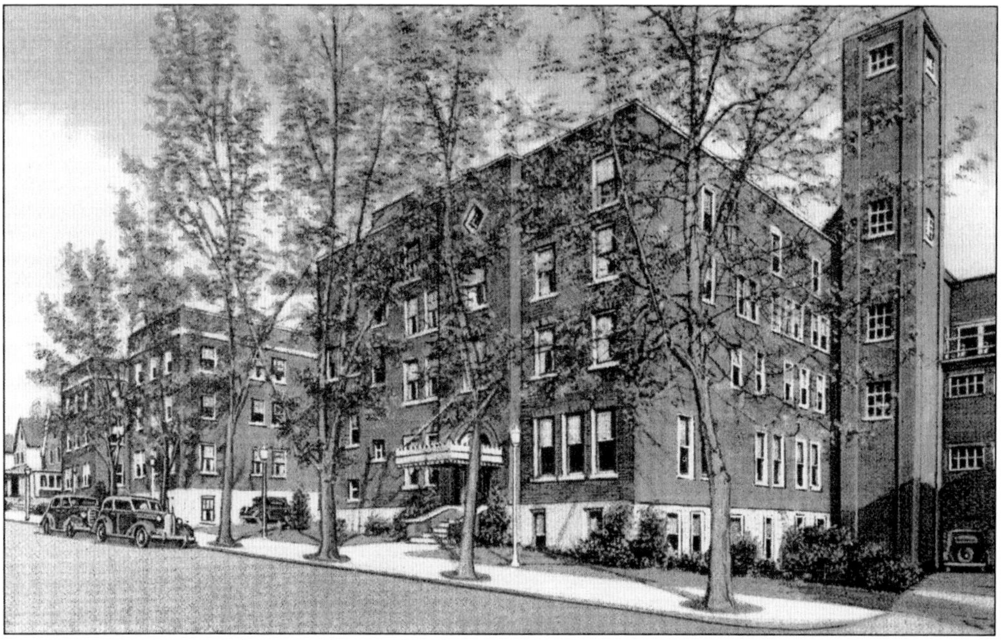

In 1905, George F. Johnson donated a house in Lestershire to begin the Kings Daughters Hospital. Dr. Charles S. Wilson purchased the business several years later and moved it to Harrison Street, renaming it Lestershire Hospital. In 1927, Endicott-Johnson purchased the hospital from the Wilson estate and deeded it to the hospital's board of managers. It was renamed in honor of Dr. Wilson. Pictured is Wilson Memorial Hospital.

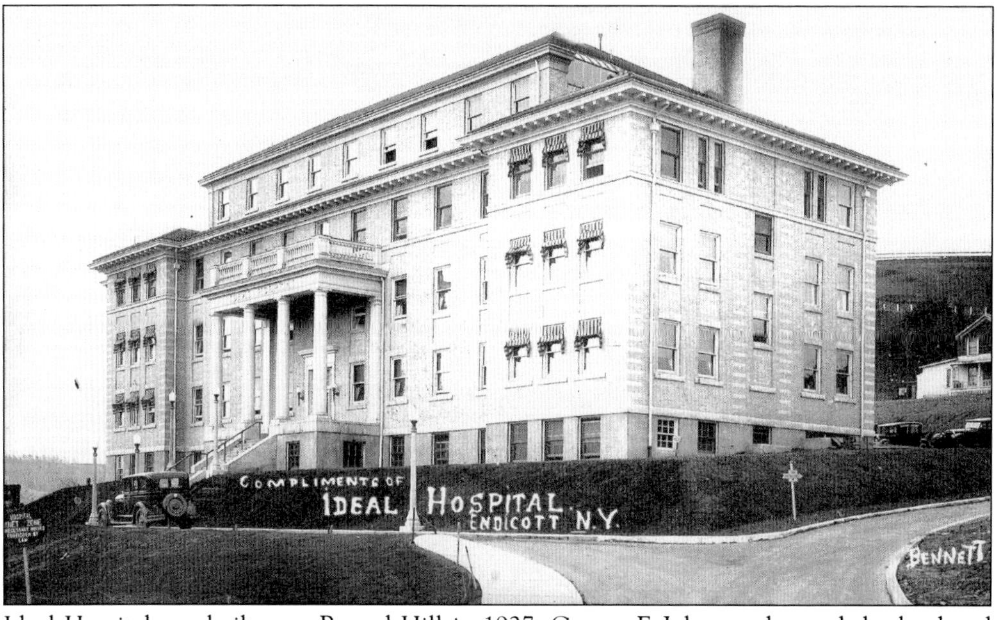

Ideal Hospital was built near Round Hill in 1927. George F. Johnson donated the land and $150,000 toward construction. The building is now a senior living center. Health care was a priority in the Endicott-Johnson plan. In one of Johnson's letters to workers, he stated, "The richest man in the world is the healthy poor man and we have happy workers in this Valley of Fair Play."

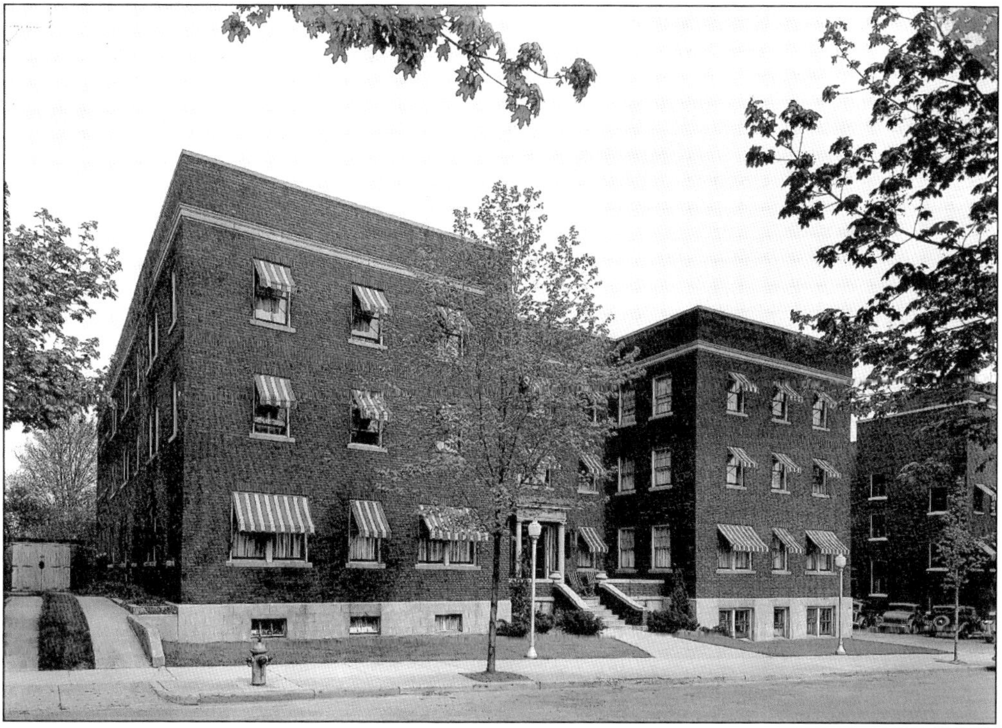

A nurses' residence was donated to Wilson Hospital by C. Fred Johnson in memory of his wife, Ida. Pictured are the exterior and interior of the residence in Johnson City. Ida Johnson's portrait is shown above the fireplace.

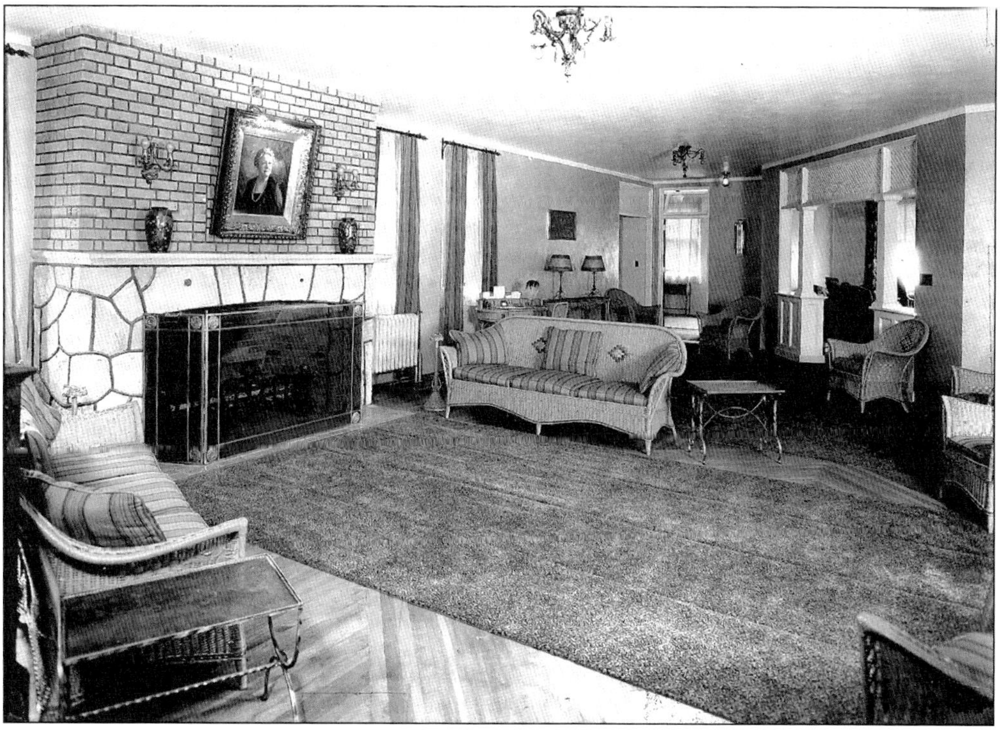

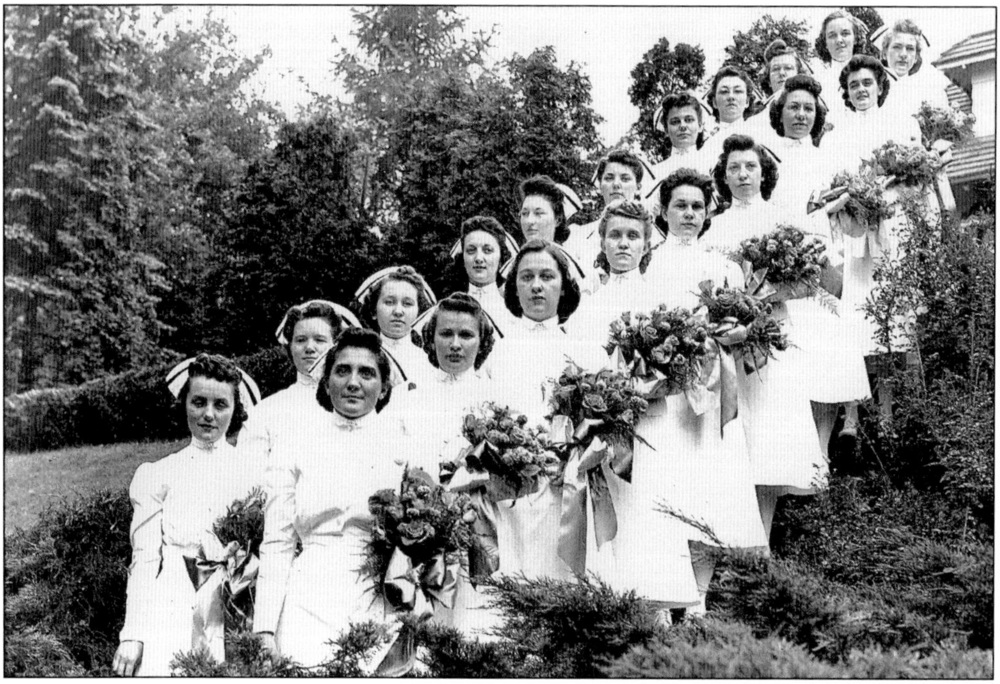

The Wilson School of Nursing graduating class attends a graduation tea party in the formal garden of Mrs. Charles F. Johnson, on Main Street in Johnson City. The tea party was a yearly event hosted with a great deal of elegance to honor the graduating nurses.

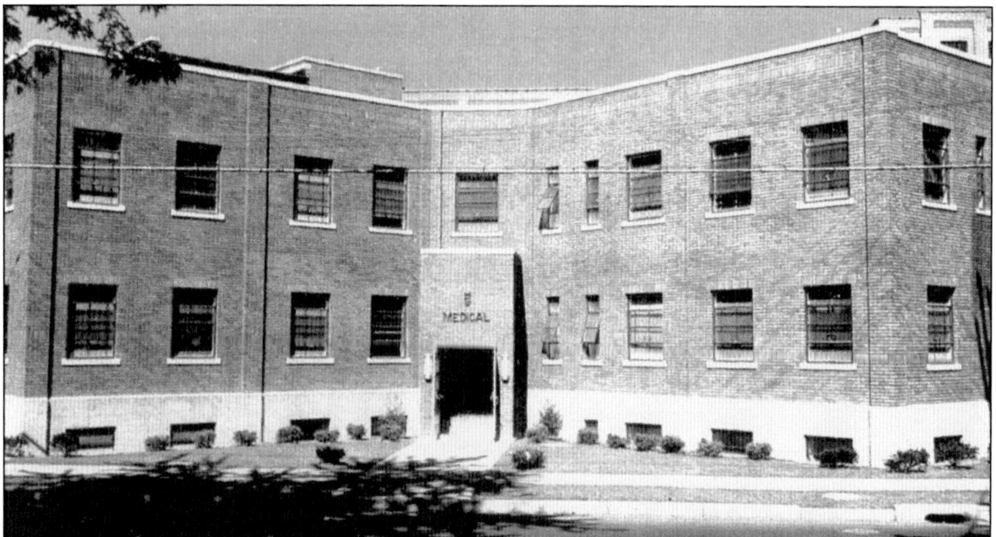

Endicott-Johnson opened a medical clinic in the sole leather tannery in 1917. A full-time nurse and doctor were hired. At the same time, another doctor was engaged to make home visits to the employees. The official EJ medical service began in 1918 and was the first established by a major American company. In 1955, more than 50,000 workers and their families were covered by a comprehensive policy, including dental, medical, and eye care. In 1940, a large medical building was constructed on North Street in Endicott in the shape of a cross. It remained in operation until EJ began to disappear in 1967–1968; medical services were discontinued at that time.

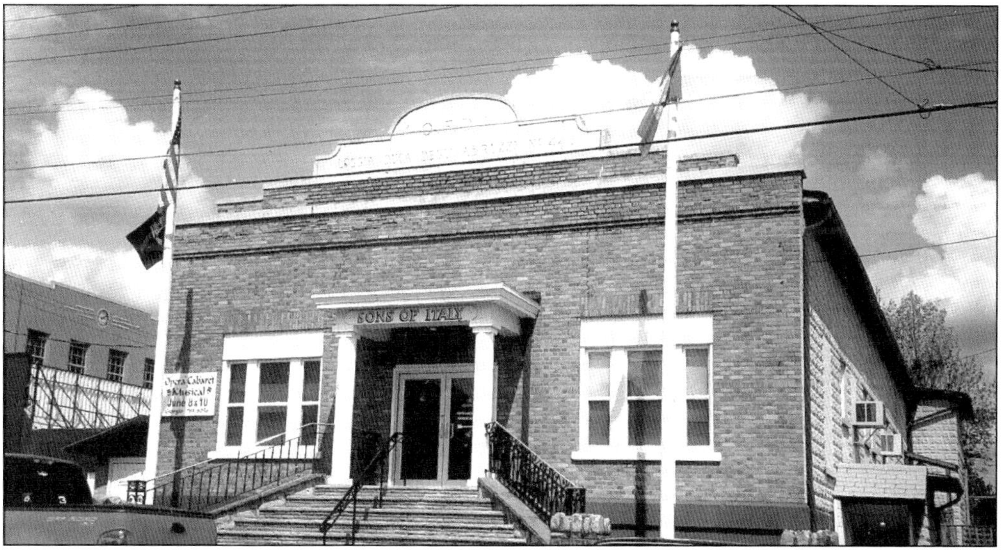

According to an article in the 1920 *EJ Workers' Review*: "One of the most progressive organizations of the New Americans is the Loggia Duca Degil Abruzzi No. 433—Sons of Italy Lodge. Of its 273 members a majority are EJ employees." When a need arose for larger space, George F. Johnson donated three large lots on Odell Avenue. The Johnsons were elected honorary members of the society. George F. was also conferred the honor as Cavaliere of the Order of the Crown of Italy by a representative of the king of Italy for his help and friendship to Italians—an honor rarely granted to non-Italians.

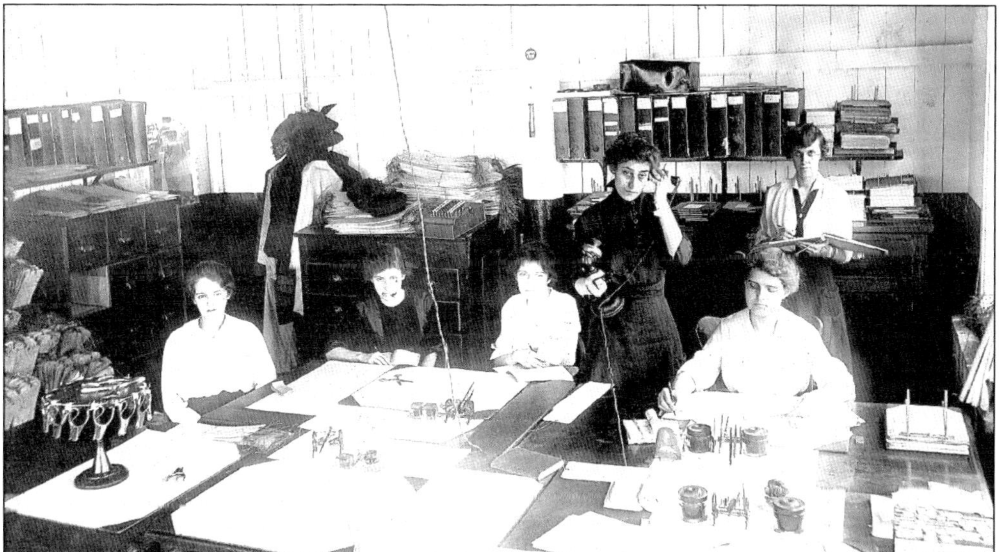

In 1892, the *Binghamton Democrat* printed a letter from the local manager of a clerical staff (not from Endicott-Johnson): "I would rather have two good men—women are more ornamental than useful—nice but very little good at business and women under 20 are no good at all to the management—they need watching—especially the good looking ones—the best typewriters I ever hired were over 35 and unattractive." Endicott-Johnson tried to give women a fair deal; there was, however, still controversy about keeping a woman on the payroll after she married. This is an EJ office c. 1915.

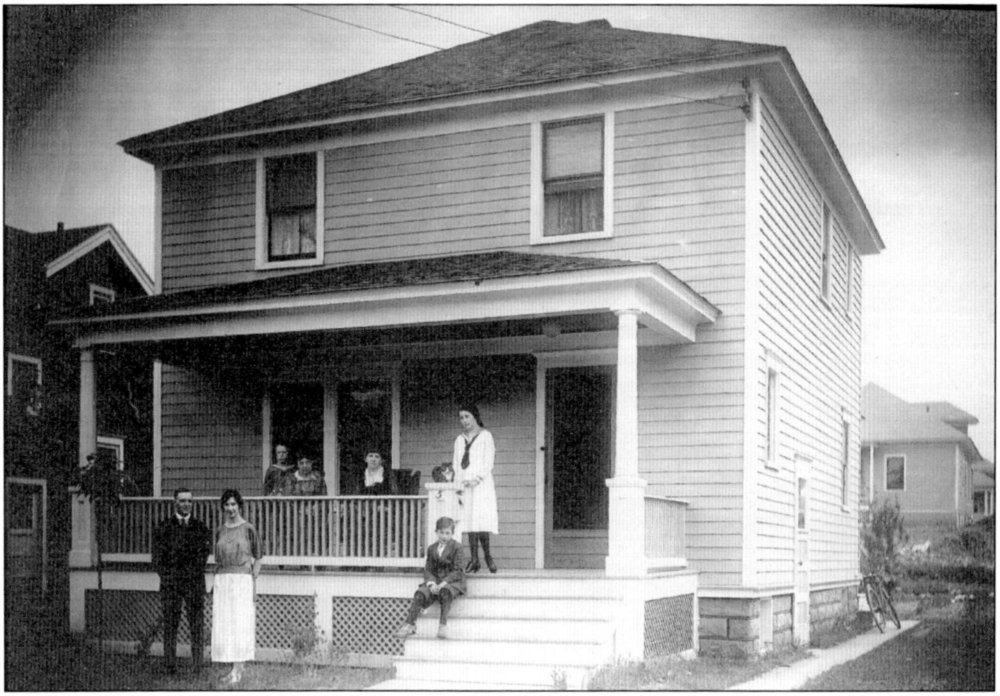

The Endicott-Johnson factories depended upon an immigrant labor force. The new arrivals needed safe, reasonable housing to keep them from the clutches of "rent hog" landlords. In 1904, EJ began building homes sold to workers at cost. A small sum was taken from paychecks each week for the mortgage. A four-room, one-bath home cost about $2,100. Housing settlements mushroomed around EJ factories, resembling early feudal villages. Affordable living was a central factor in George F. George F. Johnson's plan for a "million dollar temple of industry." In 1936, Johnson responded to Pres. Franklin D. Roosevelt's praise of Endicott: "so far we have caused more than 2,500 homes to be built in this valley . . . not exactly as fine as the White House, not quite as fine as my home, but plenty good enough." Johnson also stated, "the home is the answer to Bolshevism, radicalism, socialism and all other 'isms.' Home is the basis of all security." There were a few snags in perfection: the south side of the village of Endicott, called Endwell Terrace, began with deed restrictions allowing only Anglo-Saxons and Irish to live in the area.

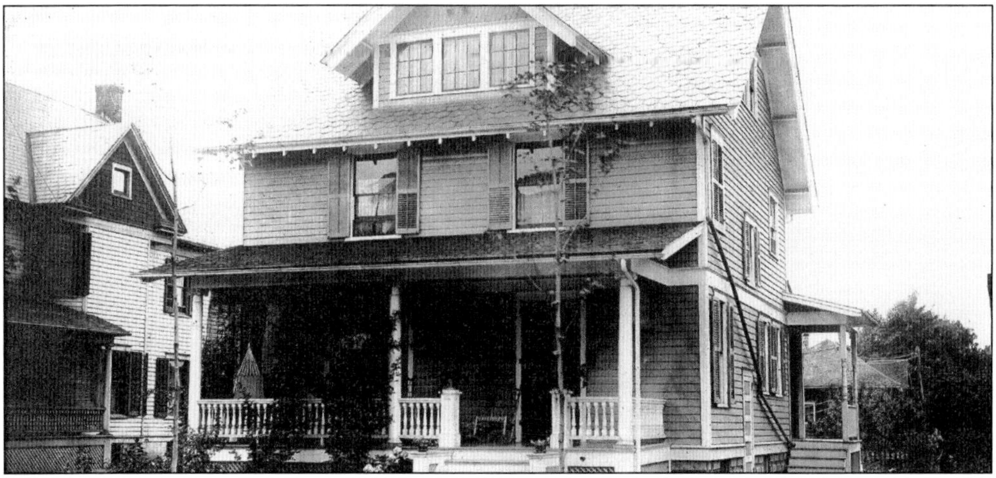

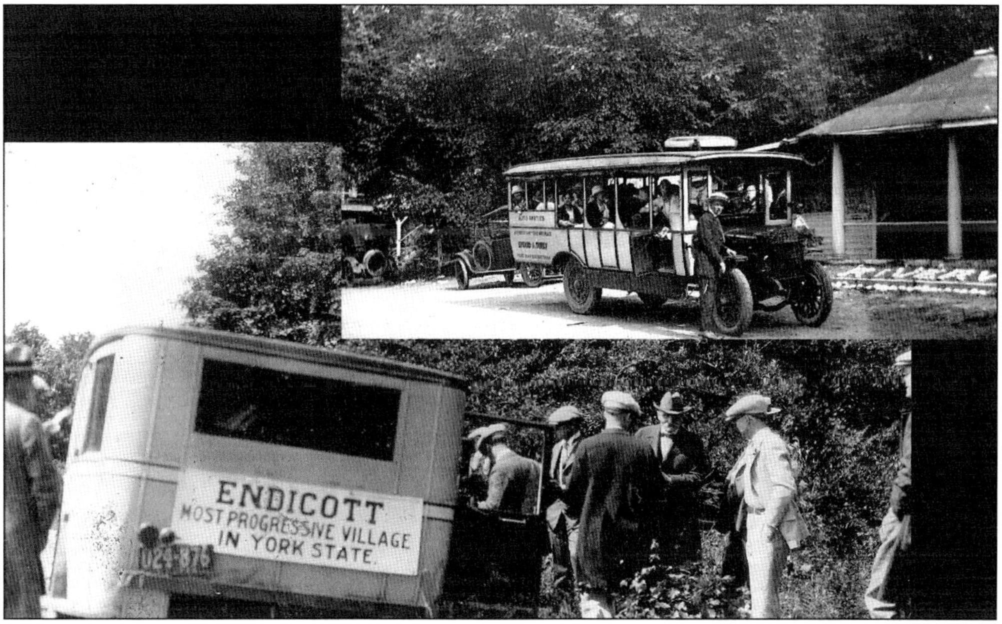

In 1926, the Endicott Board of Trade sent businessmen on a trip along the East Coast to promote the benefits of living and working in the Magic City of Endicott. The men traveled in a motor coach, stopping at cities along the way to encourage a move to "the biggest little town on the Globe" and the most "progressive village in New York State." Signs in the window proclaimed "Ideal Industrial Conditions."

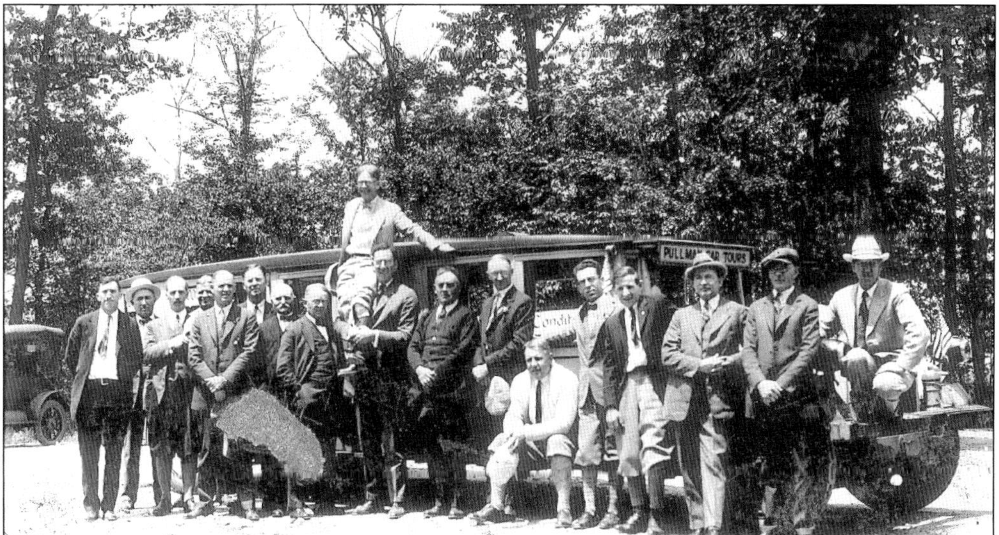

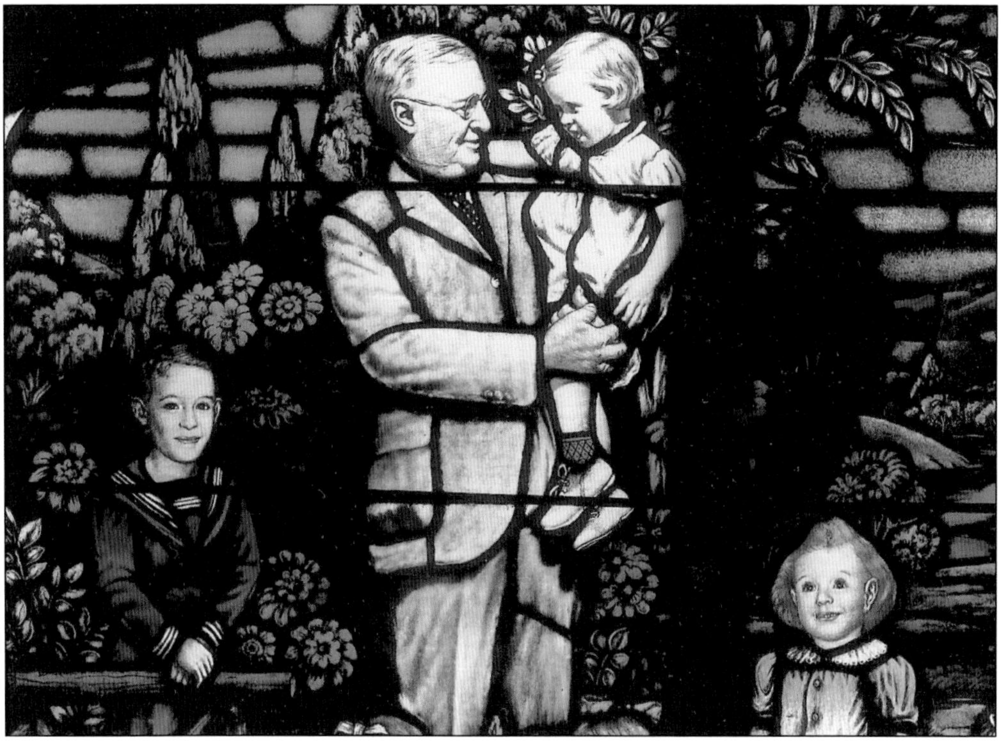

Because of the high esteem in which family and community held George F. Johnson, a stained-glass window was commissioned showing Johnson in a garden with children. The 10- by 20-foot window was placed in the First Methodist Church in Endicott in 1945. Done in brilliant cathedral glass colors, it remained near the altar for several decades. As the Johnson mystique began to fade, the gigantic work of art (strangely resembling concepts of Jesus in the garden with children), was moved to a less prominent position over the McKinley Avenue entrance.

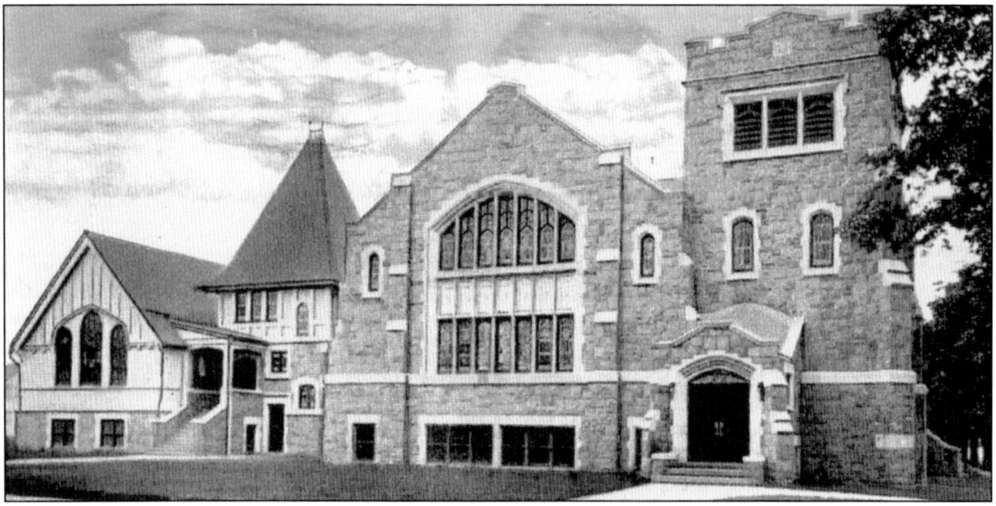

In 1919, the Presbyterian church on the corner of Floral Avenue requested financial assistance from George F. Johnson, who agreed to donate to the building fund provided that the church was constructed in Johnson City instead of Binghamton. Therefore, the municipal boundary lines were dabbled with, and the church near the EJ arch was built in Johnson City.

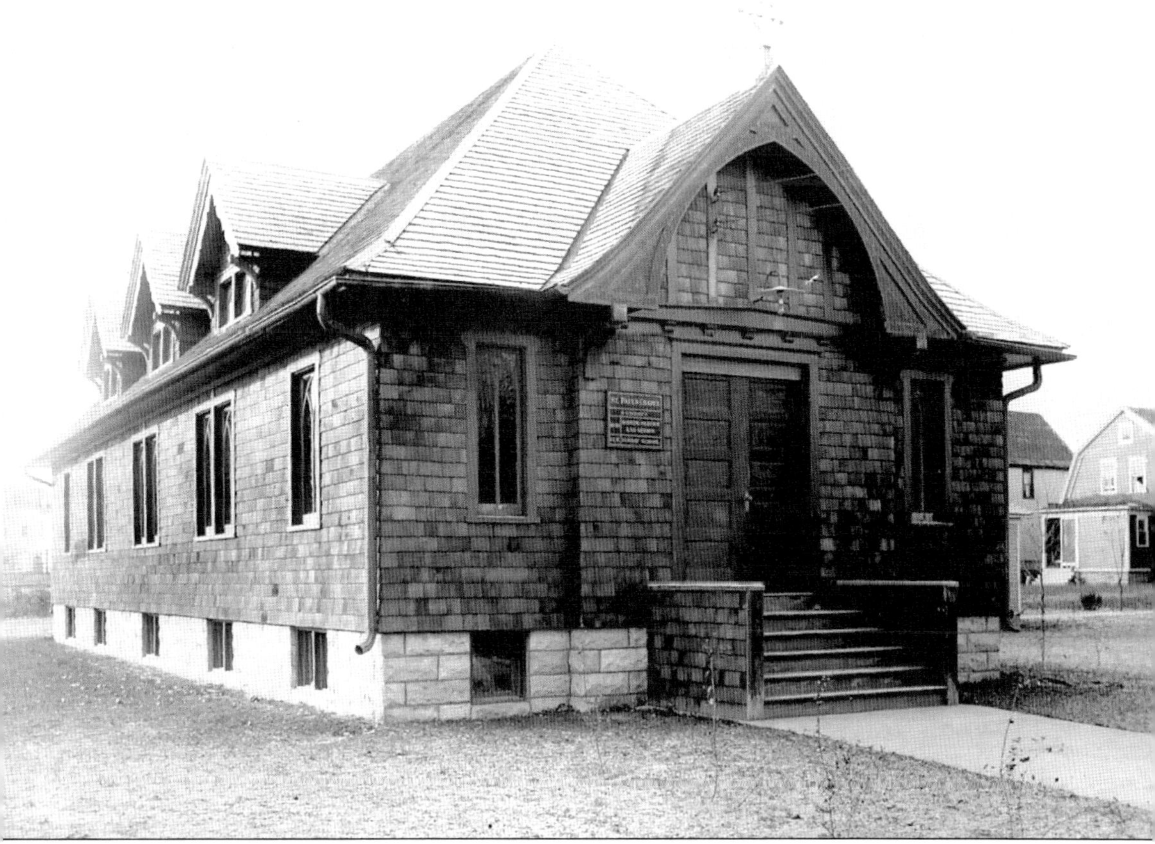

St. Paul's Episcopal Church began in 1909 in Harvey's Hall in Endicott. In 1911, George F. Johnson donated three lots on which a chapel was to be built. In 1952, construction commenced on a new larger brick structure. In an example of the community's goodwill between people of different faiths, Temple Beth-El offered room in its building so that St. Paul's could continue services during the building of the new church. This photograph is of the original church in 1911. George F. Johnson and his company donated generously to many religious organizations, but he did admit to some doubts as to their usefulness: "I have never known any good to be accomplished by the efforts of ministers of the Gospel to clean up cities . . . they are well meaning but men of poor judgment . . . to interfere with harmless pleasures. Rather than deal with real evil they close moving pictures and prohibit sports on Sunday."

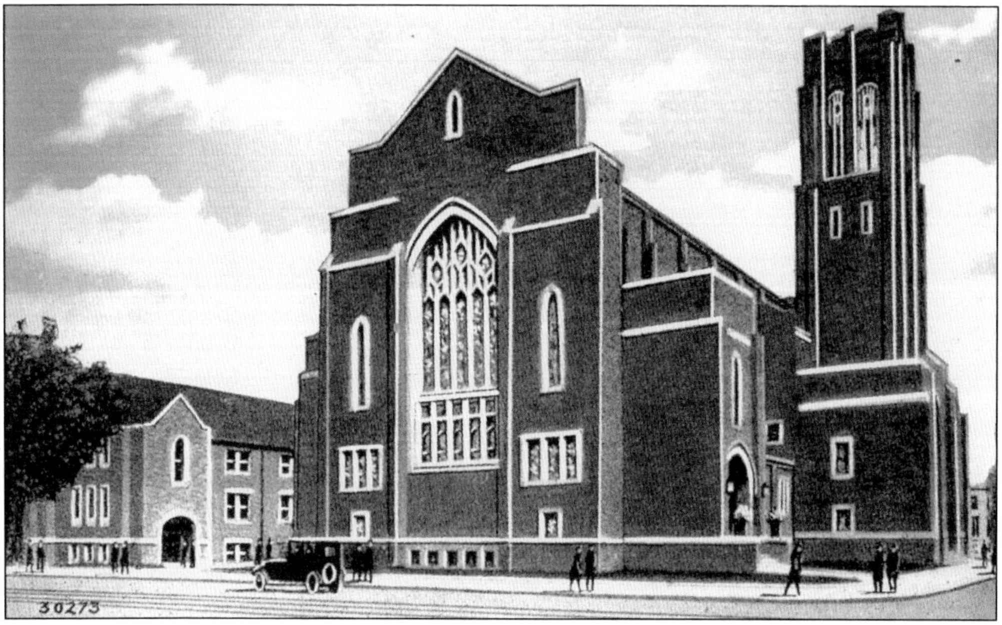

In 1890, the first services for the Lestershire Methodist Episcopal Church were held in the packing room of the Lester Shoe Factory. George F. Johnson arranged for the space; boot boxes were used as pews and pulpit. Later, G.H. Lester donated two lots on Main Street to the church, and a small wooden structure was soon completed. In 1916, George F. and C. Fred Johnson offered to finance a large part of the cost of $438,000 for a new edifice provided that the church was named after their mother, Sarah Jane Johnson. The grand new Gothic-designed church was dedicated in 1927. The carillonic tower bells were installed in the great tower of the church as a memorial to those who lost their lives in World War II; the music can be heard within a three-to-four-mile range. The church also contains a $25,000 pipe organ, donated by the widow of Harry L. Johnson.

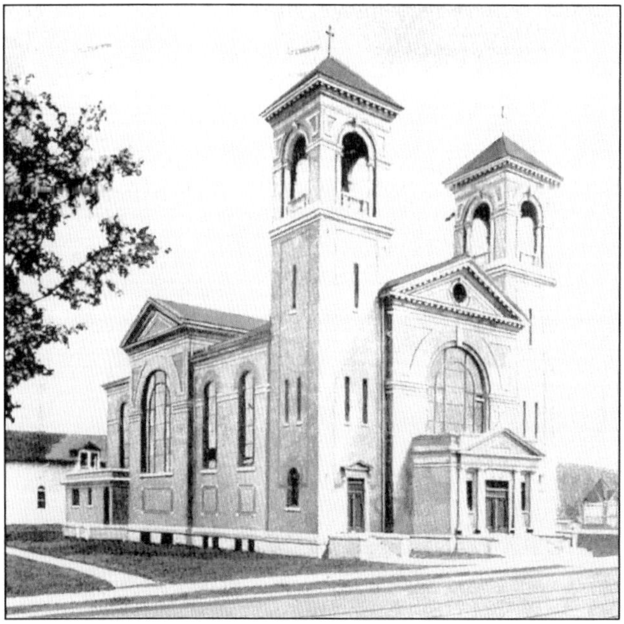

George F. Johnson and his wife donated a magnificent set of chimes to St. James Church in Johnson City. The chimes were dedicated in 1917 for the community to enjoy forever. Many of the bells are named in honor of patron saints of the Johnson family. (It has been reported that George F. gave a costly set of chimes to a leading church in Johnson City, with the stipulation that at 9:00 every night, all year round, the chimes would toll his favorite song, "Auld Lang Syne.")

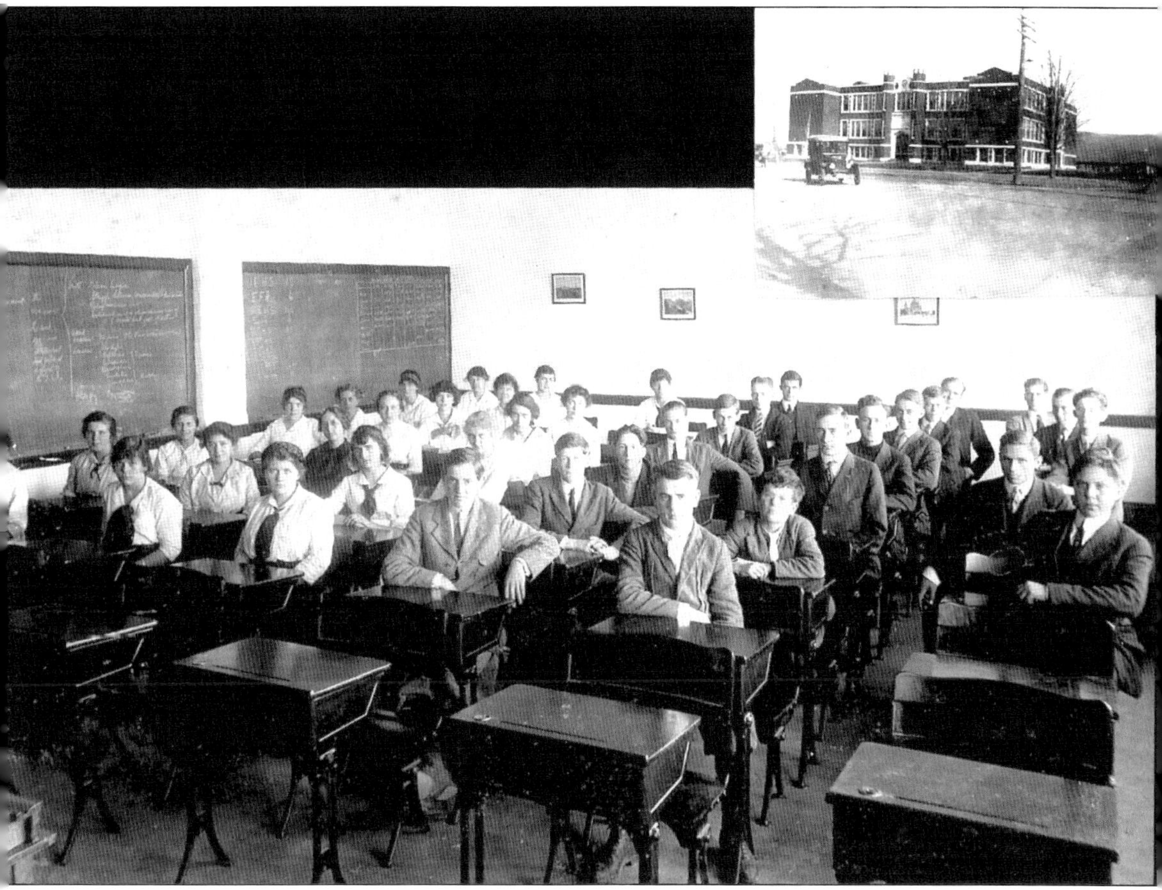

George F. Johnson once said that "higher education is a waste of time for a man in business," but he did admire the local school system for basic learning, stressing the benefits of the "democratizing effects" of public schools. He deplored efforts that separated children into groups of any kind and even refused Endicott-Johnson aid to parochial schools. He also said, "the only university needed is work, books, people. You can get all the education you can ever use from these." He once heard a college professor tell a class that "a college education is a must if you don't want to spend life working with your hands." To Johnson, this was advice to be nonproductive. When Syracuse University offered him an honorary doctorate, he refused it. Another Johnson quote was, "men do not follow knowledge, they follow personality." This attitude probably was a factor in the downfall of the company. Johnson's heirs to power did not have his business acumen, and in accord with the his dictates, also did not have formal business educations. Pictured is a Union-Endicott High School class c. the 1920s.

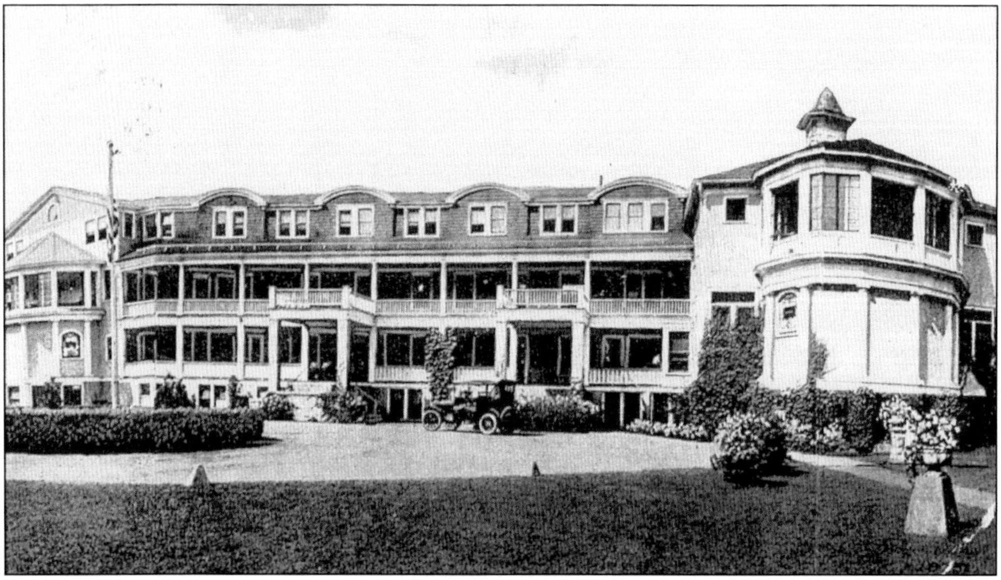

The 1920s were difficult for George F. Johnson, as he fought intolerance and bigotry. Many organizations requested financial aid from Endicott-Johnson, but occasionally assistance was soundly refused. In 1925, Johnson wrote to the Practical Bible Training School on Riverside Drive in Johnson City, "No good will come from your suggested interview. Our interest in the Practical Bible Training School came to a very sudden death when I realized that it is teaching doctrines of hate for other denominations."

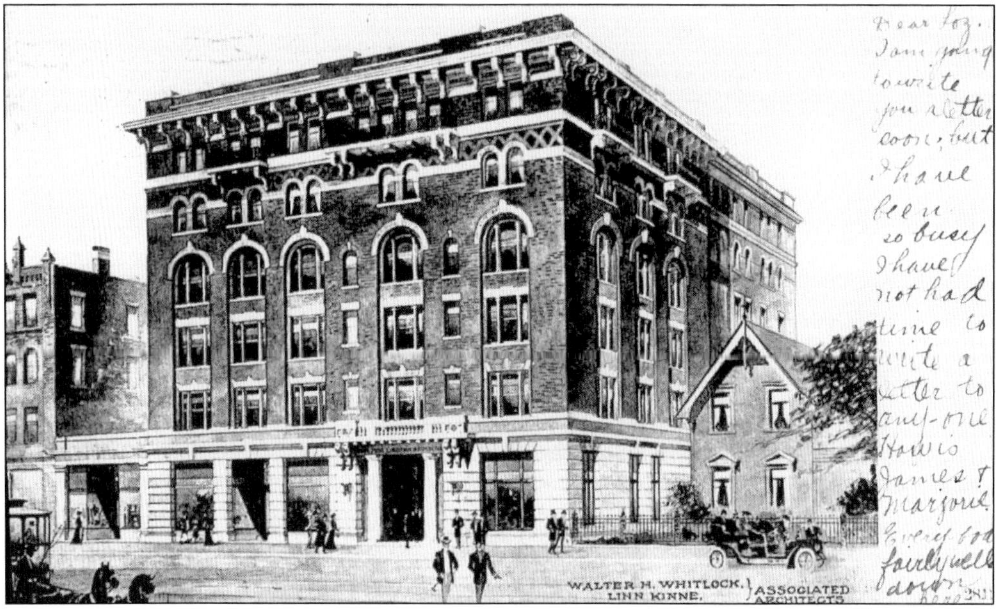

Endicott-Johnson, in the form of George F. Johnson, was usually pleased to contribute to community projects. However, there were exceptions. He refused to give anything to the YMCA, stating, "Any organization which bars Greek, Jew, or Gentile gets none of my money while I am awake and conscious . . . it is a sectarian organization . . . I haven't any money for a public organization that draws the line on religious belief." At that time, Catholics were among those banned from using YMCA facilities.

Endicott-Johnson was a veritable United Nations of workers. In 1920, at least 40 percent of EJ employees were immigrants. Among the 20,000 workers in 1955, more than 38 nationalities were represented. Through the local libraries, EJ offered classes in language, cooking, and naturalization. The October 1920 *EJ Workers' Review* has become a classic illustration of the blended community. Shown are workers posing for a photograph in native costume.

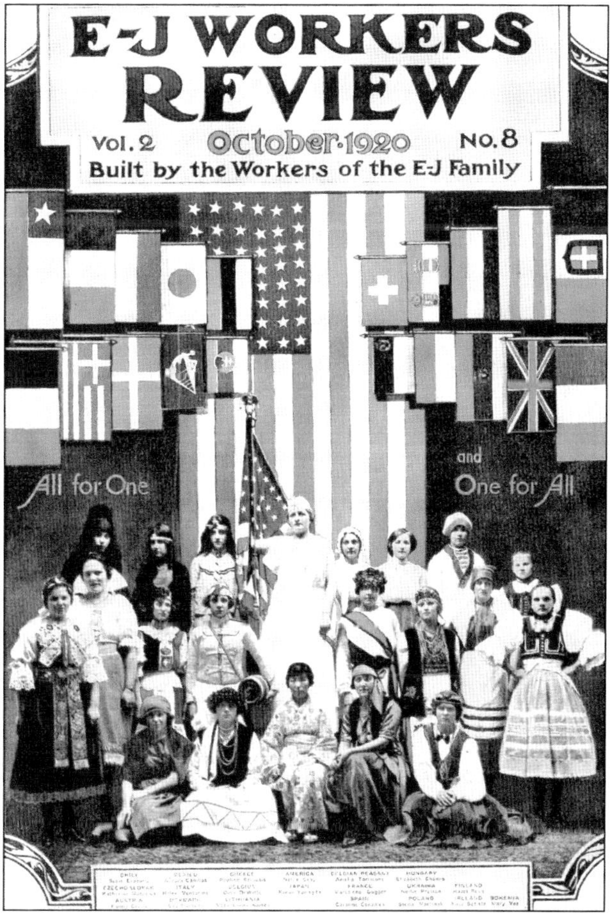

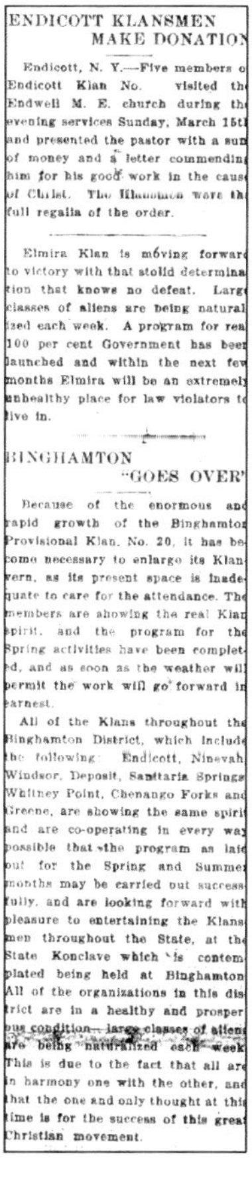

ENDICOTT KLANSMEN MAKE DONATIO[N]

Endicott, N. Y.—Five members o[f] Endicott Klan No. visited th[e] Endwell M. E. church during th[e] evening services Sunday, March 15t[h] and presented the pastor with a su[m] of money and a letter commendin[g] him for his good work in the caus[e] of Christ. The Klansmen wore th[e] full regalia of the order.

Elmira Klan is moving forwar[d] to victory with that stolid determina[-] tion that knows no defeat. Larg[e] classes of aliens are being natural[-] ized each week. A program for rea[l] 100 per cent Government has bee[n] launched and within the next fe[w] months Elmira will be an extremel[y] unhealthy place for law violators t[o] live in.

[B]INGHAMTON "GOES OVER"

Because of the enormous an[d] rapid growth of the Binghamto[n] Provisional Klan, No. 20, it has be[-] come necessary to enlarge its Klan[-] vern, as its present space is inade[-] quate to care for the attendance. Th[e] members are showing the real Kla[n] spirit, and the program for th[e] Spring activities have been complet[-] ed, and as soon as the weather wil[l] permit the work will go forward i[n] earnest.

All of the Klans throughout th[e] Binghamton District, which includ[e] the following: Endicott, Ninevah, Windsor, Deposit, Sanitaria Springs, Whitney Point, Chenango Forks an[d] Greene, are showing the same spiri[t] and are co-operating in every wa[y] possible that the program as lai[d] out for the Spring and Summe[r] months may be carried out success[-] fully, and are looking forward wit[h] pleasure to entertaining the Klans[-] men throughout the State, at th[e] State Konclave which is contem[-] plated being held at Binghamton. All of the organizations in this dis[-] trict are in a healthy and prosper[-] ous condition—large classes of alien[s] are being naturalized each week. This is due to the fact that all ar[e] in harmony one with the other, an[d] that the one and only thought at thi[s] time is for the success of this grea[t] Christian movement.

During the 1920s, Binghamton was the New York State headquarters for an organization that promoted hate on the basis of heritage, religion, and color—the Ku Klux Klan. Endicott-Johnson was a target of the Klan because of its large number of immigrant workers. In 1926, the Klan threatened a nationwide boycott of EJ products. George F. Johnson, the *Binghamton Sun* run by William Hill, and Franklin D. Roosevelt all fought against bigotry, combining to defeat the local Klan. Pictured is a Klan newsletter, the *Vigilance*.

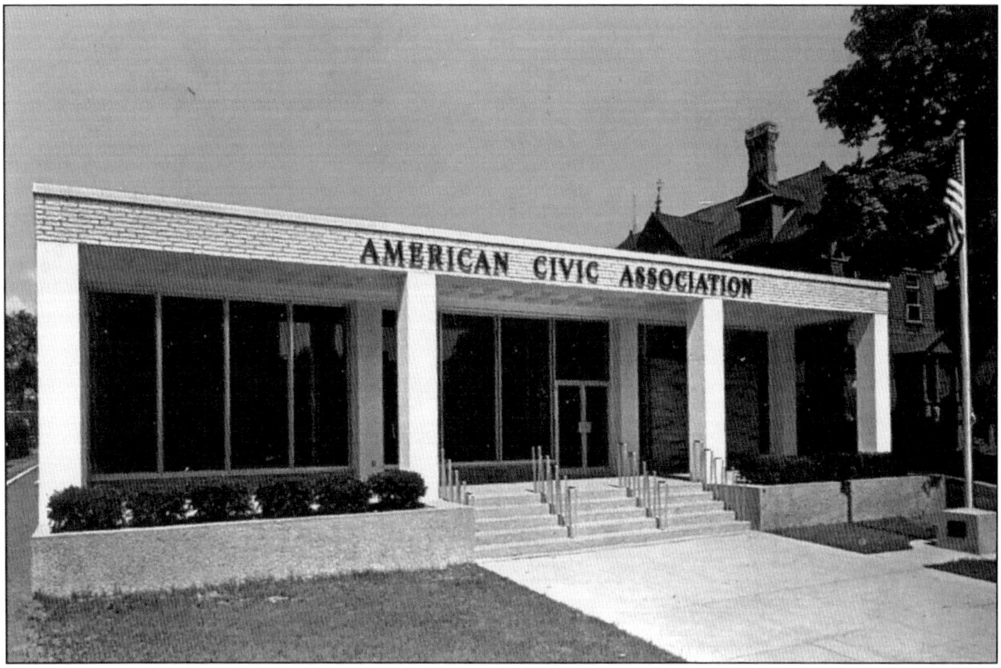

The American Civic Association, now on Front Street in Binghamton, was formed in 1939 to welcome and assist new Americans, celebrate the diverse traditions brought into Broome County, and encourage brotherhood and understanding. The availability of work in the Endicott-Johnson factories brought one of the largest influxes of immigrants into this area. Many ethnic traditions have been preserved throughout the generations and continue to enrich the local culture.

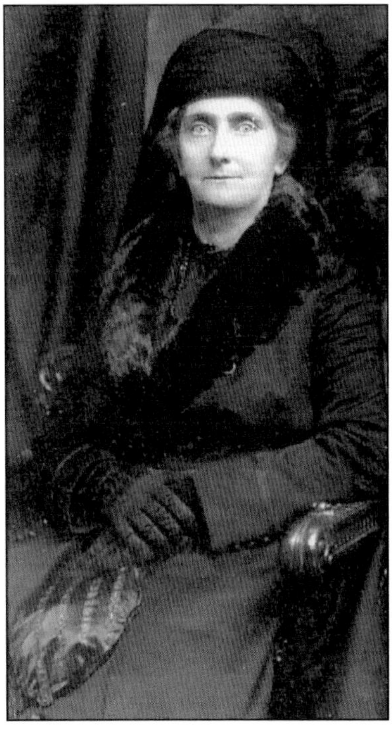

Thousands of immigrant workers poured into the United States looking for work in a booming shoe town. According to legend,"Which way EJ?" was the only American phrase most immigrants knew when arriving at Ellis Island. The great mosaic of cultures contributed to a community with a rich heritage. Pictured is a local immigrant woman in old world mourning garb.

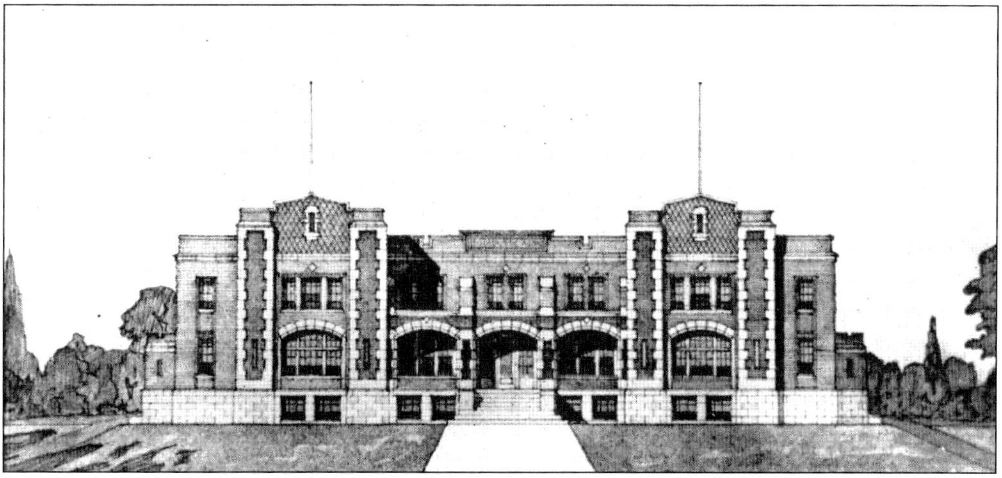

George F. Johnson believed in keeping his workers healthy through wholesome exercise and sports. Two recreation centers were eventually built for community use, one in Endicott and another in Johnson City. Included was a state-of-the-art sound system so sensitive that it could record the beating of an ant's heart. A Hammond organ was donated from the West Branch 30 year club of Endicott-Johnson workers. Plans were drawn in 1920 for the elaborate "sports temples," but economic conditions delayed the construction until 1949, when Charles F. "Mr. Charlie" Johnson, then president of EJ, built a simplified version, emulating George F. in generosity—though EJ could ill afford the expense. The yearly membership fee for employees to join the association was 25¢.

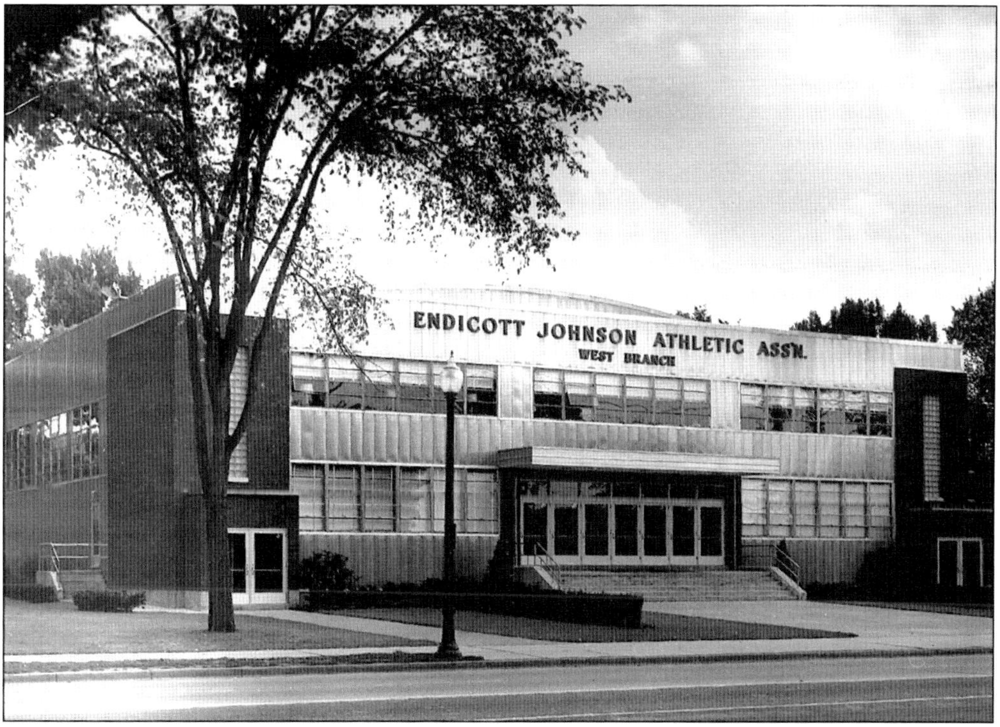

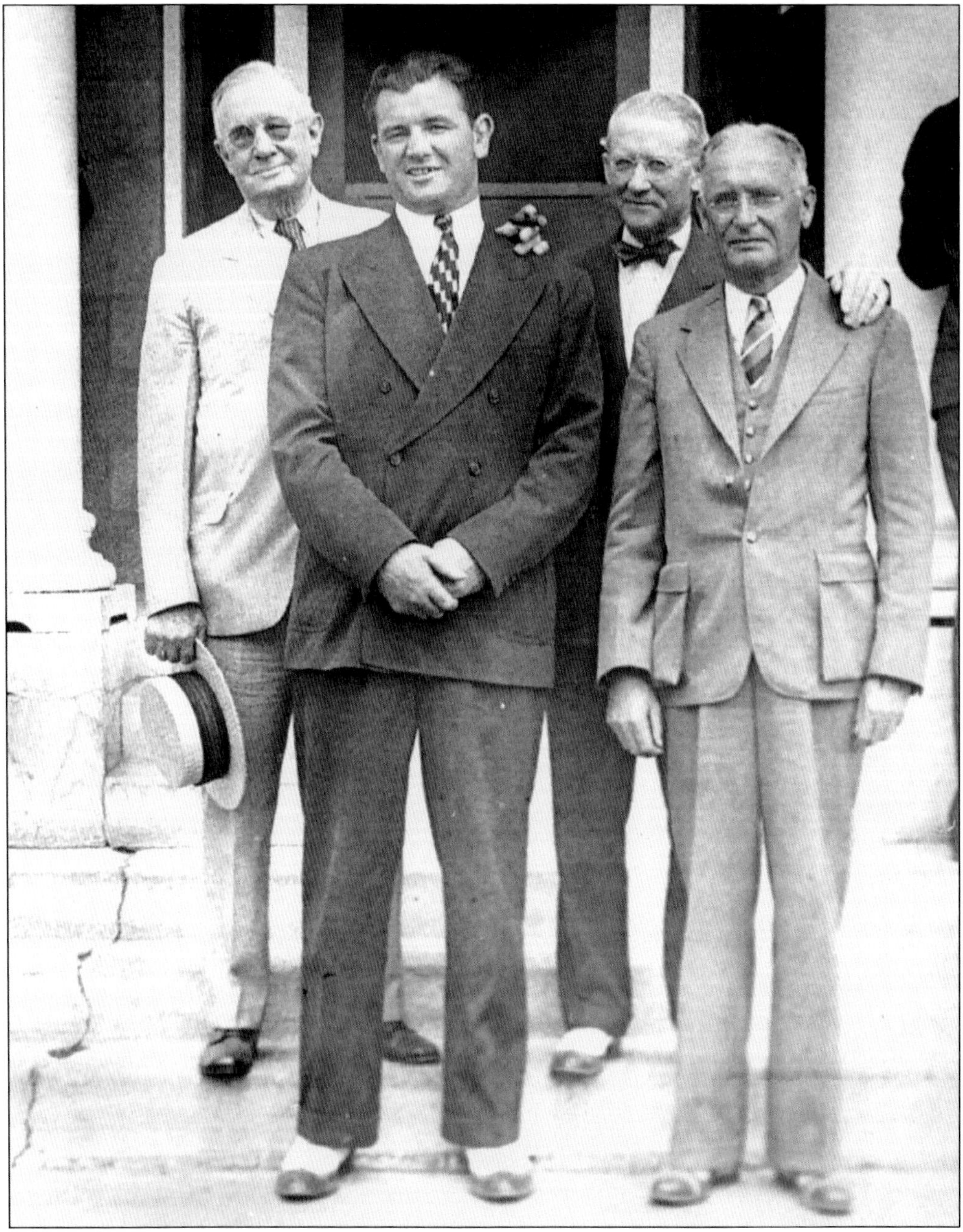

German heavyweight boxer Max Schmeling, front left, established training quarters at the Rood Farm in Willow Point, Vestal, in 1930. George F. Johnson, back left, had leased the Twin Orchards farm home and invited Schmeling and his training crew to use it as their headquarters. A training camp was set up at En-Joie Park in Endicott, where thousands of people gathered to watch the title contender exercise. Schmeling was scheduled to fight Jack Sharkey, a Binghamton native, for the world heavyweight title. Schmeling made a daily run from Vestal to Round Hill in Endicott that attracted sports enthusiasts from all over the country, including world-famous sports writers. Johnson made daily visits to the camps and had a sign reading "En-Joie Health Camp" placed at the farm.

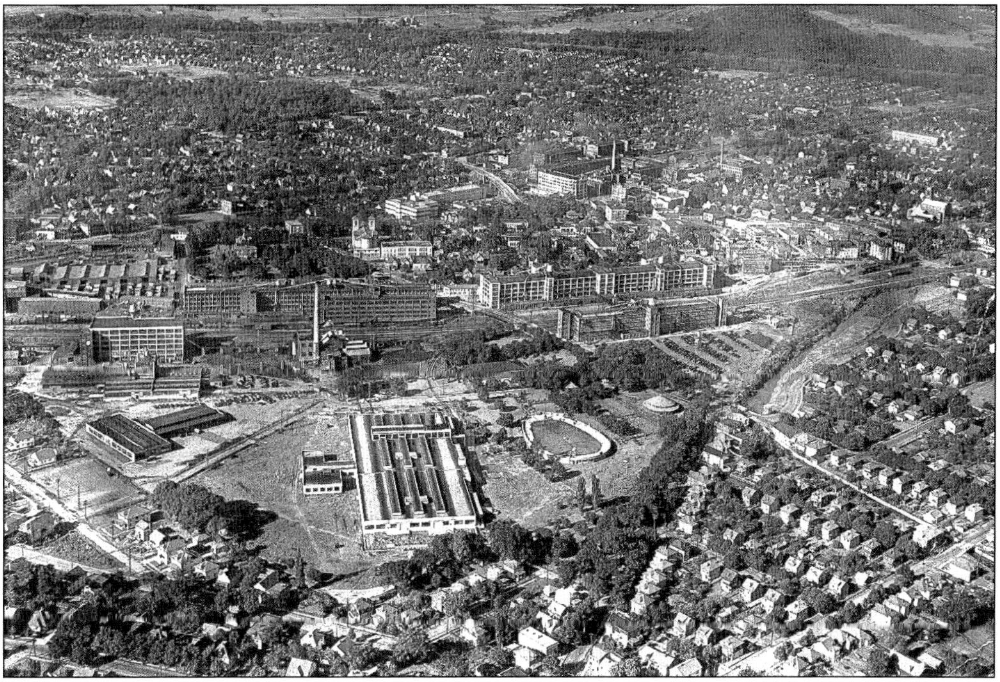

Donated by the Johnson family in 1927, CFJ Park contained a gigantic above-ground pool in which 2,000 people could swim at one time. The pool was nine feet above the ground with extensive locker rooms underneath. The largest carousel of the six in the area, featuring all jumping animals, is located at CFJ. The pool was torn down in 1982, but the carousel continues to enchant riders of all ages.

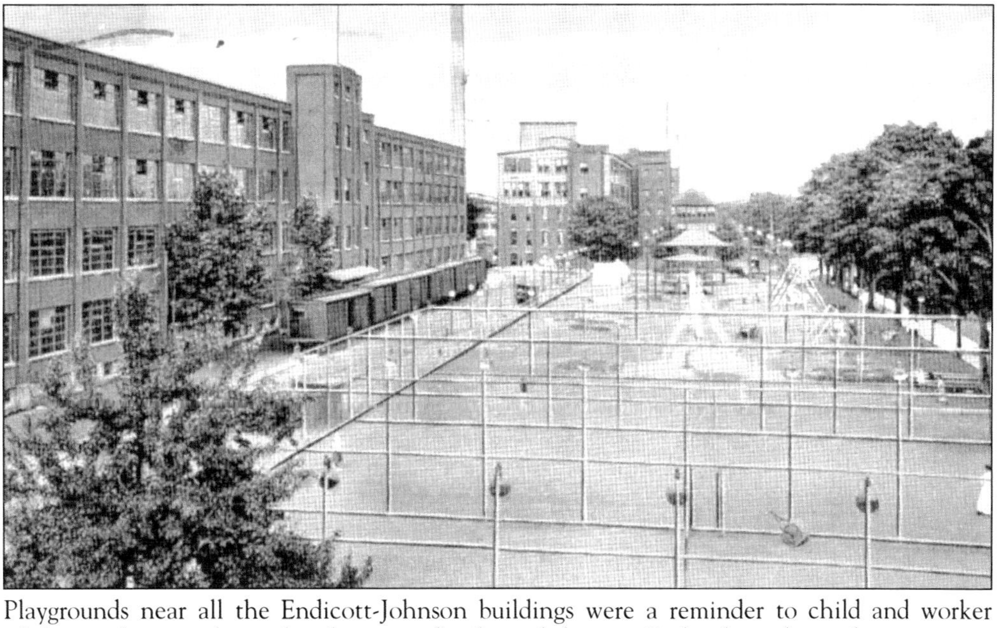

Playgrounds near all the Endicott-Johnson buildings were a reminder to child and worker of the symbiotic relationship between family and factory. Parks throughout the area were donated by the Johnson family. In the first ward of Binghamton, one such park was not called a playground—a large sign named it a "Johnsoniaum."

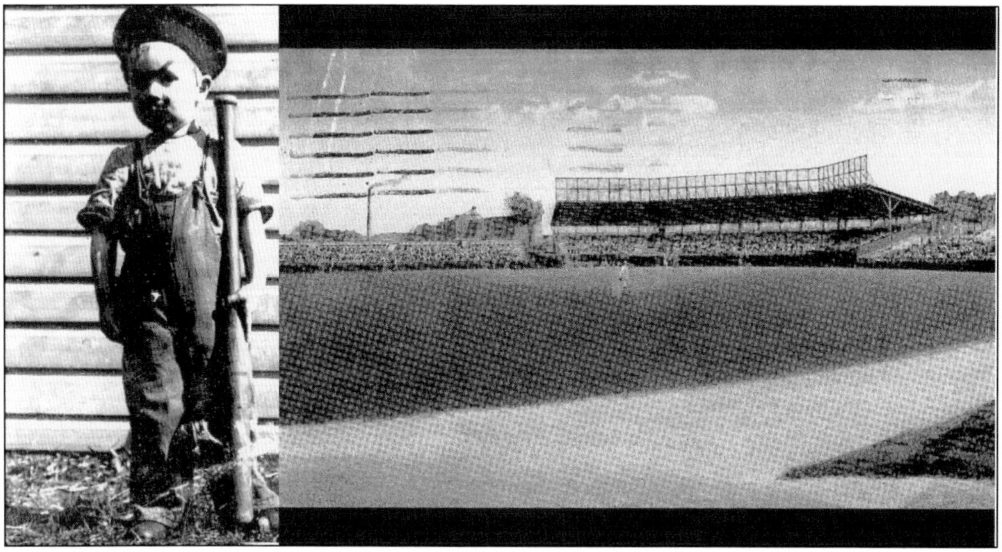

One of the few facts George F. Johnson knew about Binghamton before he arrived was the name of its baseball team—the Bingos. By 1913, he was financially secure enough to indulge his love of sports and build a baseball stadium in Lestershire. Johnson Field became the home of the New York Yankee farm team the Triplets. A very young enthusiast of the ball team is pictured *c.* 1919.

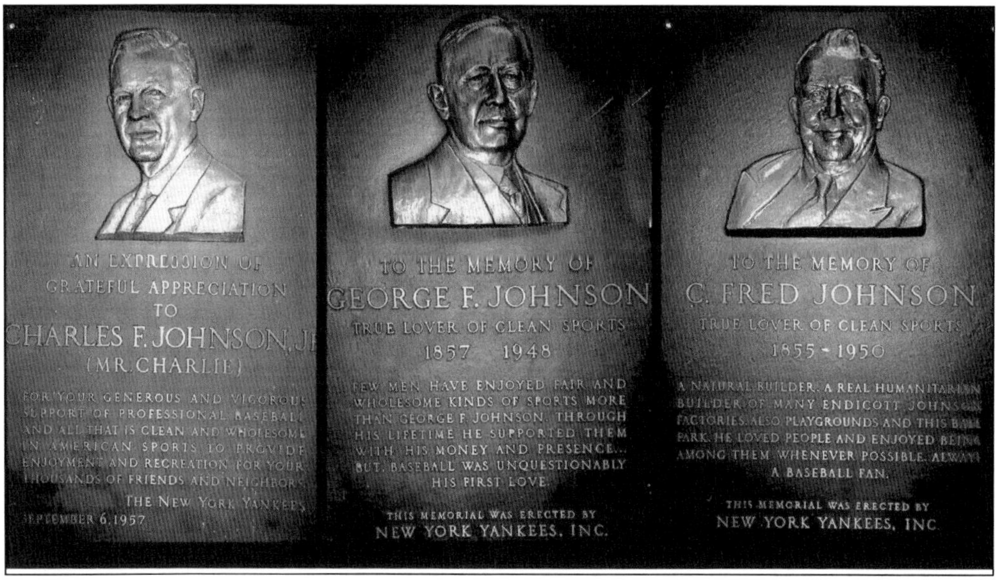

In honor of the Johnson family's love and support of baseball, the New York Yankees commissioned three three- by four-foot bronze plaques with the images of Charles F., George F., and C. Fred Johnson. The stadium was demolished in the mid-1960s, but the plaques can now be seen in a permanent exhibit at the town of Union history center, the Amos Patterson Museum.

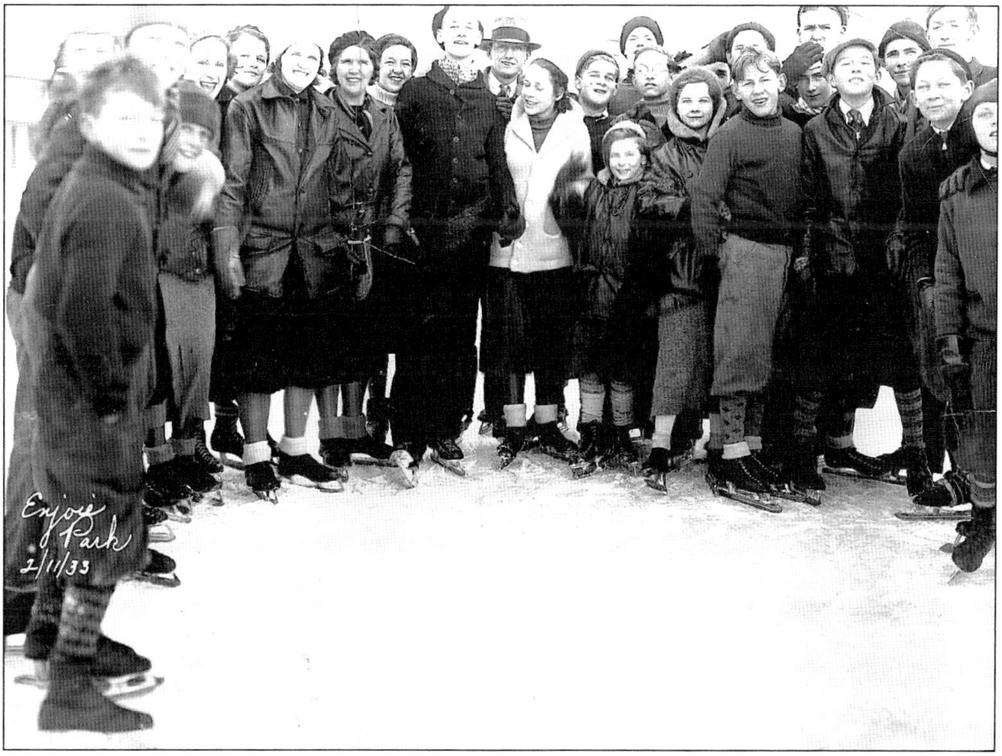

Ideal Park was the scene of happy participants in sports during every season. The center of the racetrack was flooded for winter activities. This photograph was taken of an ice-skating party in 1933. Also held at the rink were professional jumpers and entertainers on the ice and competition skating events.

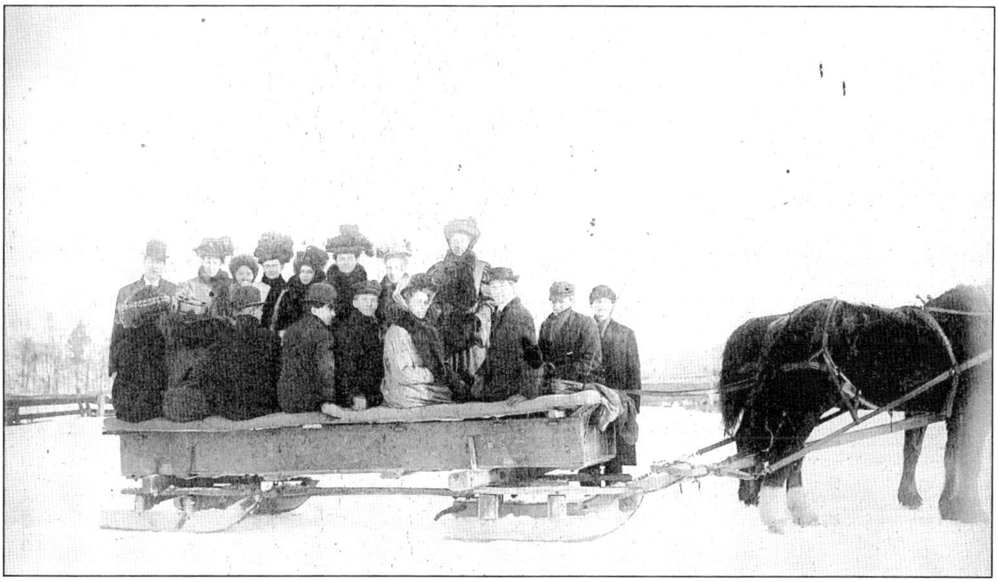

Recreation was not only for fair weather in the early Johnson era. This photograph is of a horse and sleigh party in the town of Union c. 1908.

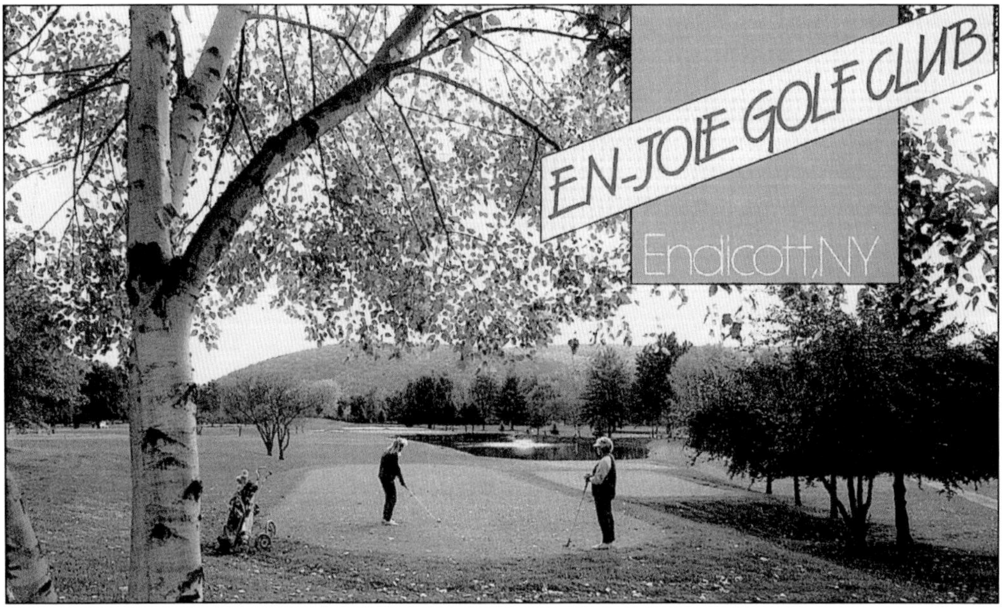

En-Joie Golf Club opened in 1927. According to George F. Johnson, "some foolish workers got it in their heads that golf was only for the rich . . . golf is just as good for hard working shoemakers as it is for a tired businessman . . . the poor can play golf just a cheaply as go to the movies and it is better for health. Give men comfort to live and play then you can work them hard and they will be ready for more." (Ed Aswad photograph.)

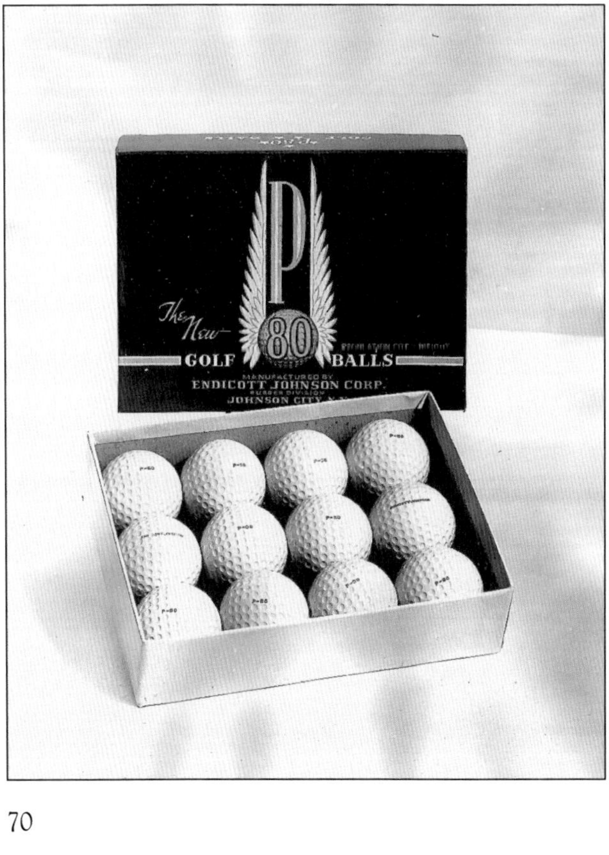

Golf balls were made by Endicott-Johnson and used on fairways that were planned smooth, with no rough places where balls could be lost. The cost of a game was 25¢; a ball, another 25¢; and a golf bag, 75¢—all affordable for the EJ worker in the 1920s.

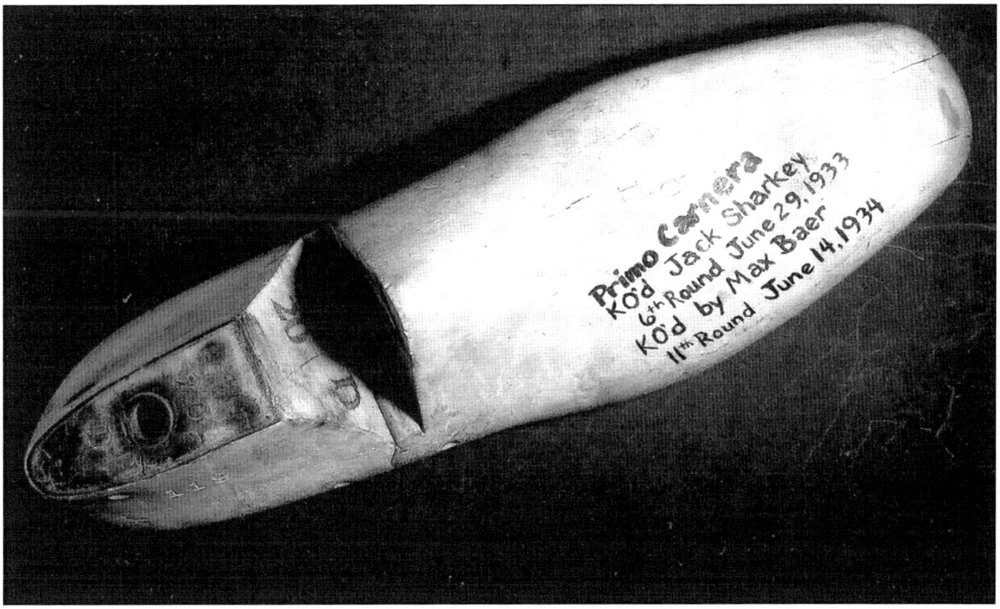

A nationally known pugilist of the 1930s, Primo Cannera had feet so large no store carried ready-made shoes. The giant boxer was six feet, six inches tall, with hands nearly as big as his feet. Endicott-Johnson made special wood shoe lasts in size 20D and custom-fashioned his shoes. Cannera won the heavyweight title by knocking out the reigning champ and Binghamton native Jack Sharkley in 1933. Because of his menacing size, Cannera became a wrestler in 1946.

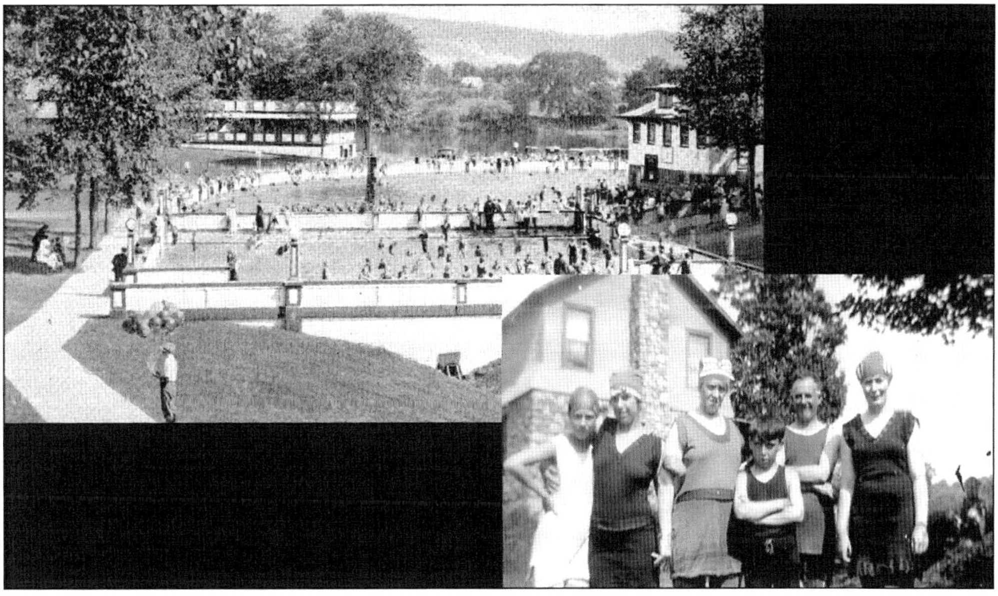

The swimming pool at Ideal Park, donated to the community by Endicott-Johnson, was so large it was called an inland sea. The pool held over one million gallons of water and was surrounded by sand beds, a toddler pool, a bathhouse, and miles of gardens along the river. Pictured is the pool and some native bathers wearing traditional wool swimsuits.

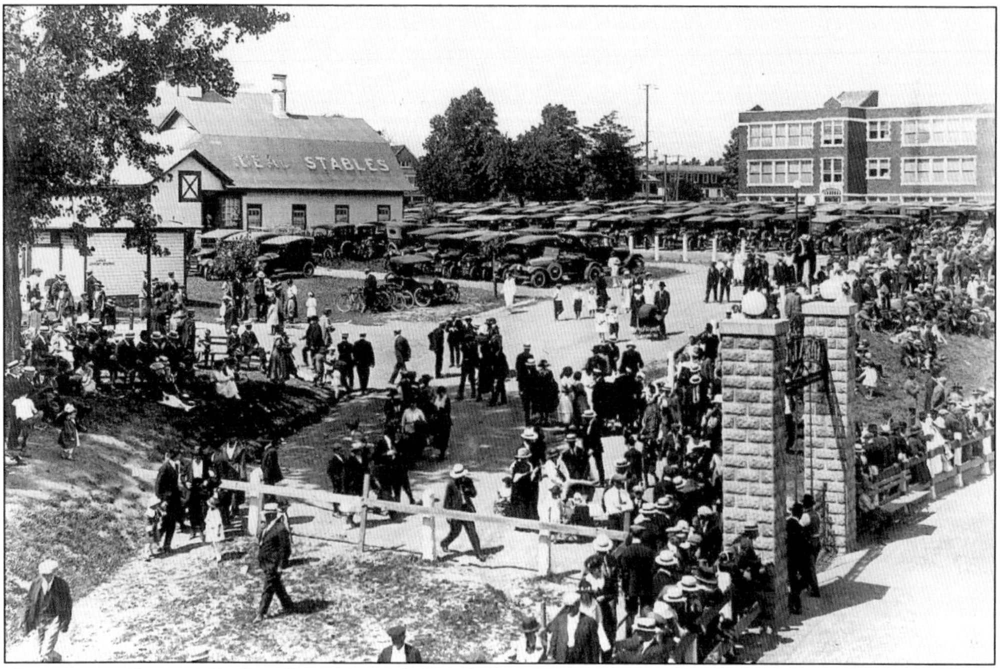

Known as Casino Park when owned by the trolley company, Ideal Park was 36 acres of recreation facilities located along the Susquehanna River. A dance and entertainment pavilion, gardens, picnic grounds, benches, electric fountains, and swimming pools were just a few of the attractions that enticed thousands of visitors each pleasant day. Cars were restricted to a parking lot. Union-Endicott High School and horse stables can be seen in the background.

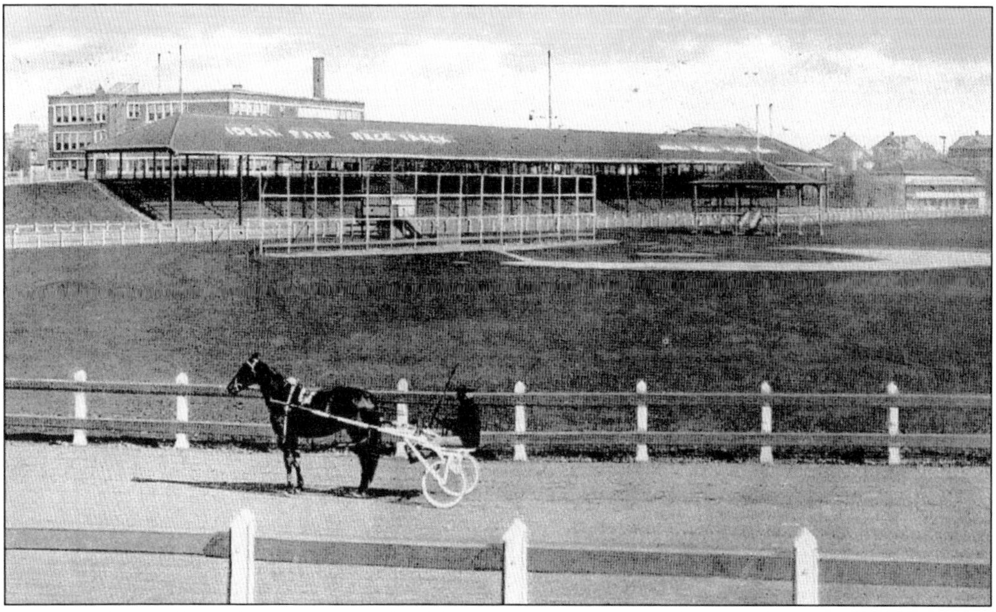

As part of its policy of encouraging healthy leisure activities, Endicott-Johnson held harness races beginning in 1920 at the Ideal racetrack, along the Susquehanna River. The racetrack contained a half-mile trotting track, where some of the best horses of the Orange County race circuit would vie for the winner's circle. The Ideal stable could house 168 horses.

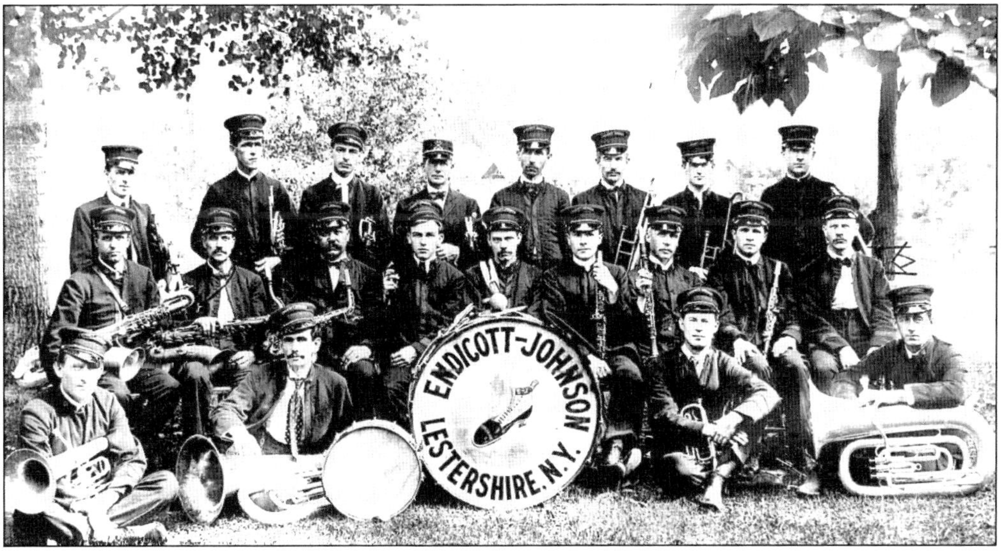

The Endicott-Johnson Shoemakers Band and Chorus consisted of factory workers. Endicott-Johnson called music "the handmaid of industry," and the best singing instructors to be found were hired to train the chorus. The groups often traveled to entertain and compete, still receiving full pay. The group was also known as the EJ Cobblers Band. A common joke at the time was "Who is playing the shoehorn?"

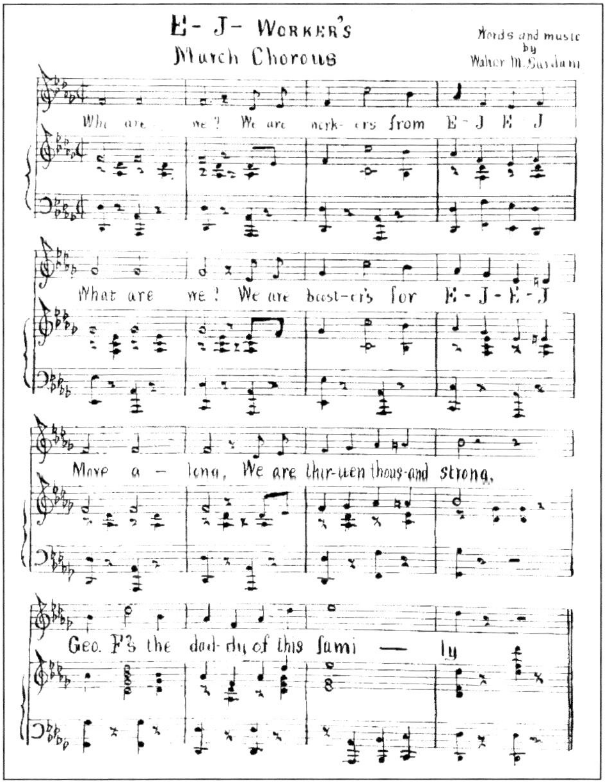

Corporate loyalty was prized at Endicott-Johnson—and what better way to express the sentiment than in music? Any gathering was an opportunity to put EJ pride on display in song, making a joyful noise to the company. Many musical arrangements were available, extolling the virtues of the Johnson family and "Shoe town U.S.A." This one was written by local composer Walter M. Surdam c. 1925.

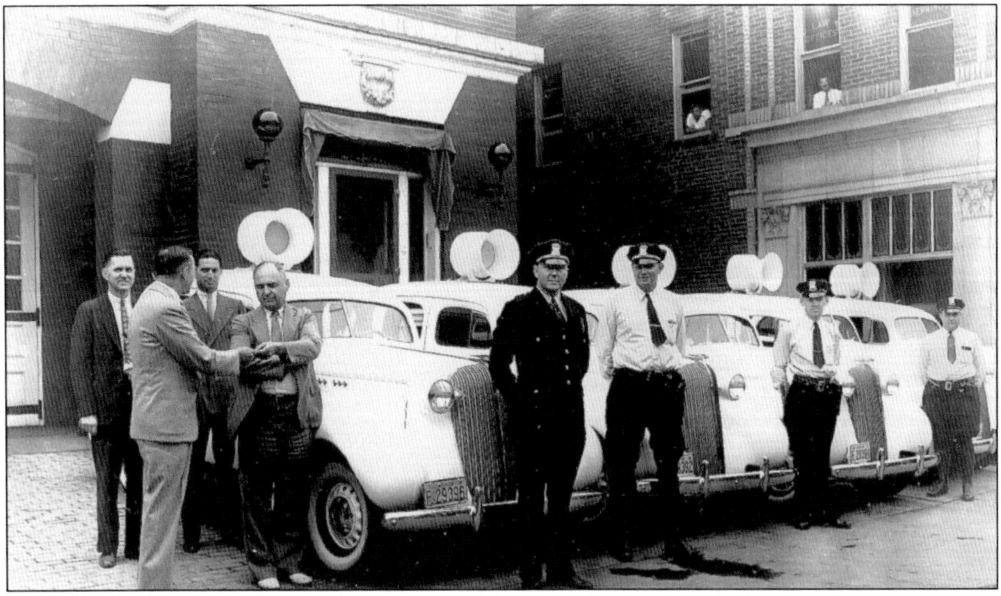

Even a Magic City needs a police force. In the 1930s, an area of Endicott known as the Old Knob was flourishing with crime: "White slavery, bawdy houses, burglary, holdups, murder and mayhem, and nefarious goings-on plagued the streets." It was known as a rendezvous for every white slaver and cutpurse in the Southern Tier. Then entered Chief Leroy Wike, who clobbered crime, and the streets became "safe and comparatively dull," according to news reports. The photograph above was taken in 1936.

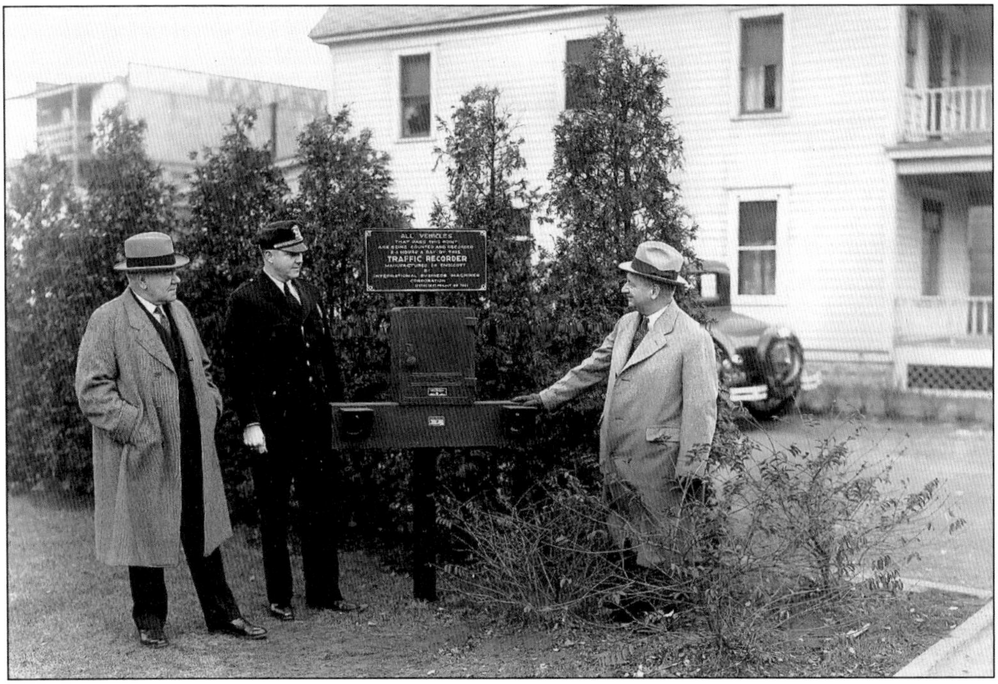

Traffic control experiments were conducted in Endicott with the full cooperation of the police force and a device invented by the IBM Corporation. Chief Wike is pictured with a prototype traffic recorder machine.

Three

EJ Worker and Workplace

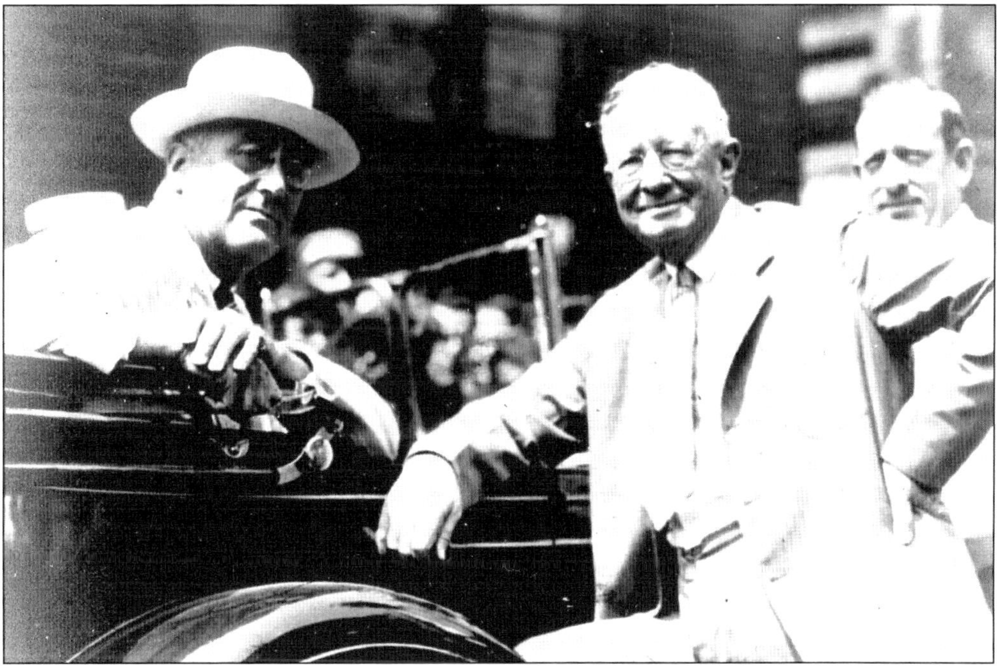

George F. Johnson, center, was outspoken about protecting his business and workers from "politics." In a letter written in 1919, he expounded, "A professional legislator is a thing to be dreaded. His idea for correction of evil is 'law' (laws, and more laws); laws themselves creating the very evil (or at least aggravating the very evil) which they seek to prevent—nagging, repressive, interfering, meddlesome, aggravating laws, which make people impatient and sore." However, over the years, he did support Franklin D. Roosevelt, left, Al Smith, and Woodrow Wilson for president, as he felt they would create policies good for the common man.

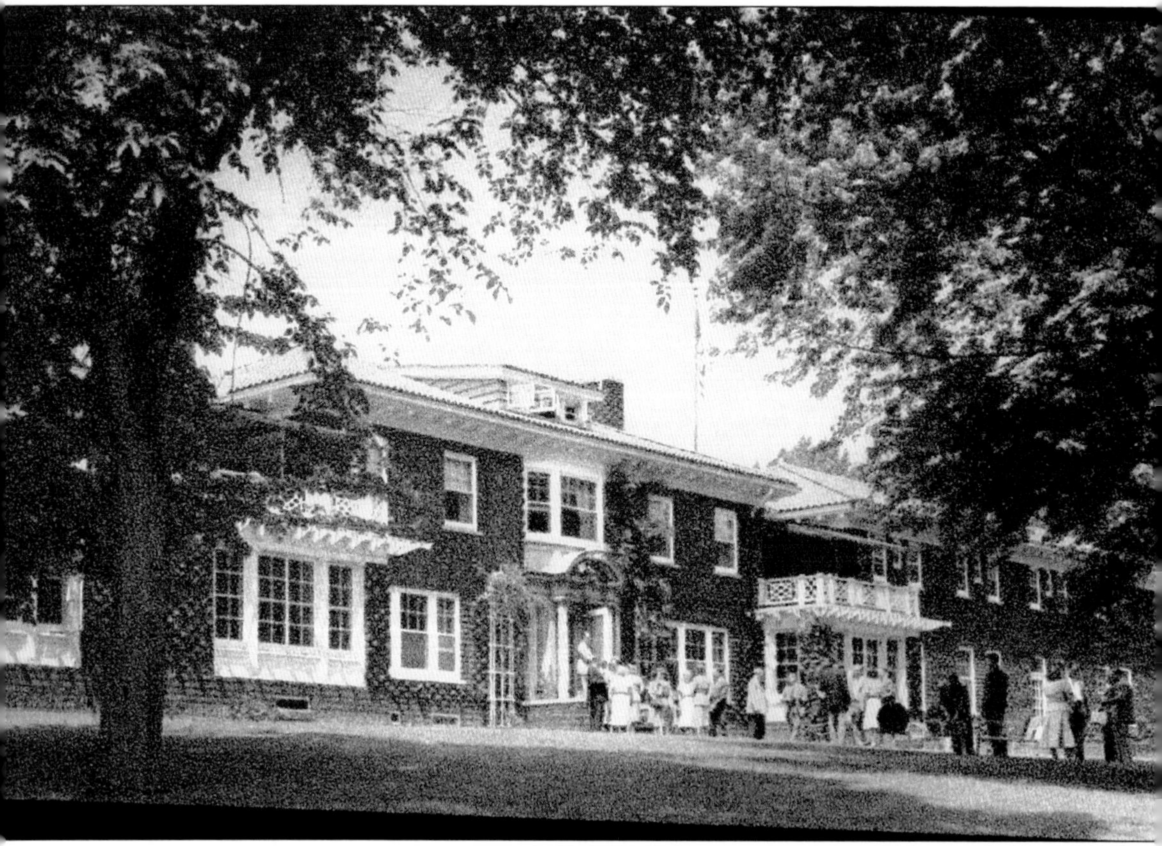

George F. Johnson believed all employees of Endicott-Johnson should live well but modestly. The company treasurer, Eliot Spaulding, did not fit the corporate profile. Spaulding's abode was an elaborate mansion on a hilltop in Endwell. Letters from Johnson to H.B. Endicott speculated that something would have to be done about Spaulding and his ostentatious lifestyle, noting that Spaulding employed four women in the house to take care of only three people. "He is putting himself where his up-keep will just about take all his income. This man must be crazy." Johnson wrote that Spaulding was "out of line and out of harmony with company policies regarding labor, and is shaving the interest on Liberty Bonds" and "he is more harm than help, and not our kind of fellow. The best interests of this concern are served by such men as Harry and George W. They are not served by such men as Eliot." In later years, the Spaulding estate became the Kahulura Country Club and then the IBM homestead. Spaulding left EJ to become a bank president.

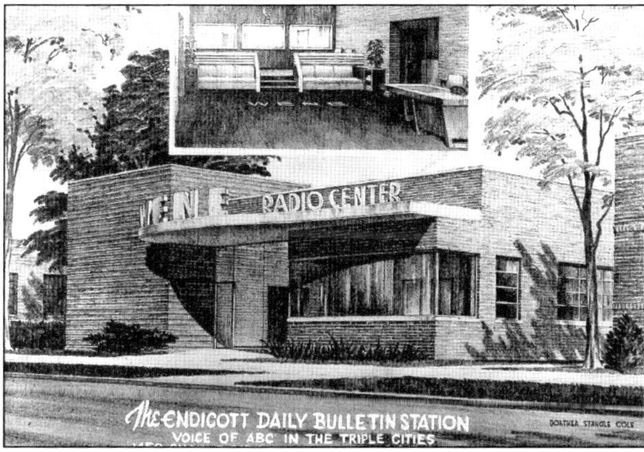

ENDICOTT DAILY BULLETIN

Published by
EMPIRE NEWSPAPERS-RADIO, Inc.
Operators of Radio Station WENE
909-911 E. Main St., Endicott, N. Y.
Owego Bureau, 44 Lake St., Phone 341
Vestal Bureau: Westfall Bldg., Phone 2497

The Endicott Times Established in 1851 Was Combined With The Endicott Daily Bulletin June 1, 1940.

JAMES H. OTTAWAY, Publisher
BYRON E. FRENCH, General Manager
WILLIAM C. LUNDQUEST, Business Manager
HARVEY W. TRAVIS, Editor
Official Paper of the Village of Endicott

MEMBER OF THE ASSOCIATED PRESS
The Associated Press is entitled exclusively to the use for republication of all the local news printed in this newspaper, as well as all AP news dispatches.

The Bulletin is delivered to all homes in Greater Endicott by carrier boys at 30c per week or $15.60 per year. Published daily except Sunday. Entered as Second Class Matter Oct. 15, 1937 at the Postoffice at Endicott, N. Y. Under the Act of March 3, 1879.

"We never know anything until we know the truth." —George F. Johnson.

William Hill was postmaster of Lestershire in 1896. He worked to keep the mail rates low so that the young Endicott-Johnson factory could send advertisements and mail at a cheap rate. Hill was removed from office amidst rumors of postal fraud and went on the become the youngest mayor of the village of Lestershire, elected at age 21 in 1901; he served three terms. He was the nephew-in-law and lifelong friend of George F. Johnson. He had a stellar career as a politician and as the owner of the *Endicott Daily Bulletin*. The editorial page of the newspaper for many years carried the banner quote from Johnson, "We never know anything until we know the truth."

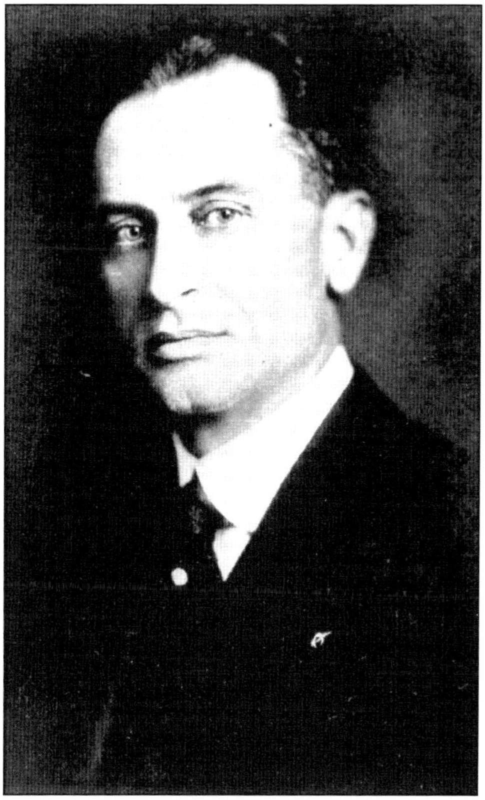

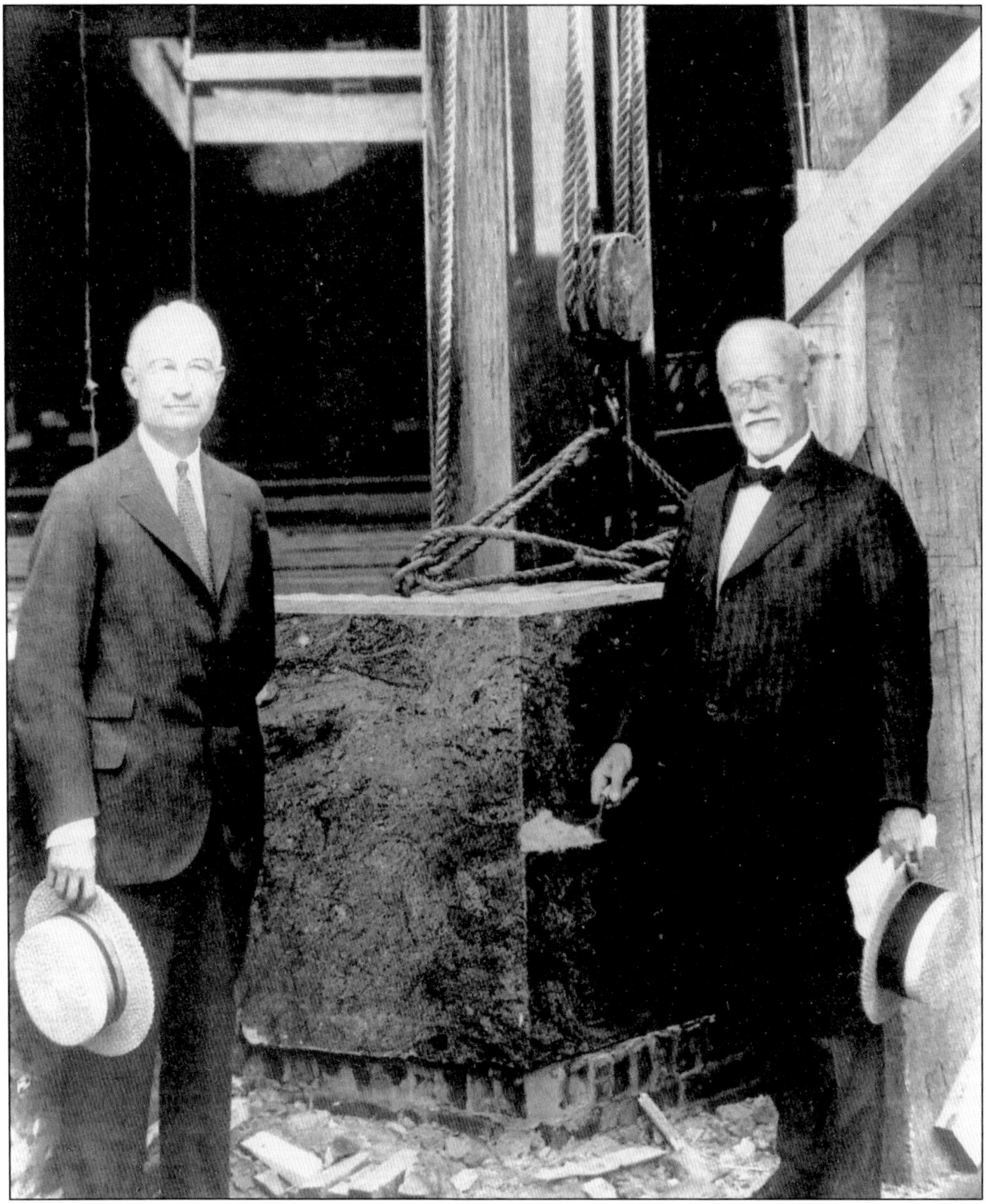

Born in 1875, Chester B. Lord, left, stands with banker Sherman Phelps. Lord was the vice president of Endicott-Johnson and on the board of directors until 1927. In his letter of resignation, Lord cited several reasons for leaving: first was George F. Johnson's treatment of EJ executives, using them only as figureheads and not as part of the decision-making process. He also stated, "a serious breakdown in EJ is that GFJ dominates the entire business which may be guided by the 'Golden Rule' but it is the GFJ rule . . . board members are unable to offer a different opinion or they will be humiliated by GFJ. We should have had an organization of executives who can run the business . . . not one person to direct all the operations." The dominance of Johnson continued, and the company survived because of his innate business sense; however, the next generation could not fill these EJ shoes in instinct or intellect, and once the guidance of Johnson declined, so did the corporation.

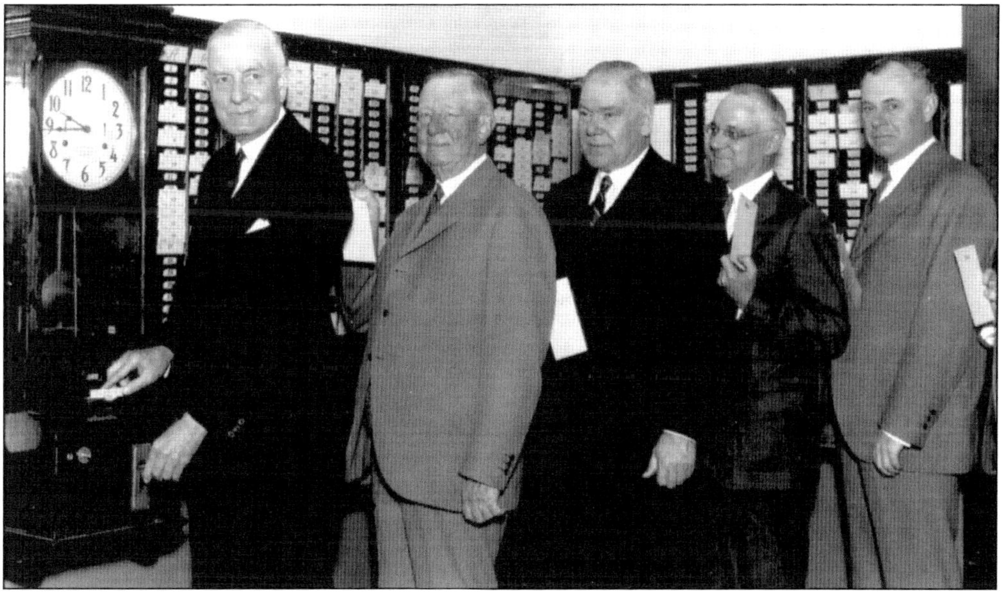

Among those punching cards at a time clock in 1932 are T.J. Watson, left, followed by George F. Johnson. Johnson wanted IBM to remain in Endicott. In 1927, he wrote to Watson, encouraging him to build and grow in Endicott. He suggested Watson offer decent wages and benefits to attract a quality work force. Later that year, Watson replied with thanks. For many years, Endicott-Johnson sent workers to IBM classes to learn successful sales techniques. Pictured below is the Class of 1942 in front of the IBM Endicott education building.

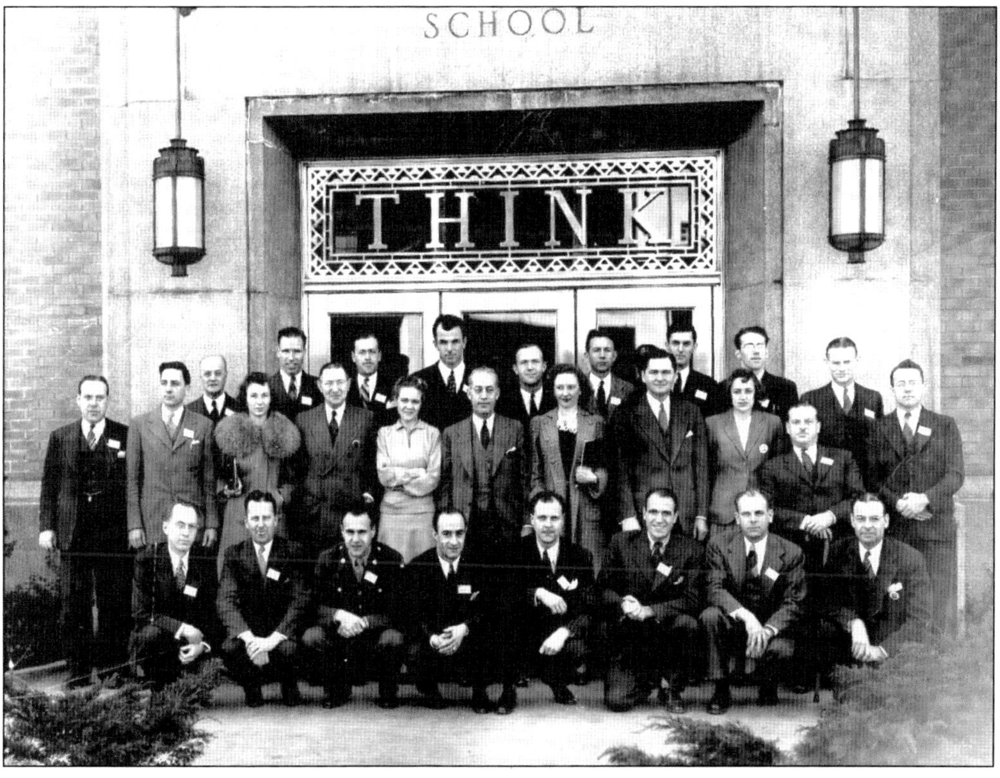

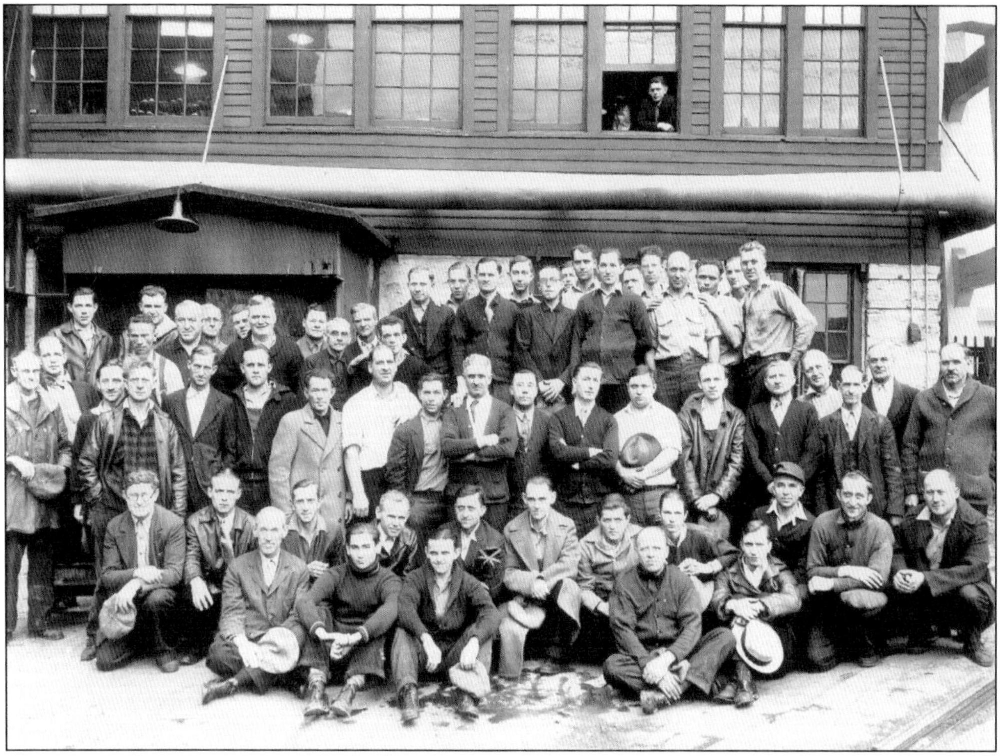

George F. Johnson supported both the National Recovery Act and the reelection of president Franklin D. Roosevelt. To further these goals, the largest shoe in the world was created in 1935 by Endicott-Johnson to be the centerpiece of a parade to support the NRA of 1933. The legislation was supposed to restore confidence in the economy and reduce industrial unemployment. The local parade was spectacular, but the law was declared unconstitutional in 1936. Shown is the EJ bottoming room in 1933.

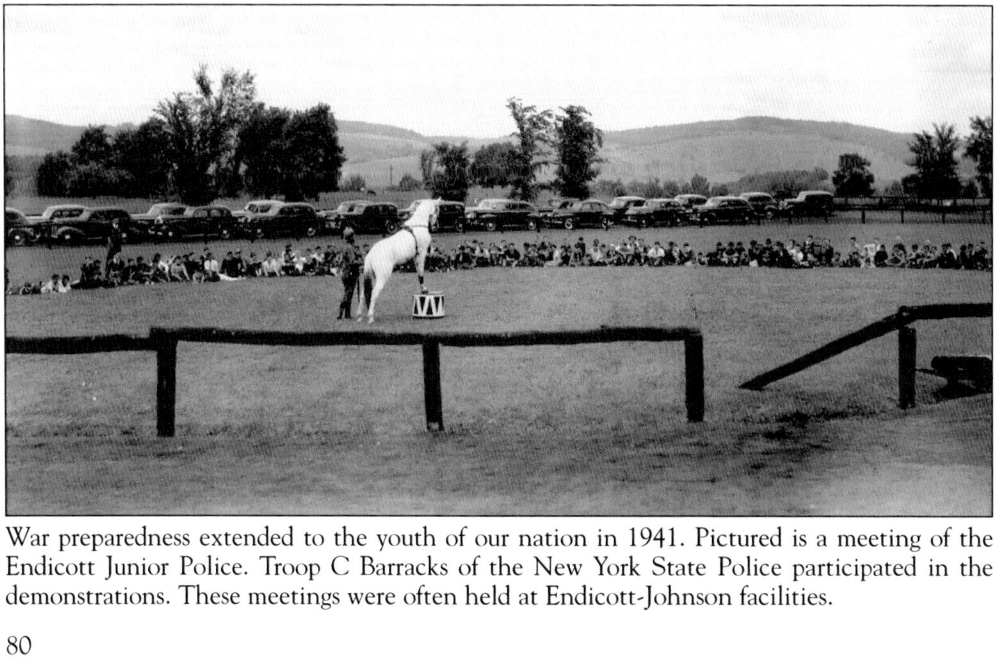

War preparedness extended to the youth of our nation in 1941. Pictured is a meeting of the Endicott Junior Police. Troop C Barracks of the New York State Police participated in the demonstrations. These meetings were often held at Endicott-Johnson facilities.

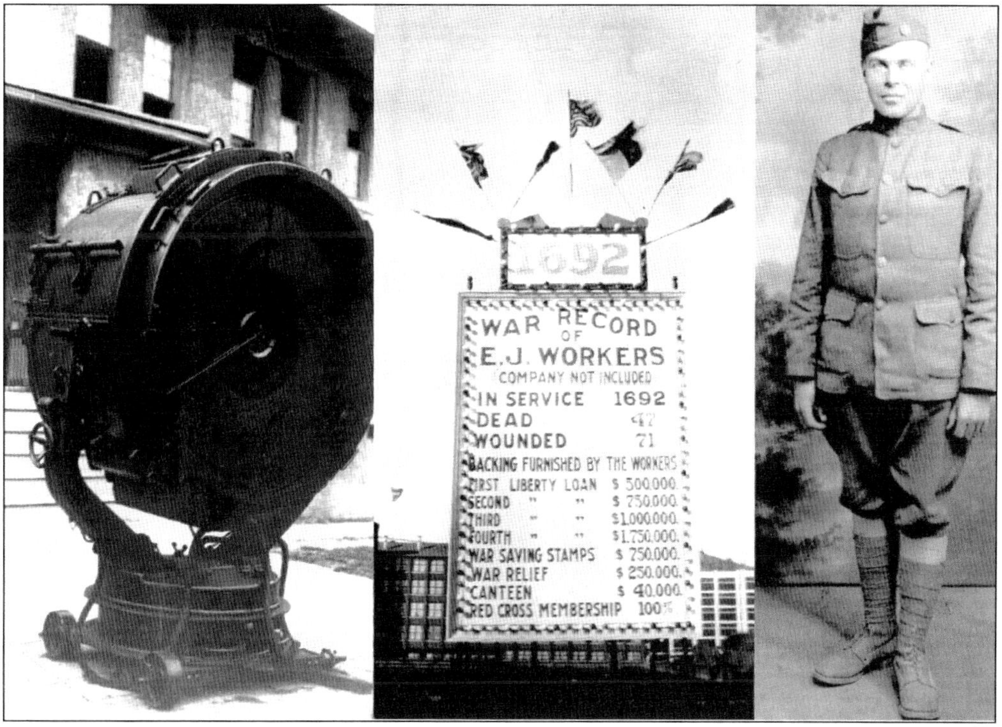

Endicott-Johnson worker Archie Peck was one of 54 men in the United States (at that time) to be awarded the Congressional Medal of Honor. He also won the French Medal Militaire of the French Legion of Honor and the Palm and the Silver Medal of Montenegro. Only a few people in the world wore the Montenegrin honor. The World War I hero returned to EJ after the war and breasted heels in the fine welt bottoming room in 1919. The photographs show a World War I soldier, a massive spotlight for plane watching, and the EJ War Record.

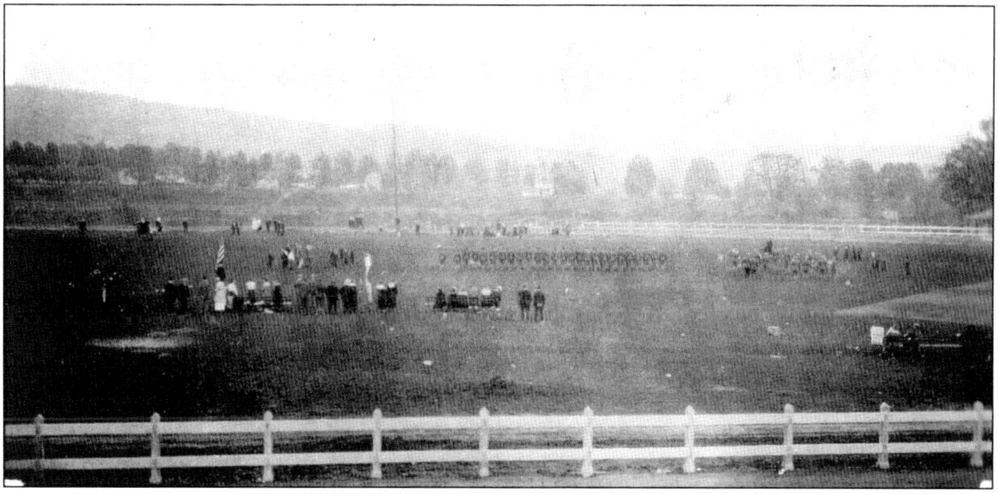

This photograph shows the new racetrack at Ideal Park in Endicott at the beginning of World War I. The space was also used as a drill field for the home defense guard formed in the Magic City. Four Broome units were active, attending practices at the EJ field, all using weapons furnished by George F. Johnson.

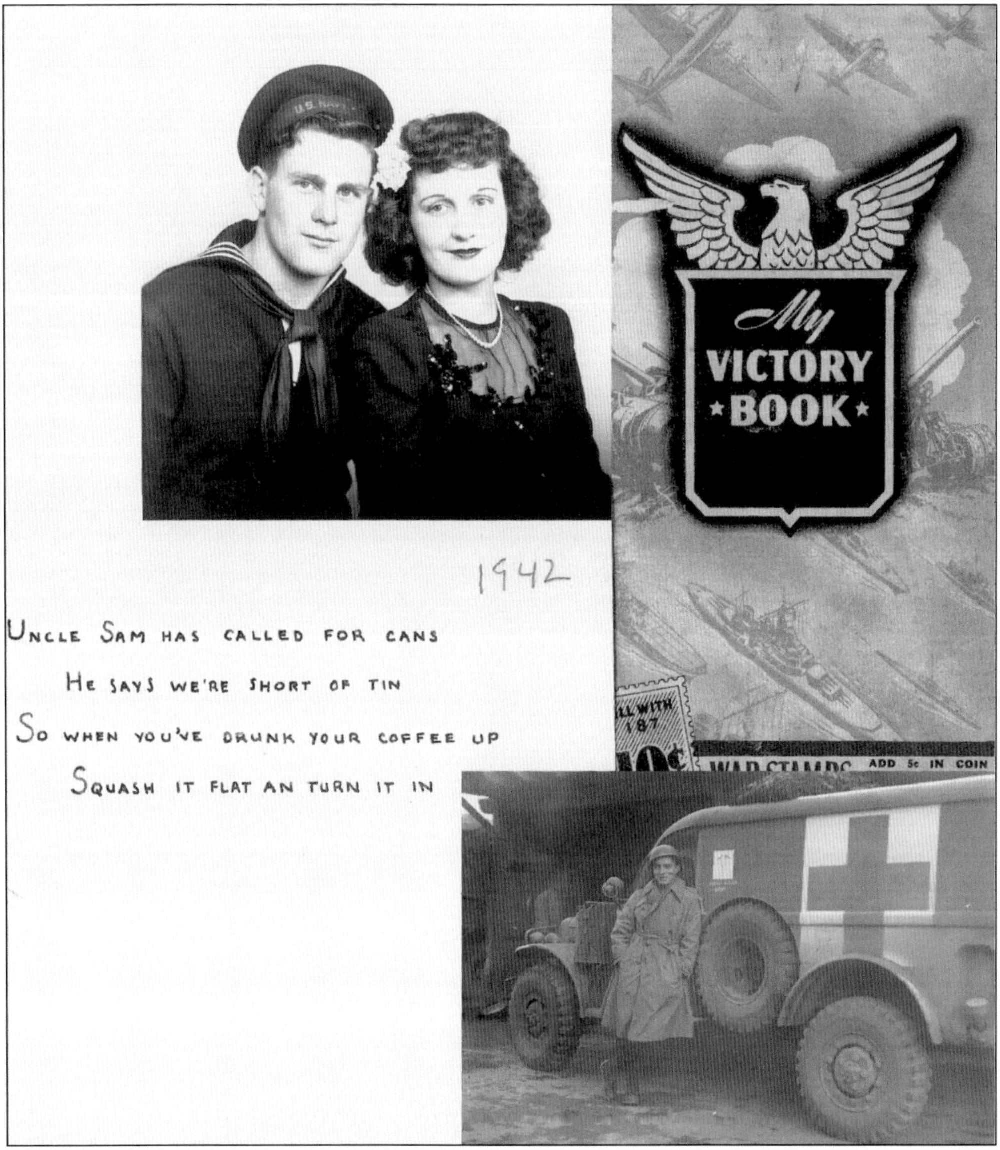

Full support for military personnel was provided by Endicott-Johnson during World War II, beginning with farewell breakfasts for departing service people and continuing with welcome home programs, bond drives, and guarantees of employment upon return to EJ. Vacation pay, gift boxes, and the regular delivery of hometown newspapers to soldiers cost the company $1.2 million. The company made 25 million pairs of rugged boots for the military during World War II. Today, Len Robenolt, the 83-year-old father of author Suzanne Meredith, still wears a pair of his EJ World War II army combat boots when working in the garden. The corporation also assisted veterans hospitalized with serious physical difficulties. George F. Johnson sent the EJ aircraft to transport veterans home for visits and to return them to the hospital without any cost to the employee. A full-time veteran coordinator was appointed to assist with transition to private life. This collage of photographs opens a window to wartime America.

From the 1920s to the 1930s, George F. Johnson contributed approximately $350,000 to build local American Legion posts. He often stated that the American Legion was "the largest force in America for good." Three houses and $150,000 in Endicott-Johnson stock were donated to the local posts. The legions returned the praise, stating, "George F. is the veterans' best friend." At the end of World War II, Johnson City Post 758, with the assistance of the Johnson family, sponsored the largest welcome home reception for veterans in the entire United States. Shown at the right are the interior and exterior of the Endicott Legion. Pictured below are the Johnson City and Binghamton American Legion buildings.

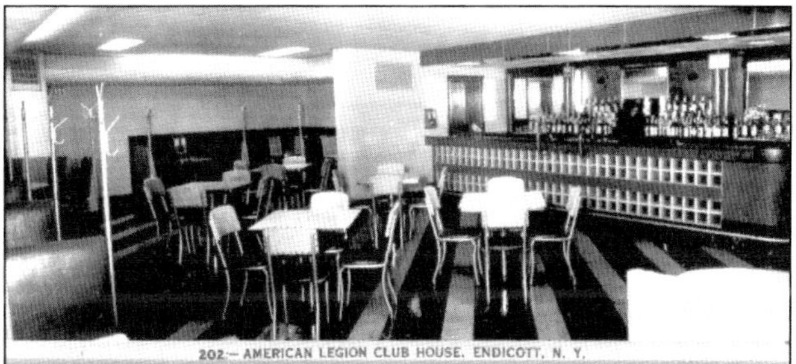

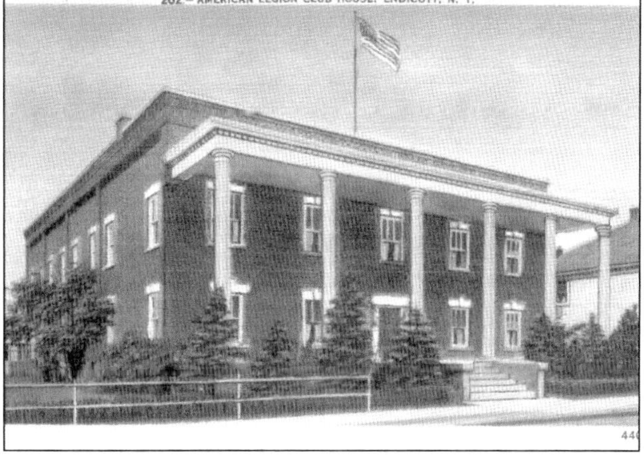

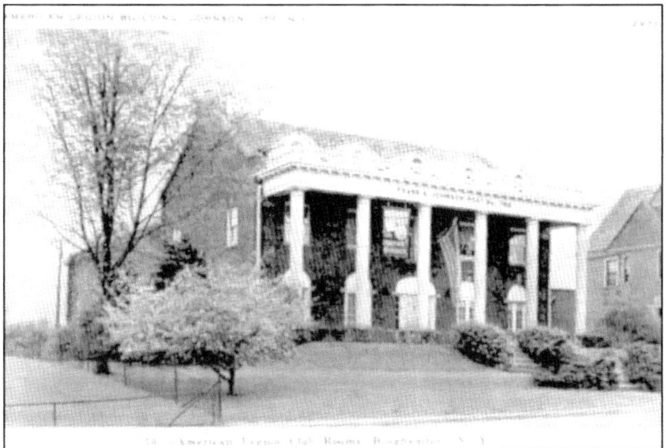

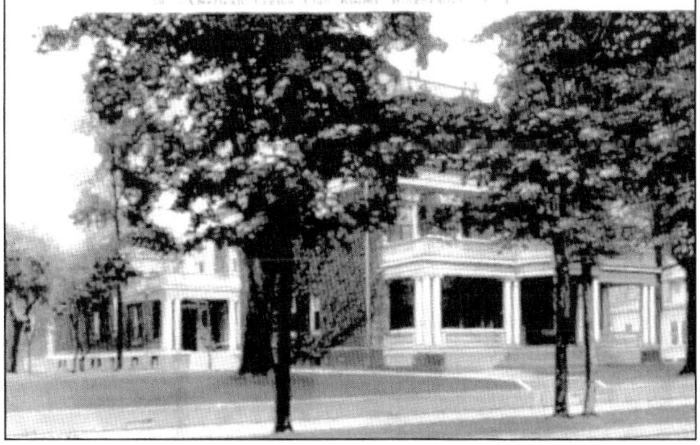

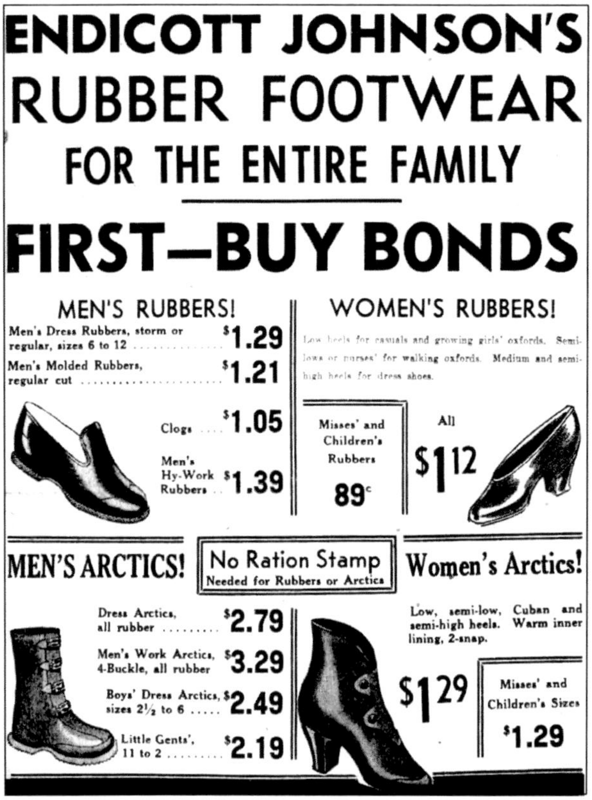

The advertisements Endicott-Johnson produced during World War II reflected corporate patriotic beliefs. The company prominently advised customers to purchase war bonds first—and then shoes. The advertisements also reminded patrons that no ration stamps were needed for rubbers and arctics. This is a typical newspaper ad of the war years.

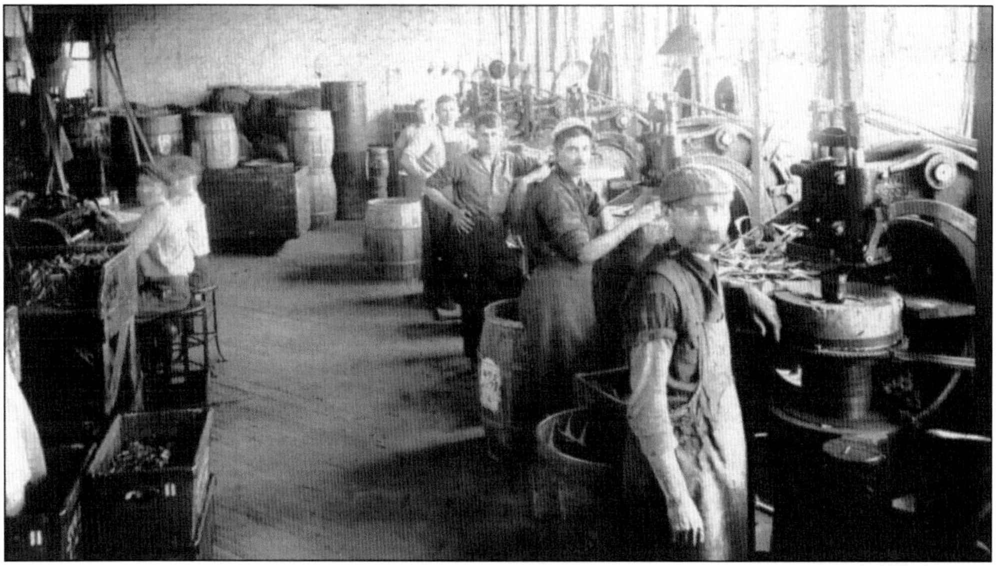

Visitors of any age were always welcome at the Endicott-Johnson factories. An elderly man remembers a room in the tannery containing huge vats of melted wax used in the finishing process of one of the cheaper leathers. Visiting children were allowed to dip their hand in the wax and repeat the process as many as four or five times, building a cast. As the mold cooled, the hand could be pulled from the model—a wondrous souvenir sculpture of a small hand.

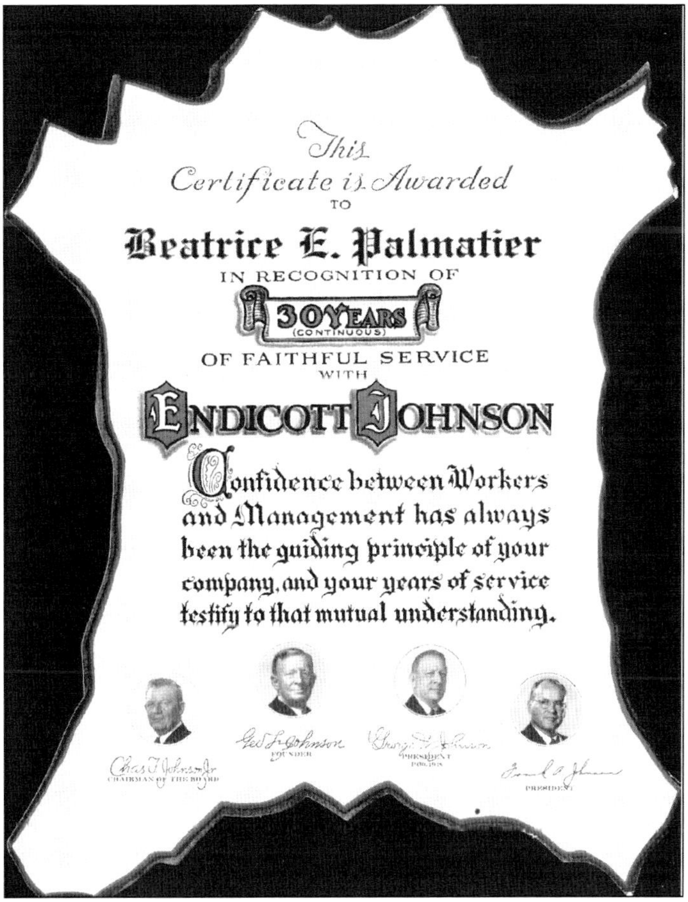

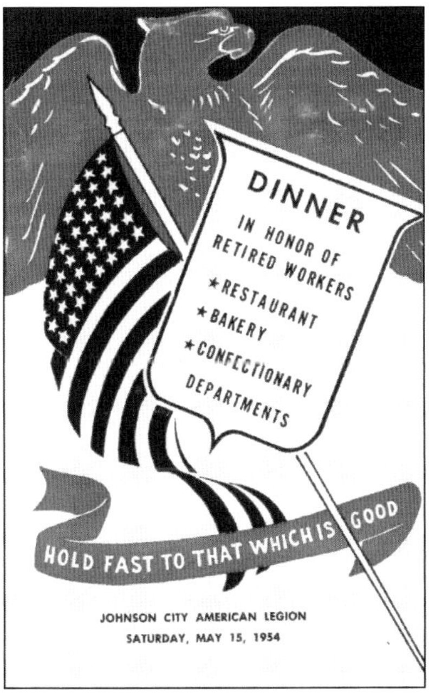

There was no fixed year for Endicott-Johnson workers to retire. As long as employees felt fit enough to work, they were welcome in the factory. In 1955, Charles F. "Mr. Charlie" Johnson had been working at EJ for 50 years, and 59 other workers matched or beat that record. The all-time record for service was that of William E. Mitchell, who clocked 68 years of work at the Scout Factory. When he and his fellow employees began working, a 60-hour workweek was normal. The above certificate, in the shape of a cowhide, was awarded for 30 years of "faithful service." The cowhide became an EJ logo, and thousands of these items still exist in the Triple Cities as treasured mementos. The company provided yearly retirement banquets. The program at the left is from 1954, honoring the restaurant, bakery, and confectionery departments. Displayed is a company motto "Hold fast to that which is good."

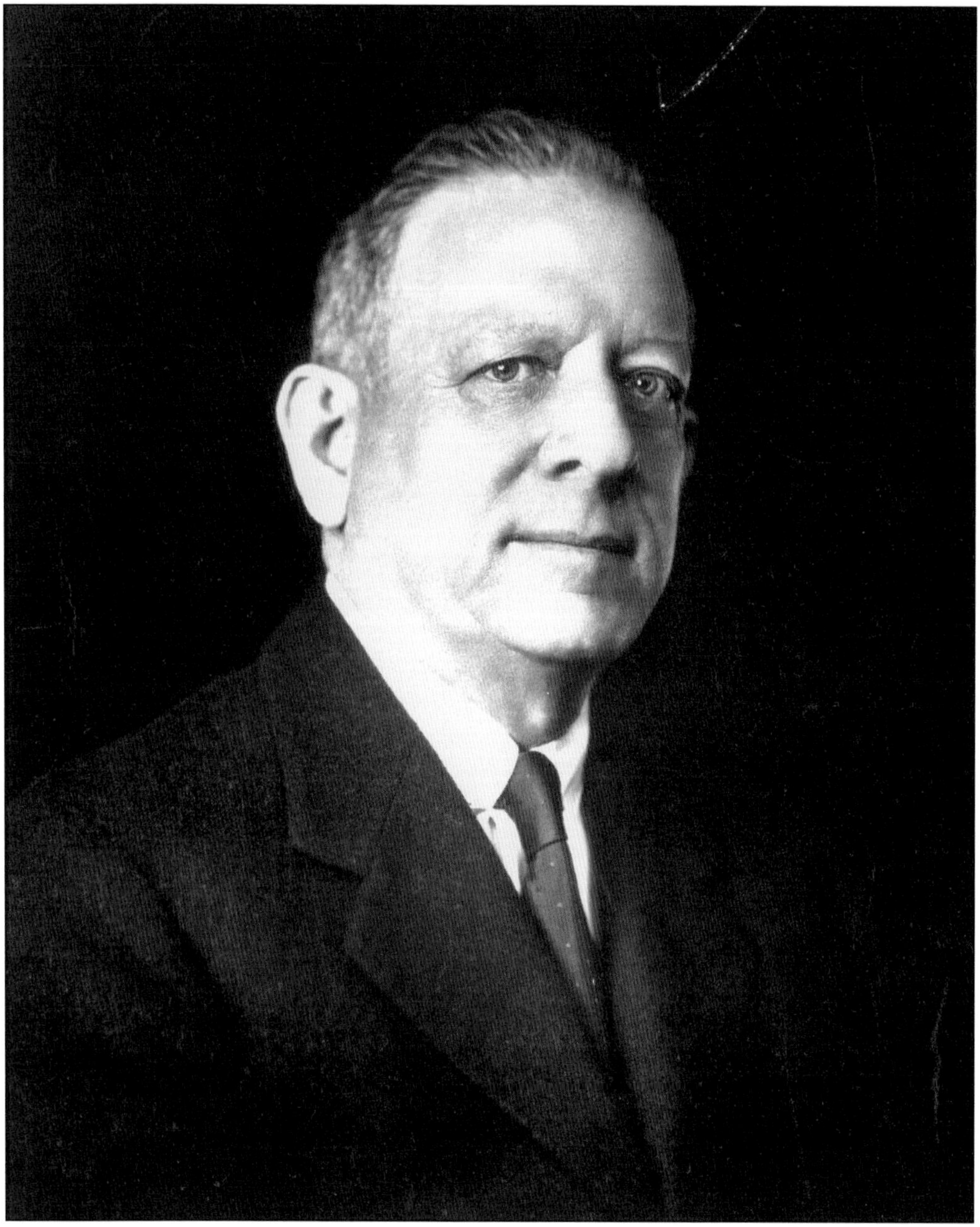

George W. Johnson, son of legendary industrialist George F., was born in 1880. He was known by employees and the community as George W. At the age of 18, he began working in the Endicott-Johnson factory, where he remained for nearly 55 years, learning to manage his father's shoe industry. His first job paid 5¢ an hour for a 60-hour workweek. His father once claimed responsibility for his son's success, saying, "I saved George W. from college and put him to work." The son learned every facet of the business, and in 1905, became superintendent of the sole leather tannery. When EJ incorporated in 1919, he was elected to the board of directors and vice president of the tanning division. He became president of EJ in 1930 and chairman of the board in 1948. His love of sports and service to the community equaled the Johnson family heritage. He died in 1953.

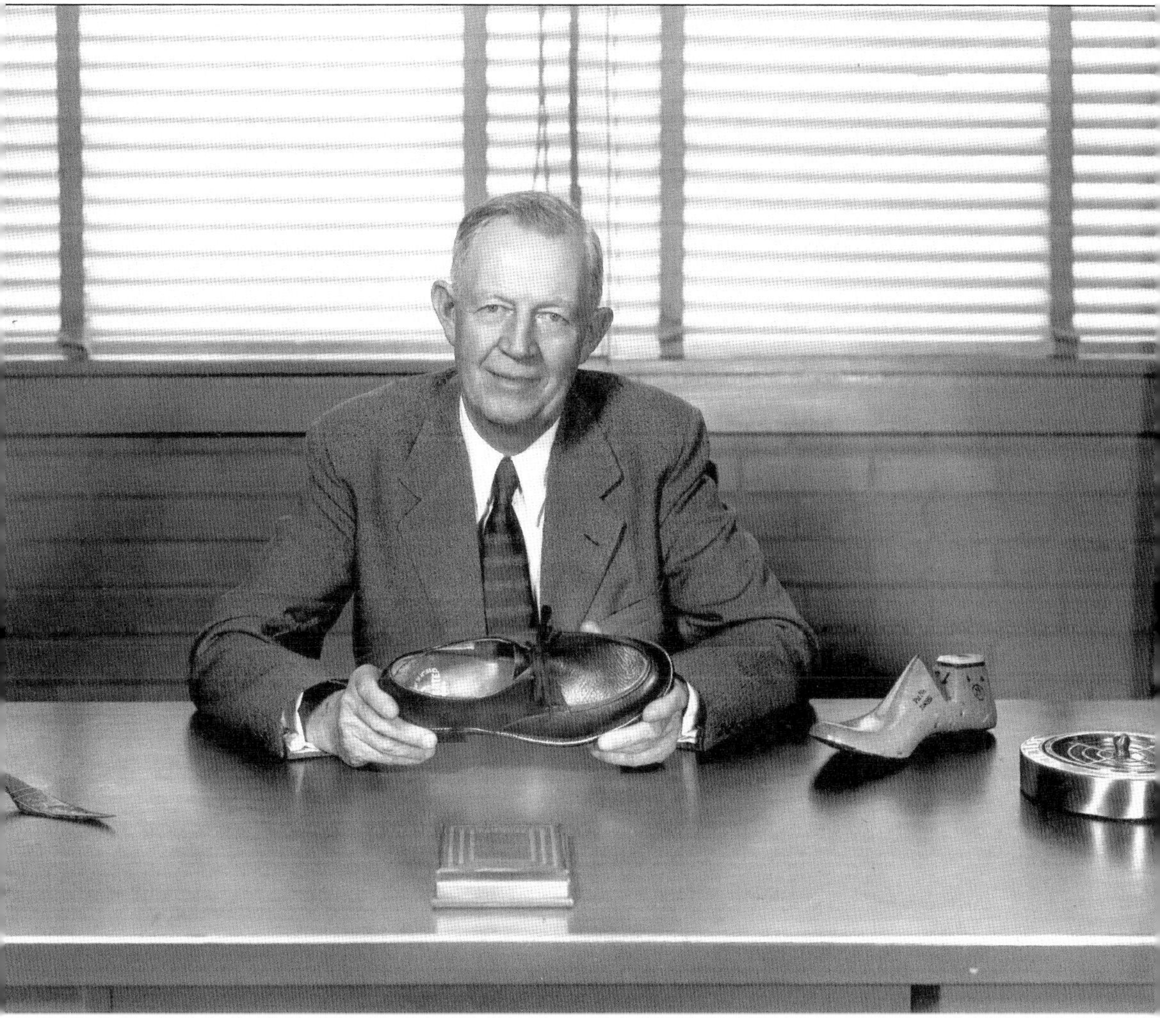

Charles F. Johnson Jr., known as "Mr. Charlie," was the son of C. Fred and nephew of George F. Johnson. In 1948, he was elected to the presidency of Endicott-Johnson. He was interested in continuing the Johnson legacy no matter what the cost to the corporation. Although well-regarded in the community, he did not have a grasp of total economic conditions or the vision to deal with putting EJ in a position to compete with offshore manufacturing. In 1948, he built two EJ recreation centers, spending millions of dollars to continue the "square deal" image. Unlike his uncle, he accepted an honorary doctorate degree bestowed by Colgate University in 1952. In 1955, the community celebrated his 50 years with the company, and in 1956, he succumbed to a cerebral hemorrhage.

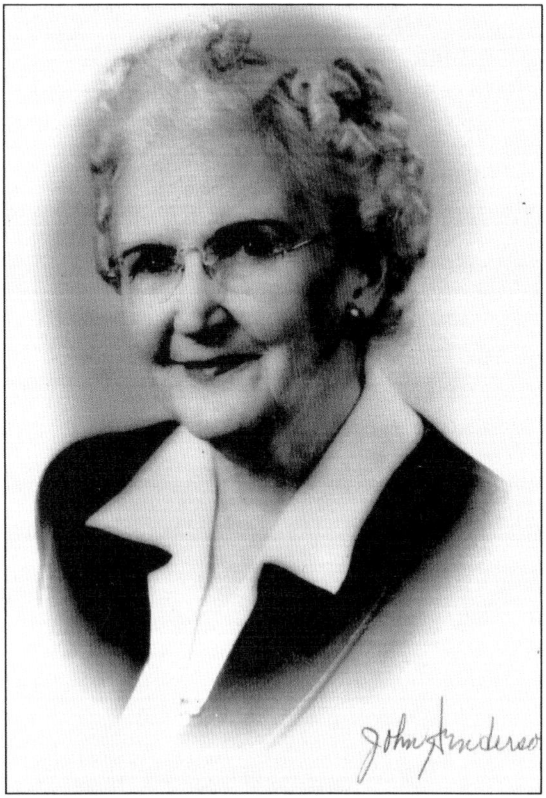

A five-year domestic science course called the Ideal Training School was open to all girls in the community from the age of nine. The the materials and the instruction for the course were provided free of charge, sponsored by Mary Ann McGlone Johnson, left, wife of George F. Johnson. The homemaking course was meant to Americanize children of immigrants. Many mothers of the children also requested access to the classes so that they could learn to "cook American." For many years, the school was located in rooms over the stables at Ideal Park in Endicott, pictured below in 1922.

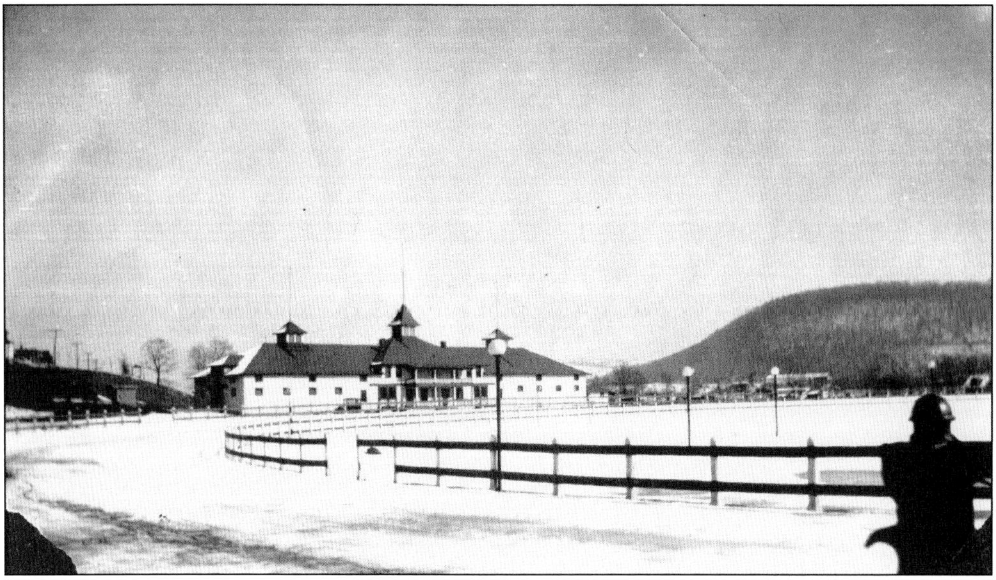

George F. Johnson's views on politics were passed to his daughter Lillian. In 1924, she wrote a letter giving her opinion of politicians: "Politicians are becoming so intense over their own party and their own selfish ideas that they are willing to let everything else attend to itself or not at all. Politics is the only word in their vocabulary nothing else matters . . . the country can not go on unless these so called representatives of the people change their method of representation."

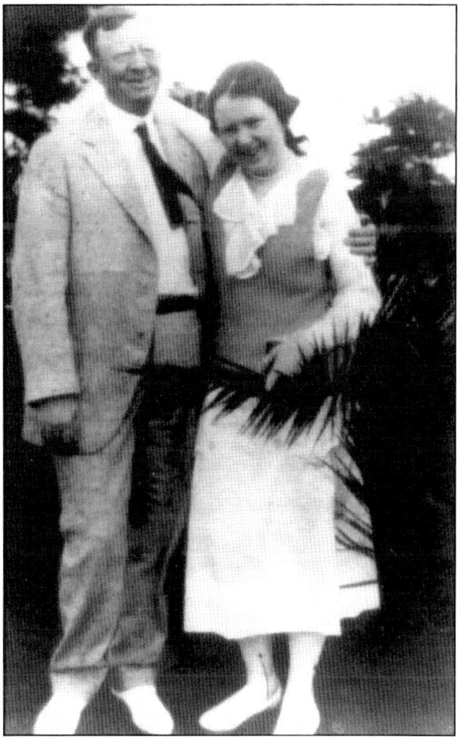

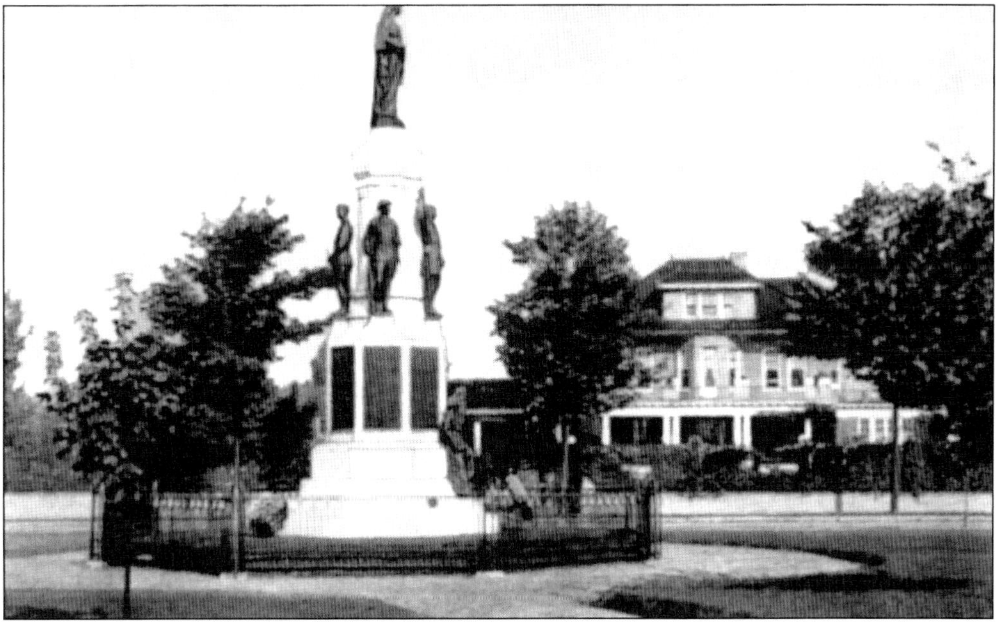

The Johnsons erected a World War I monument in honor of Endicott-Johnson workers who served in the military. At the pinnacle is a Red Cross nurse to honor Mrs. George F. Johnson's sister, who died of the flu when serving as a World War nurse. Statues of soldiers adorn the second level of the monument, and EJ workers cast in bronze sit at the base of the structure near plaques containing the names of soldiers. Mrs. Johnson also contributed to building and furnishing nursing residences at Ideal and General Hospitals.

A PLEDGE AND THE REPLY

Expression of Perfect Confidence Makes it Possible to Go on to a More Hopeful and Happier Future

TO THE WORKERS:

Confidence in the management was demonstrated again today when petitions, signed by practically all E. J. workers, were presented to officials of the company, under the following caption:

"Faith in our Leaders. E. J. Workers pledge Loyalty to their leaders, Mr. George F. Johnson, Mr. George W. Johnson and Mr. Charles F. Johnson, Jr. This pledge is our homecoming greeting to Mr. George F. Johnson. At this time when industrial strife is rampant throughout the nation, when Capital and Labor are in the throes of suspicion and distrust with each other, hurling open accusations at the other and attempting to impair the security of industry by their efforts to dominate, we want to stand by that old proverb 'Hold Fast to That Which is Good' so, with this, we, the Endicott Johnson Tanners, Shoemakers and Rubber Workers desire to PLEDGE OUR LOYALTY AND GOODWILL to our leaders, and express our complete confidence in their leadership, and our willingness to abide by whatever decisions they may consider necessary."

OUR ACKNOWLEDGEMENT

We are more than complimented, under existing conditions, to have such a splendid indorsement by and from the workers. Nothing in the world could be stronger, or express loyalty better. We may now feel certain that we have our workers' perfect confidence, and will go on to a more hopeful, and we trust happier future, for our entire organization. No further answer is necessary. The Workers have said it all.

GEORGE F. JOHNSON
GEORGE W. JOHNSON
CHARLES F. JOHNSON, JR.

March 20, 1937

In 1937, supervisors at Endicott-Johnson circulated a loyalty pledge, recommending that all workers sign the documents. EJ did not publicize antiunion views, but workers knew the company's opinion when they were given a paid holiday after a vote not to unionize was passed. After a vote in 1940, workers danced in the streets and held a mock funeral, including a casket for the AFL-CIO. A letter to employees from George F. Johnson stated, "In God's name don't forget that pledge. Stand behind your leaders. I don't think any stranger can tell you what is better for you than I can. I who has known you for 50 years and who has carefully thought and studied just what is the greatest good for the greatest number." The union responded, "Thanks both to the EJ company and its stooges and staff for attempting to destroy our union . . . this vicious and uncalled for attack by the supervisory staff of EJ has aroused every member . . . they said that communism has infiltrated into the labor movement . . . but even the powerful national association of manufacturers has its share of stinkers."

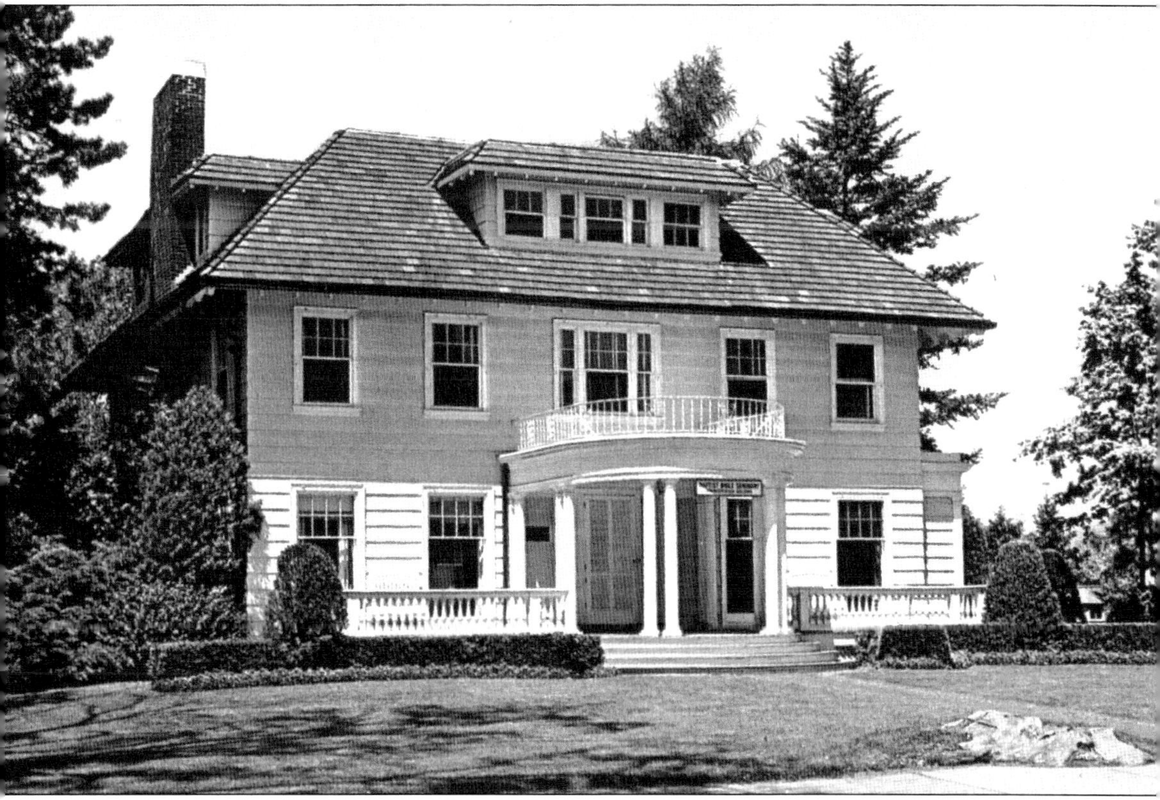

In 1913, labor "agitators" threatened to organize a strike at the Endicott-Johnson factories. George F. Johnson promptly met the challenge by promising to close the factories down until the workers returned to their senses. To remind employees of the possibility of a shutout, Johnson kept a large pile of placards announcing "Factories closed due to Union activity." According to a retiree of EJ, the signs were left for years in readiness in a prominent office where they could be easily seen as a reminder that EJ would not give in to force. In a great irony of fate, the home of Charles F. Johnson Jr., on Main Street in Johnson City, became offices for the Baptist Bible Seminary and is now union headquarters for the Broome County Federation of Labor.

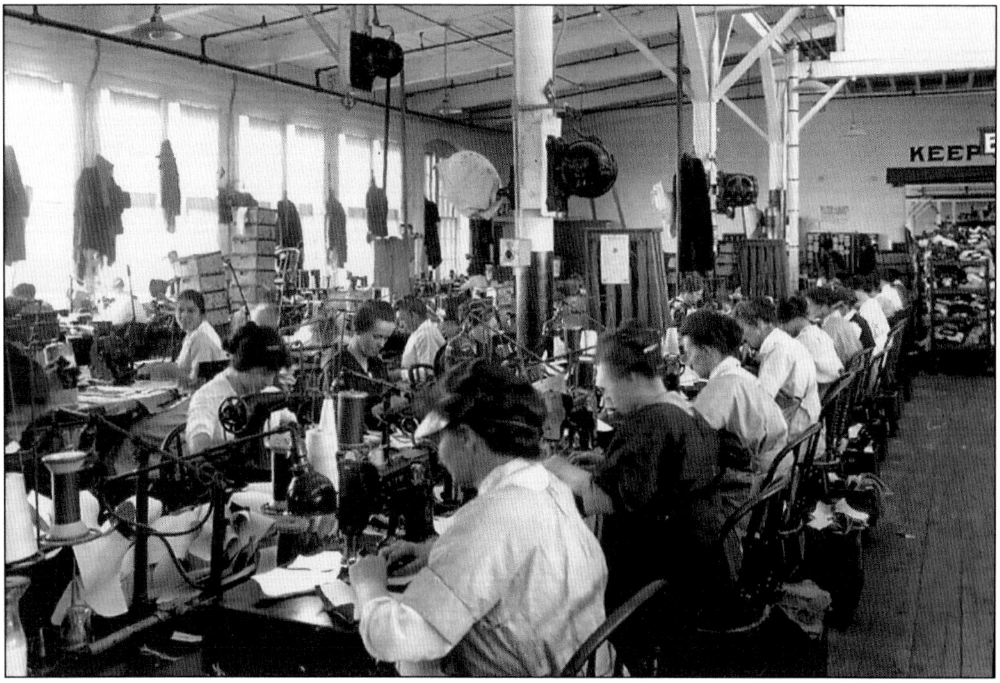

These photographs show the Endicott-Johnson stitching room. The picture above is from a glass lantern slide in the collection in New York State Archives in Albany. On a romantic note, George F. Johnson met his second wife, Mary Ann McGlone, when she worked in the stitching room at an Endicott-Johnson factory.

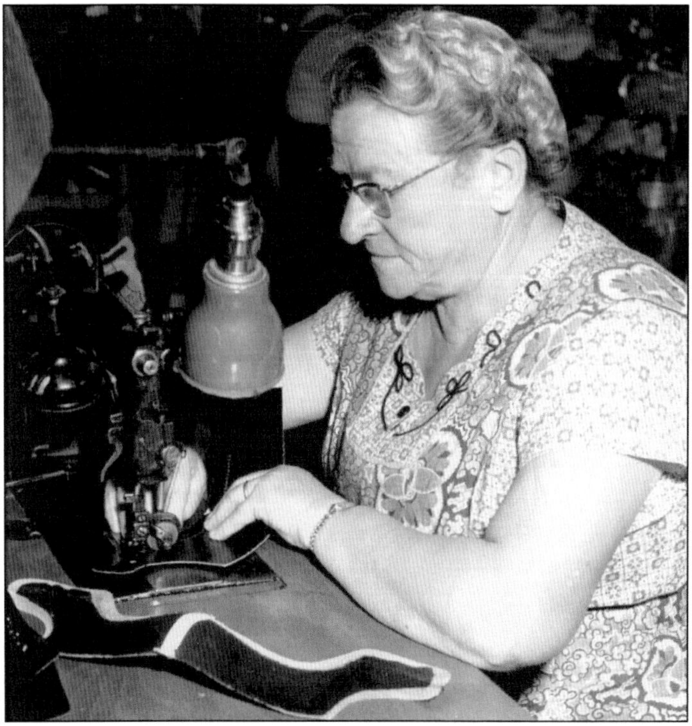

Pictured is an Endicott-Johnson worker in the fancy quarter stitching department c. 1935. In 1927, George F. Johnson complimented the majority of employees who appreciated the EJ profit-sharing plan, and to the dissatisfied he recommended, "I wish you would quit. I am sincere in this wish. Behave or get out!"

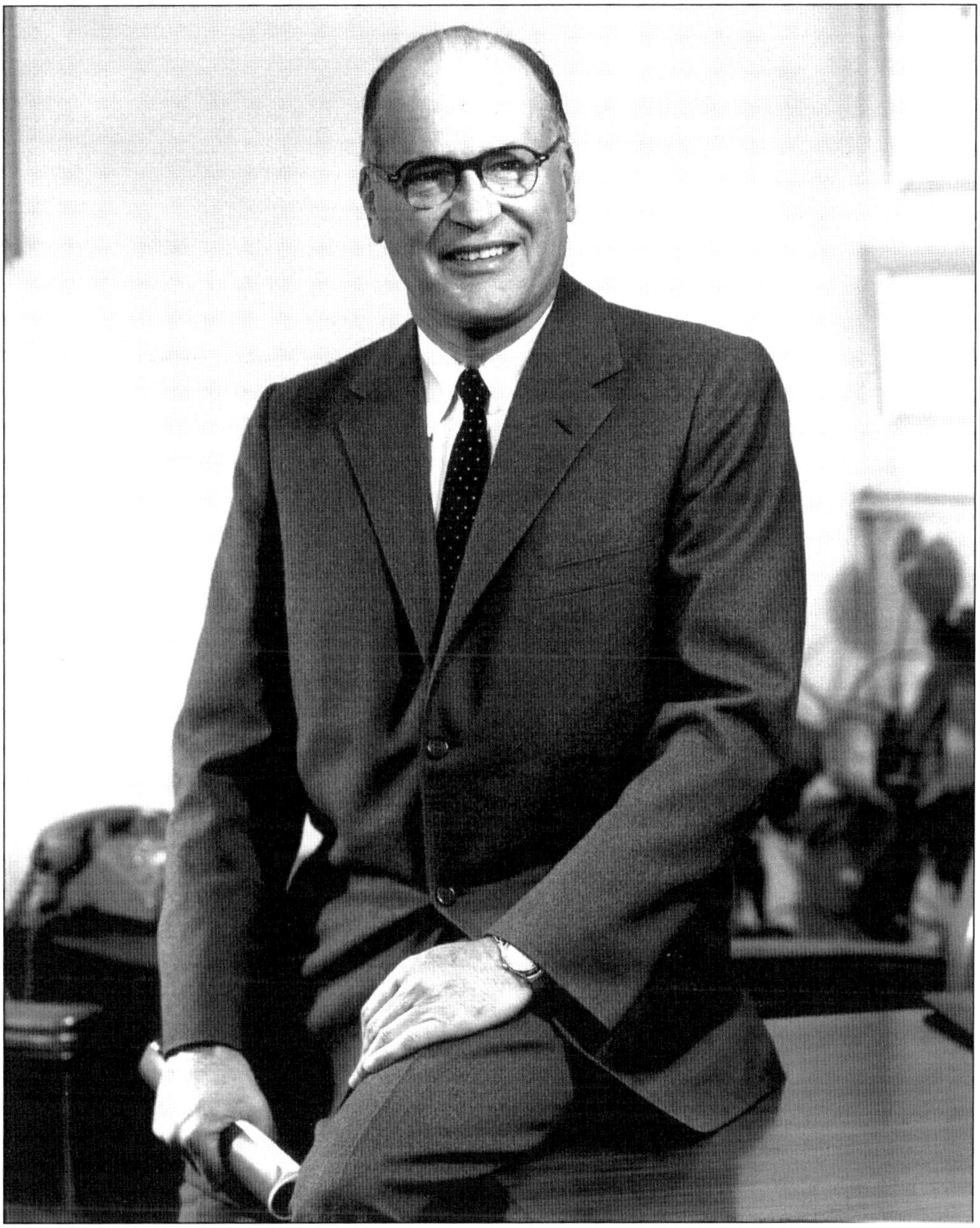

Frank A. Johnson was the son of George W. and the grandson of George F. Johnson. In 1957, he took the place of Charles F. Johnson Jr. as president of Endicott-Johnson. By now the company was in serious difficulty. Management was in disarray because there was no one person able to oversee all areas of the business and none of the Johnson descendants had been taught to delegate responsibilities to competent managers. Without George F. Johnson's guidance, progress floundered. By the time of the 1961 financial report, the company had lost $12 million. The machinery was outdated, as were the styles of shoes produced. Still, EJ tried to function on memories of the EJ days of glory. In spite of the good intentions of Frank Johnson and a new board of directors, what began as a Johnson dynasty turned into disaster as the EJ factories began to close.

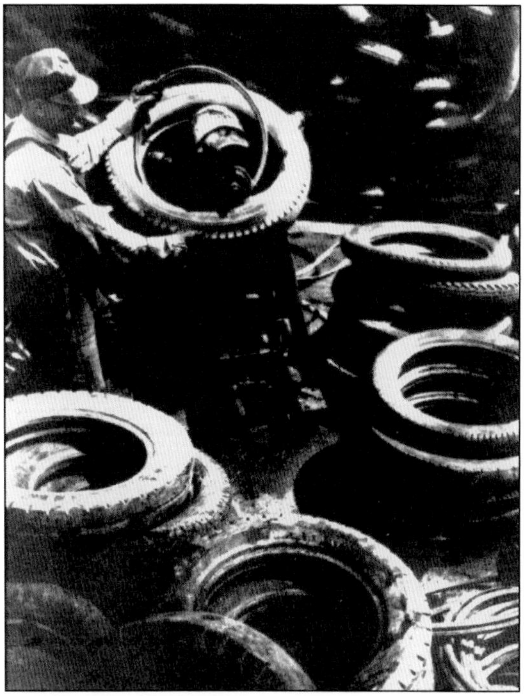

Recycle and reuse was a cost-saving plan instituted by Endicott-Johnson to minimize waste and maximize the financial benefit from waste products. In 1938, some 24 tons of old rubber tires were put through the reclaiming mill every day and used for many purposes, including heels on new shoes and boots. Another by-product the company sold at cost to employees owning EJ homes was its own "leather coat paint" made from the by-product of shoe dyes. The photograph shows the tire recycling process in 1939.

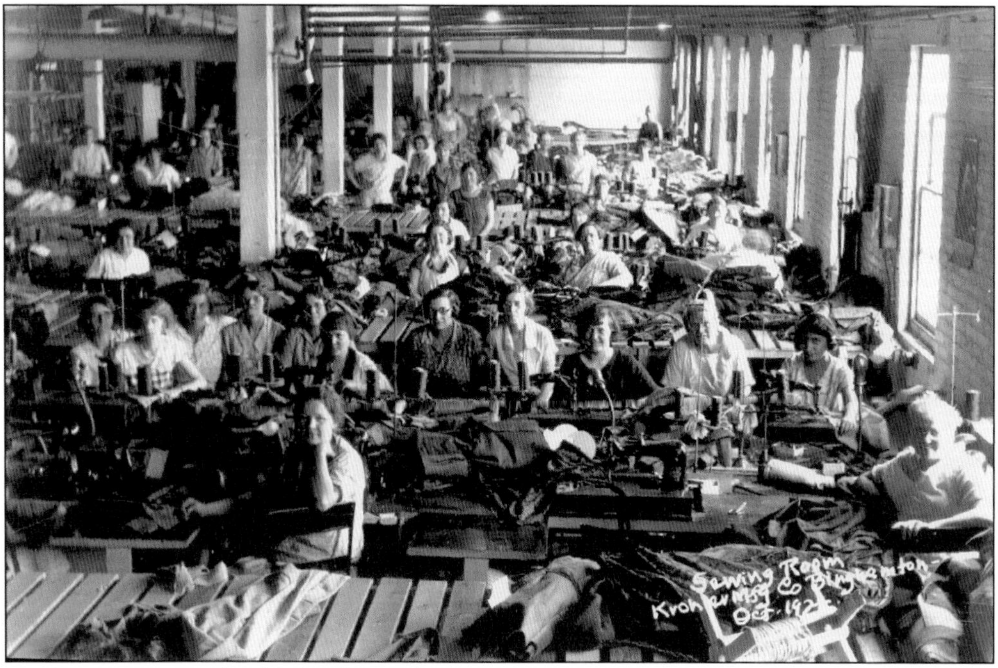

Leather scraps were shredded and turned into a nitrogen-producing compound sold for fertilizer. Acetone fumes from the rubber processing plants were gathered with a special machine and turned into liquid acetone for reuse. Hair scraped from thousands of hides during the tanning process was accumulated and sold to furniture companies to be used as stuffing—the local Krohler Manufacturing Company of Binghamton produced furniture during this era. This rare photograph shows the interior of Krohler in 1920.

SPECIAL NOTICE

TO THE WORKERS:

The United States Supreme Court having decided that the New York Law for the Garnishment of wages is Constitutional, it will be necessary for us to recognize Garnishee executions (if served in a legal way) against our workers.

We refuse to be a "debt-collecting Agency." We advise **strongly** against foolish debts; **and most debts contracted by E-J workers are unnecessary.**

Therefore, any "Garnishee Executions" served on our Officials for debts contracted by our workers **after** this Notice, will be **cause for dismissal** from the service of the Company, and the loss of all privileges.

A worker thus discharged, **if rehired,** will come in as a new man; and only **after** the "Garnishee Execution" has been withdrawn and Judgment satisfied.

ENDICOTT JOHNSON CORPORATION

November 19th, 1924. President.

George F. Johnson opposed the Garnishment of Wages Law of 1924, claiming it was inequitable legislation: "My opinion is there should be no garnishee law. This should be handled between private persons. It is made to collect debts from laborers who have nothing but their wages." In November 1924, he sent a letter to his workers advising against foolish debts: "Any Garnishee Executions served on our company will be cause for dismissal from EJ and the loss of all privileges." His thoughts were, "Debt is never justified. . . . Paying cash is a valuable habit. Try it!" and, "A man in debt is a slave." In 1915, Endicott-Johnson was approached by a coal dealer requesting garnishment of pay for a worker whose bills were overdue. Johnson decried the "unlawful" process of garnishee but considered coal a necessity if families were not to suffer. EJ agreed to pay the bills if the employee could not comply. In 1922, Johnson explained that EJ would no longer "guarantee" payment, saying workers were able to afford their own bills or look to the Humane Society . . . and the company would still not enforce garnishee executions.

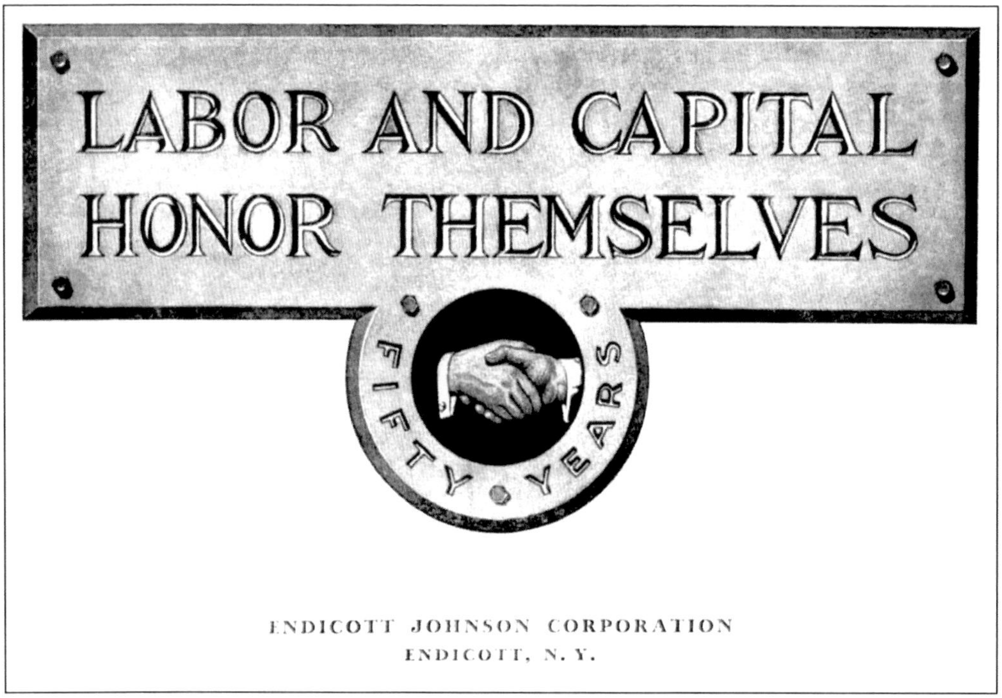

A great celebration entitled Labor and Capital Honor Themselves was organized in 1931 commemorating the 50th anniversary of the arrival of George F. Johnson. The seven-mile long parade featured 160 floats, 20 marching bands, and 40,000 people. About 150,000 spectators viewed the show. It was a holiday for the community in which Johnson was regarded a hero. The clasped hands became a corporate logo signifying cooperation between management and labor.

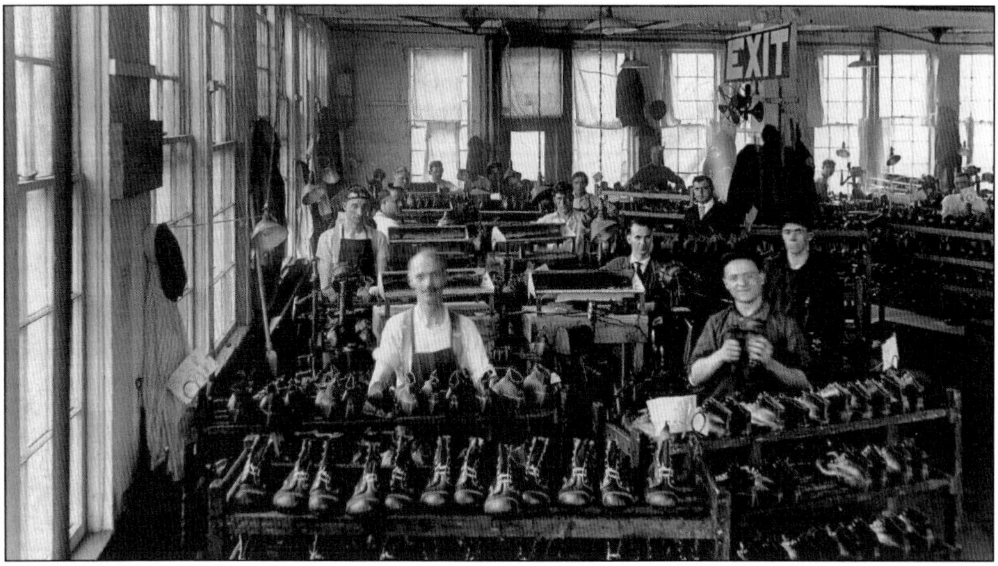

"Chasing down the cripples" was the job of Anthony Battisti. He pushed a rack through the Endicott-Johnson factory during the 1930s and 1940s, collecting all the shoes with dings, dents, and defects. Footwear with scrapes and slovenly stitches was restored to the high EJ standards and made fit for sale in his fix-it department.

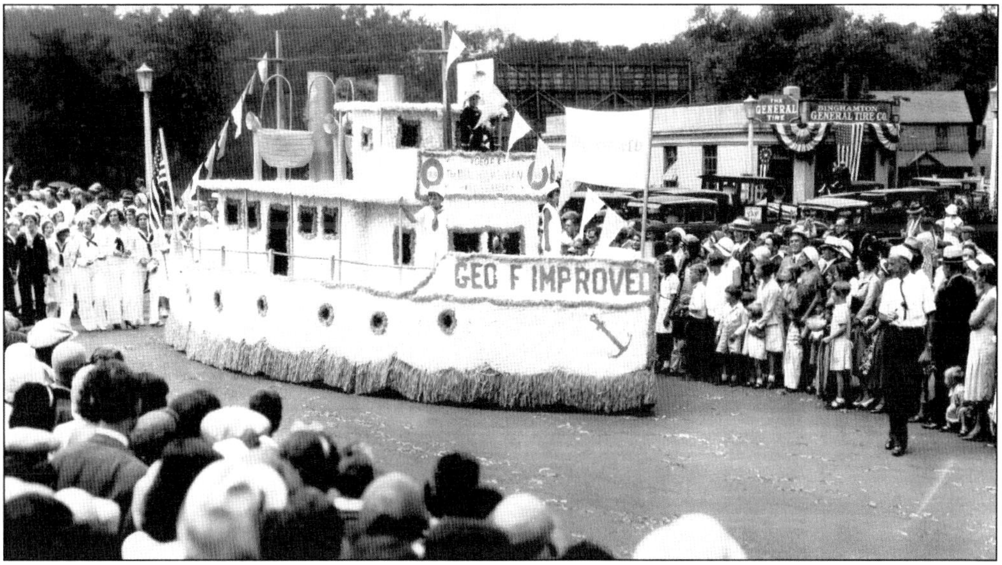

Extravagant parades became part of the local culture. Many occasions were greeted with elaborate fireworks displays and lengthy parades. The Fourth of July, Labor Day, Memorial Day, local centennials, bicentennials, effigy burnings, and welcoming George F. Johnson home from his Florida estate could all be cause for celebrations. In 1919, the first annual "George F." Day parade included an Endicott-Johnson payroll float decorated completely with one-dollar bills. That parade was only five miles long. Pictured above is an EJ float in the George F. Johnson 50-year parade; below is one in the 1952 parade for the 60th anniversary of Johnson City.

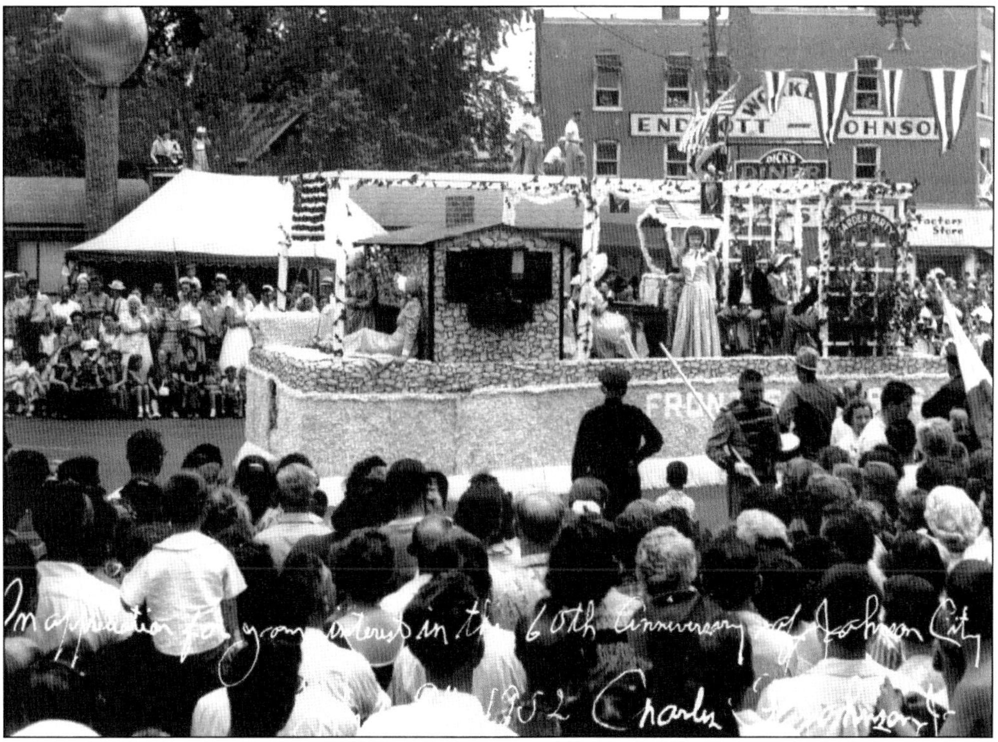

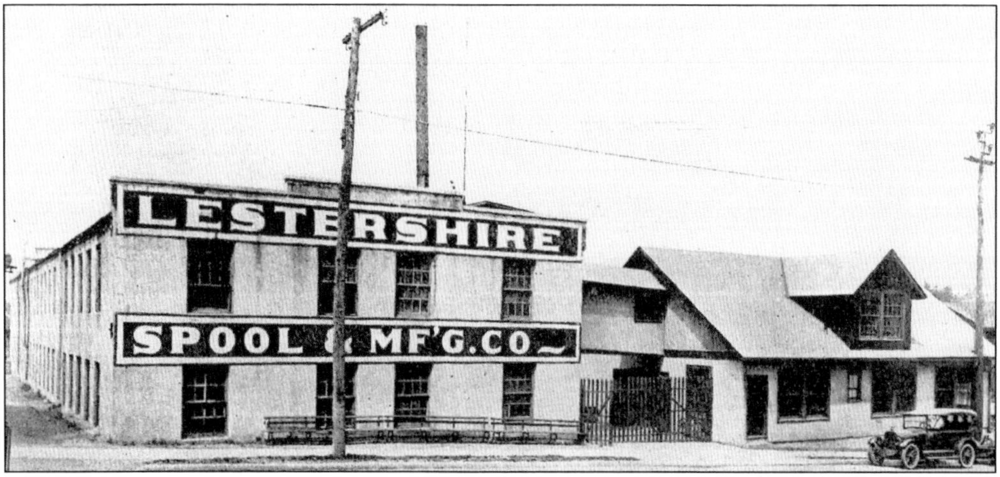

Many local industries developed to support the needs of Endicott-Johnson. The Lestershire Spool and Bobbin Company, located on Baldwin Street in Lestershire, was kept in business for many decades, supplying a variety of spools for the more than 5,100 miles of thread EJ used every day in the making of shoes and boots. Traveling through Johnson City, the smell of ripe bananas emanated from this factory, adding to the mixture of aromas of industrial prosperity. Banana oil was used as a preservative on the wooden spools. The photographs show the exterior and interior of the company *c.* 1916.

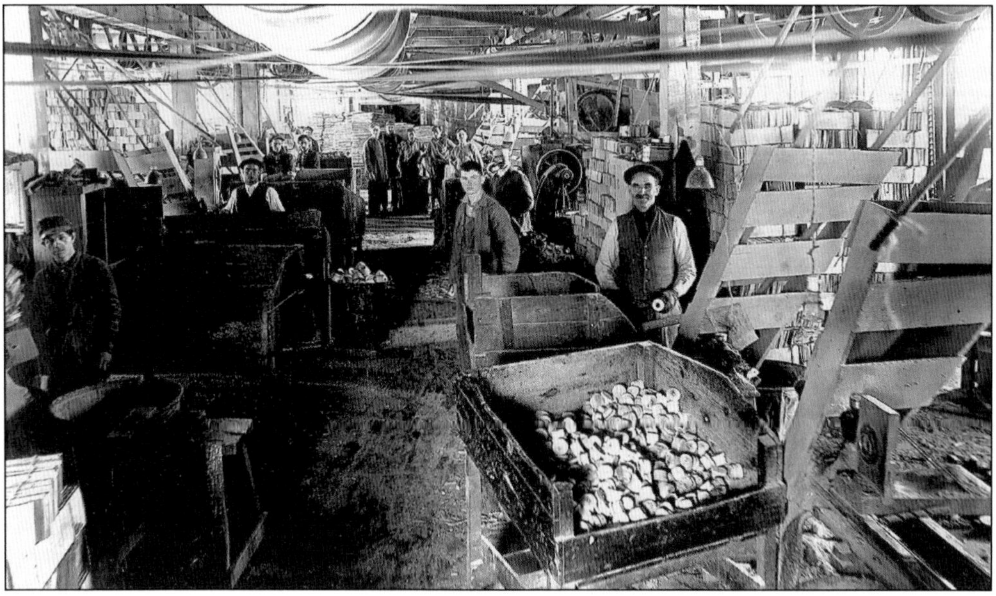

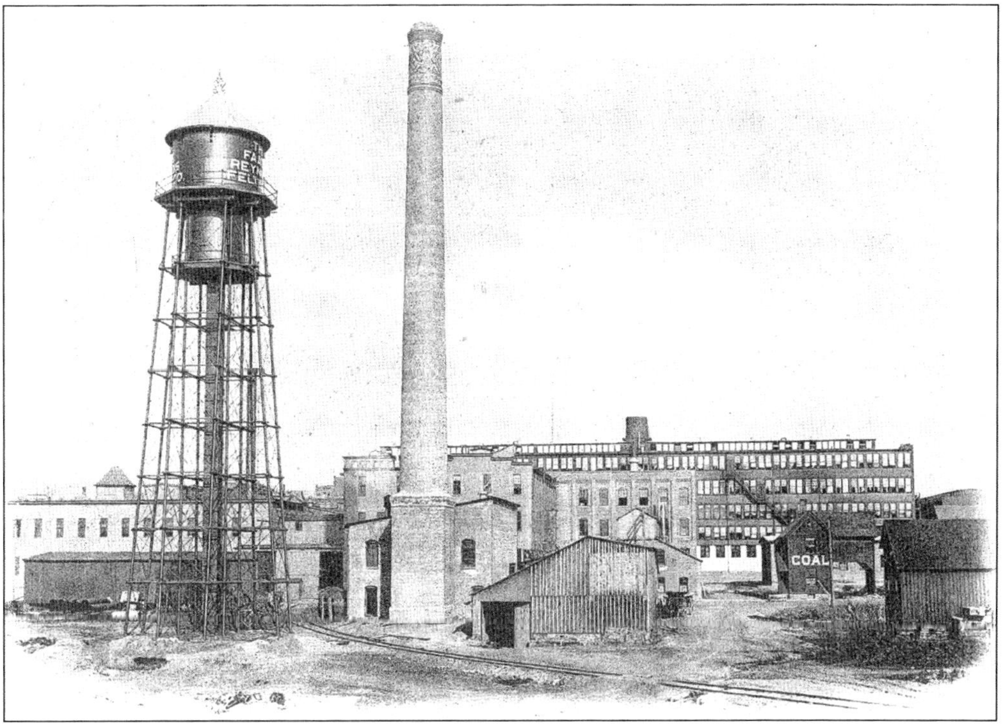

Felt is a soft but tough flexible sheet made of fibers of wool, hair, and fur matted together, compressed, and rolled flat. Sizing was added to stabilize the product. Endicott-Johnson used it in uppers of shoes, as insoles, and underneath the outer soles. Pictured is another industry that depended on EJ business—the Faatz Felting Company of Lestershire.

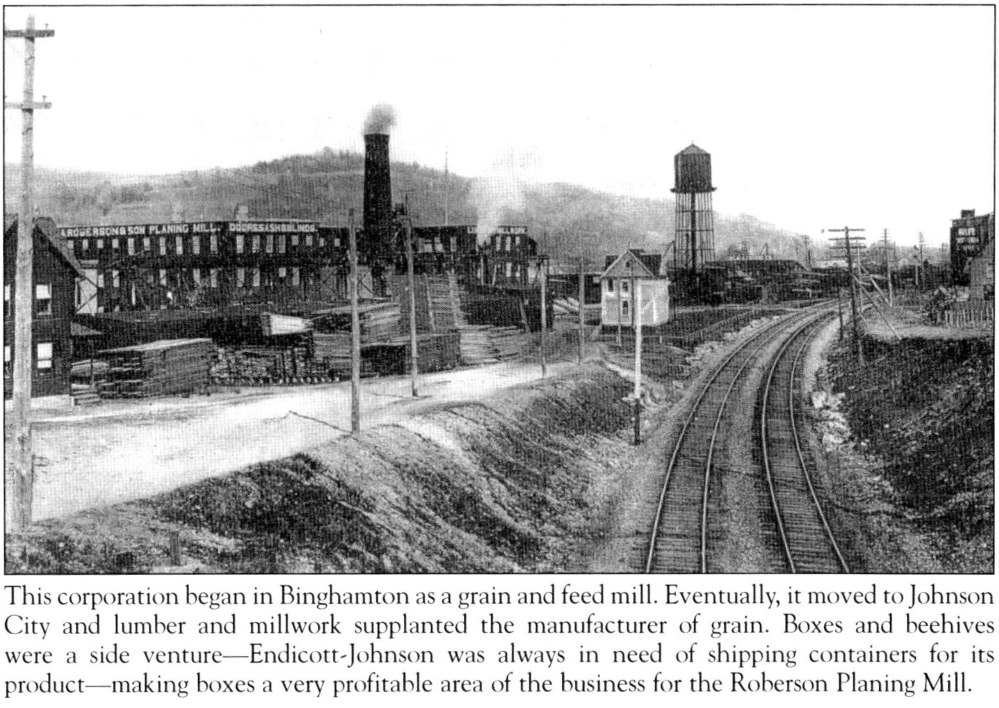

This corporation began in Binghamton as a grain and feed mill. Eventually, it moved to Johnson City and lumber and millwork supplanted the manufacturer of grain. Boxes and beehives were a side venture—Endicott-Johnson was always in need of shipping containers for its product—making boxes a very profitable area of the business for the Roberson Planing Mill.

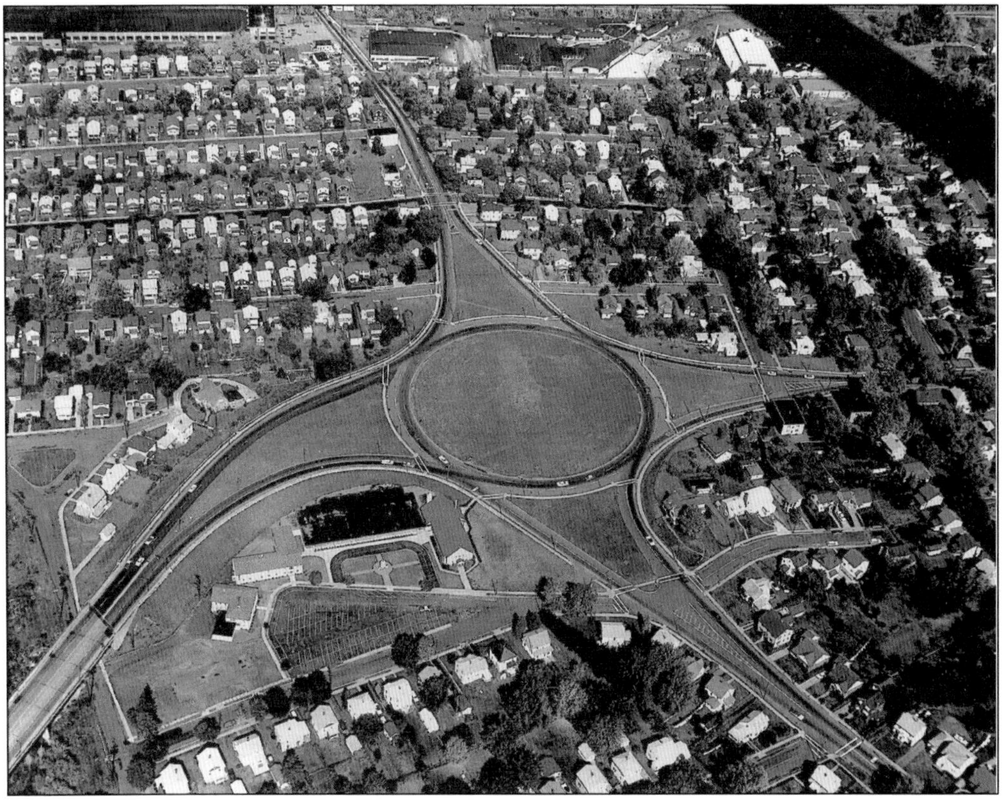

The Vulcan Corporation and Sweets Foundry buildings are shown at the top right of this aerial photograph. Both companies were part of the support system for Endicott-Johnson, manufacturing necessary products for the shoe industry. Easily identifiable are the streets laid out for EJ homes. Harry L. Johnson was in charge of building this neighborhood.

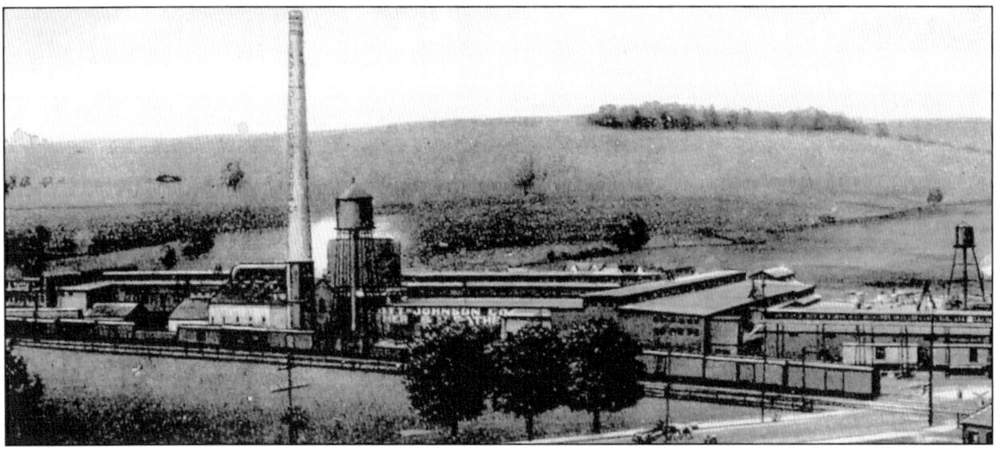

Progress sometimes has an environmental price tag. According to people who lived in Endicott, the Endicott-Johnson chimneys emitted soot that coated every item outside and sifted into homes and automobiles. Laundry dried on backyard lines had to be brushed before bringing it into the house, and the gritty ash on sidewalks crunched underfoot. Soot became thicker during chimney cleanings when steam pressure forced excess grime into the atmosphere. The pictured tannery closed in 1966 and was torn down in 1968.

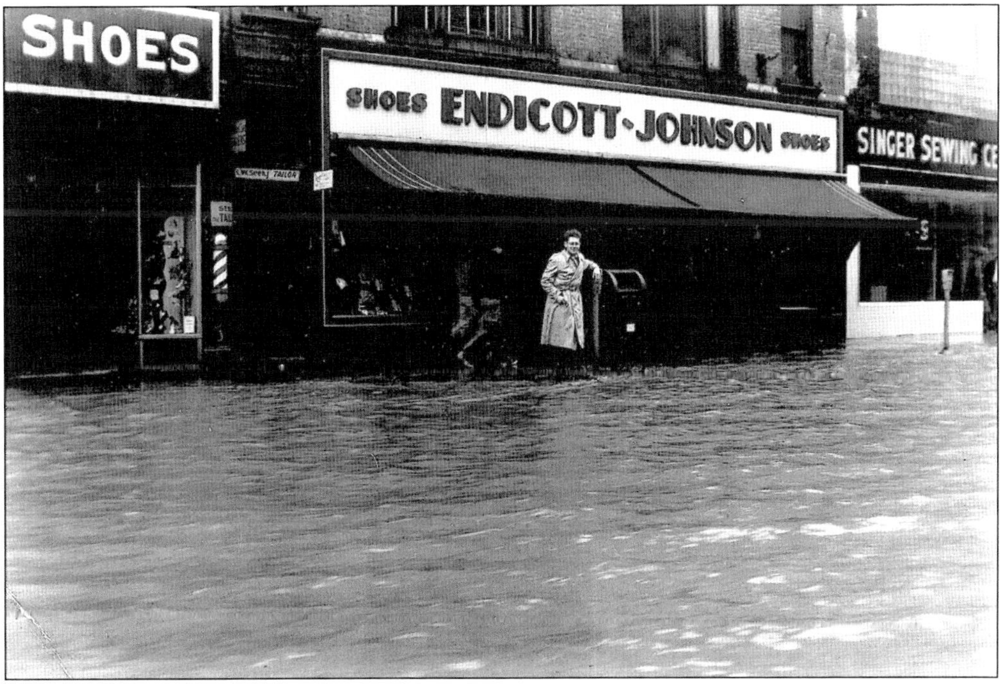

Before a flood control system was installed, devastating freshets were a fact of life in this twin river valley. In 1935 and 1936, floods swept the Southern Tier. In both years, George F., George W., and Charles F. Johnson Jr. set an example by donating money, goods, food, and personal time. Each man donned boots and pitched in during the physical cleanup. Endicott-Johnson workers gave $25,000 to the Red Cross for flood relief, and free medical services to anyone in the community needing help was available through EJ clinics. The Frank A. Johnson Post 758 American Legion was open night and day to all seeking assistance and was the headquarters for distribution of food, clothing, and household supplies. The picture above is of Washington Avenue in Endicott, and the one below is Ideal Park—both inundated with the floodwaters.

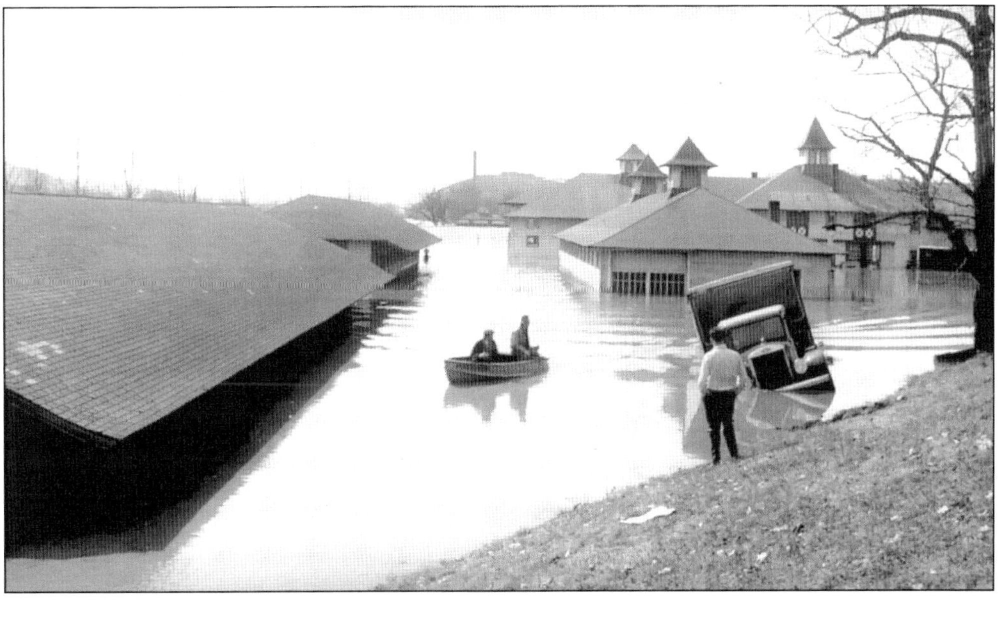

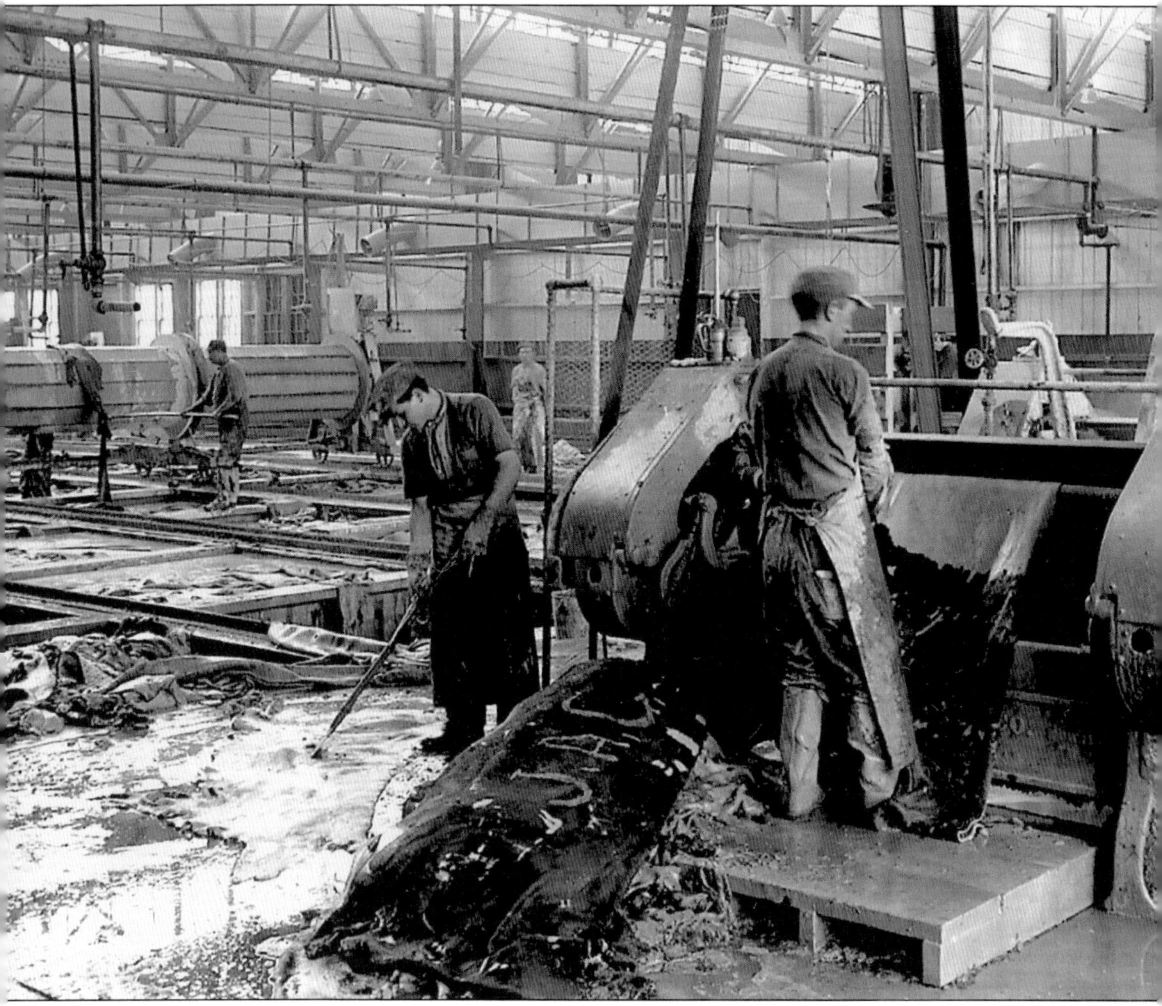

"From hoof to foot" was an advertising slogan at Endicott-Johnson. The process began with obtaining raw hides for the tanning factories. Huge vats of tanning acid filled the buildings at the end of Washington Avenue in Endicott, infusing the air with an acidic odor. The company controlled the entire process of shoe production, cutting out middleman profits and gaining industry prominence. Long before workplace regulations restricted access, Evelyn Rose, now 83 years old, remembers numerous visits to the tannery as a child of eight. She and school friends easily balanced on the narrow "duck board" walkways between vats of toxic liquid, entering and leaving the building by the outside open staircase. In 1926, EJ boasted a daily output of 130,000 pairs of shoes and 20,400 sides of leather produced daily by 17,000 employees. In an atmosphere reeking of tanning acid, a brotherhood of strength developed between tanners. It was physically challenging work that only the toughest immigrants could handle. Each man was initiated with a nickname befitting his station in the factory.

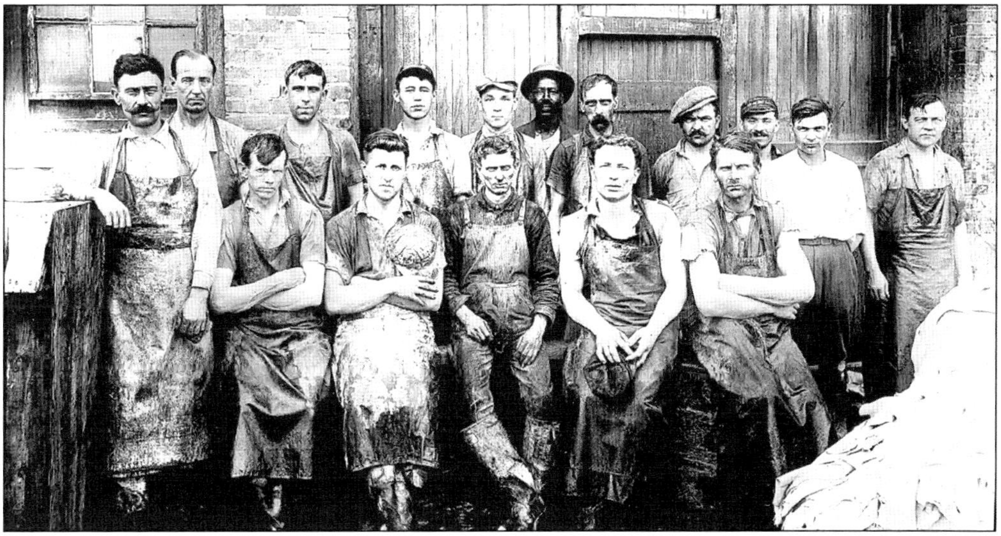

By 1927, the Endicott leather tannery was the largest in the world, containing 900 vats of tanning liquor. Men in "wet work," called "reelers," manned long hooked poles to transfer hides from one vat to another. Floors were slippery and filled with tangled hose. Often, a laborer would fall into a vat of caustic acid, crawl out of the pit, shower, and return to work. Chemical splashes could cause holes in clothes and burns on skin—but the pay was the highest in the factory.

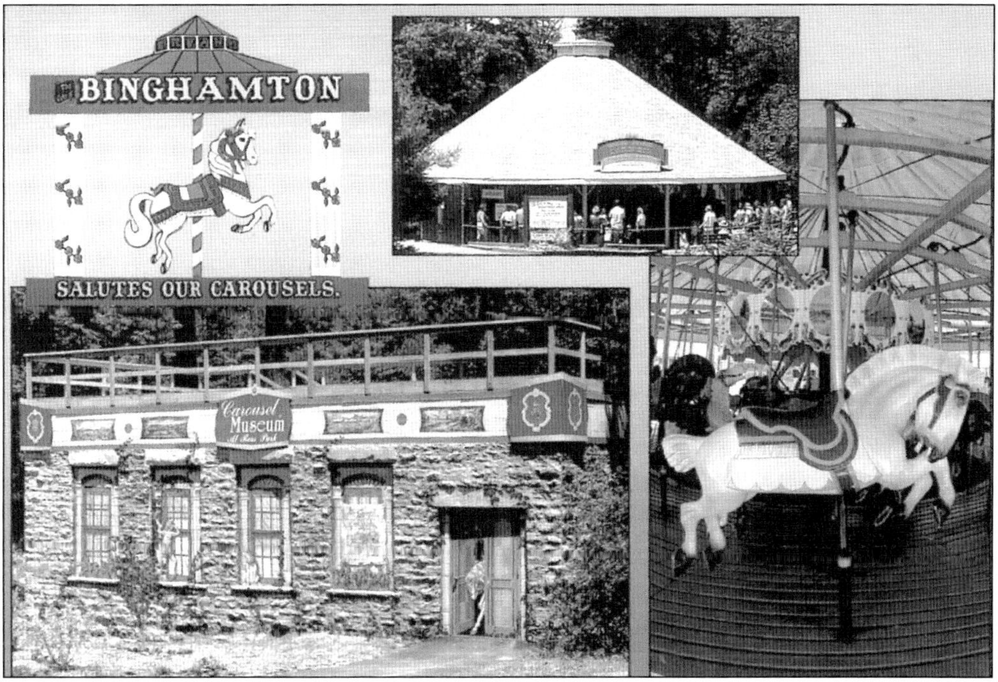

Extreme poverty as a child robbed George F. Johnson of the opportunity to purchase a few moments of pleasure on a carousel. To ensure that the children of the Magic City area would always be able to ride steeds of dreams, the Johnson family donated six Alan Herschell merry-go-rounds to Broome County between 1919 and 1934—no admission could ever to be charged. The carousel pictured is in Ross Park in Binghamton. All of the machines are listed on the National Register of Historic Places. (Ed Aswad photographs.)

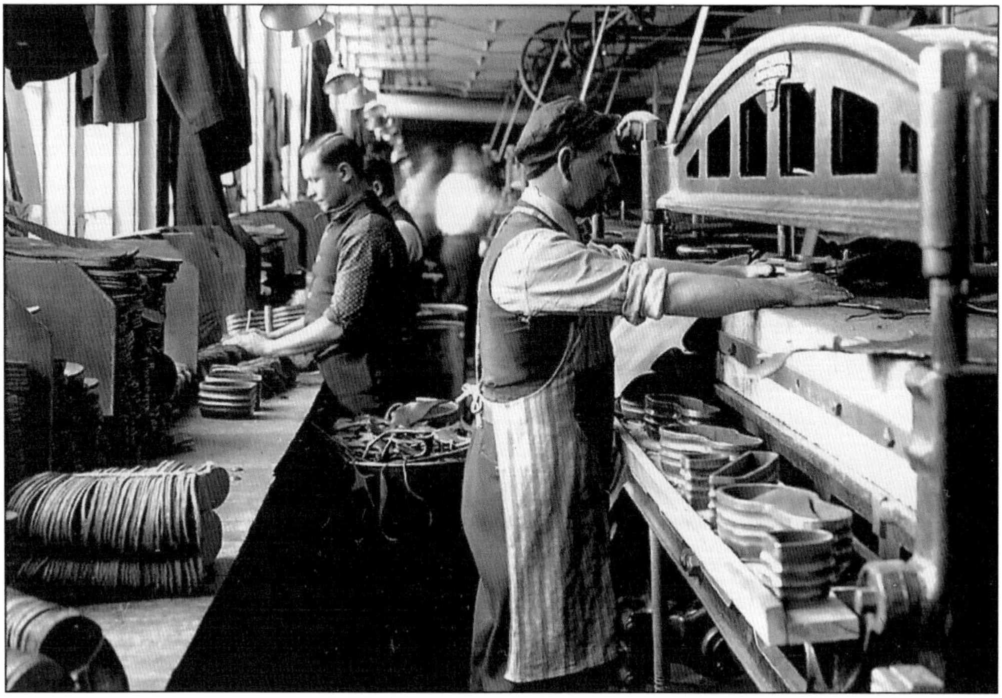

Steel dies were used to cut pieces of leather for the construction of footwear. It was an exacting process to place the dies so that there was a minimum of waste from each hide. These photographs are from the New York State Archives collection of glass lantern slides taken in 1919.

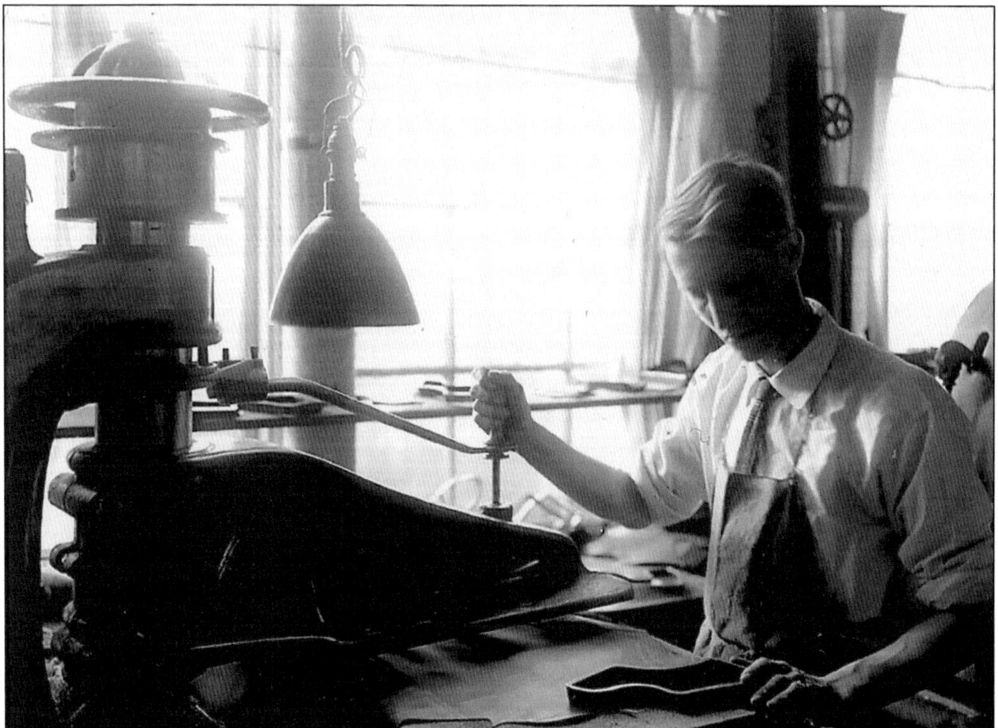

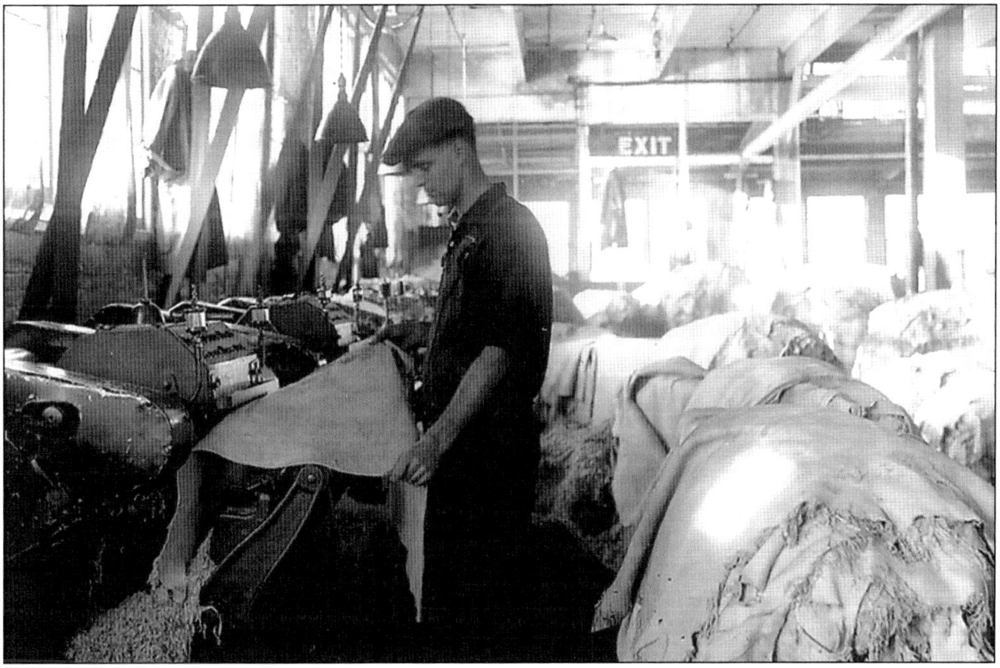

Shaving machines removed any leftover hair and flesh from hides and evened out the thickness of the of the leather. The shaving scraps were swept from the floors on a regular basis and sold for use as fertilizer.

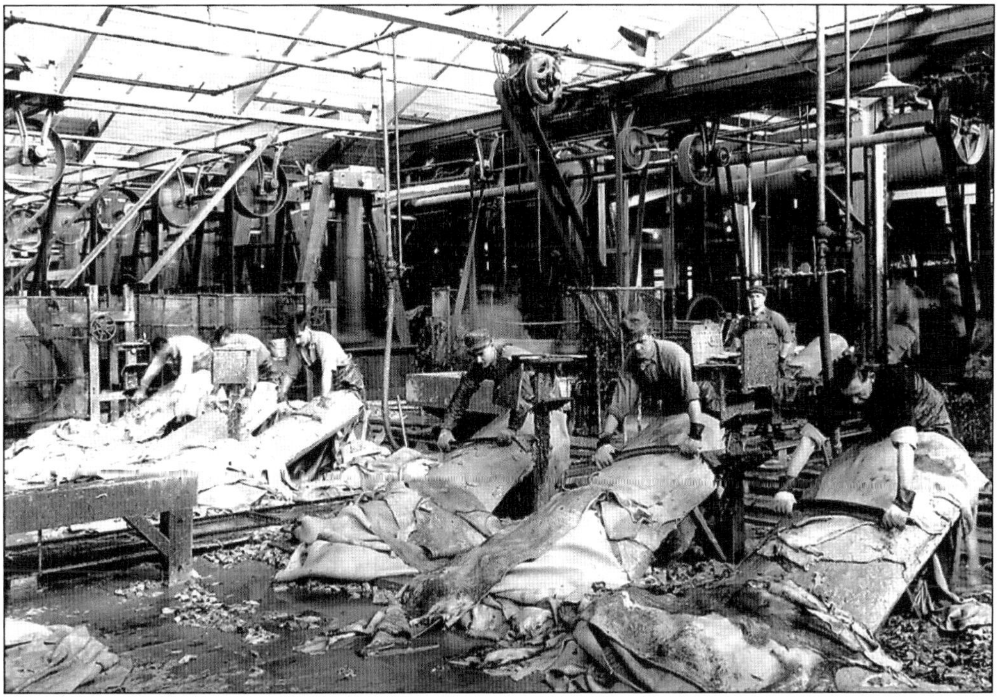

This photograph taken c. 1919 shows the hand-beaming process of scraping the hides to remove any leftover hair or flesh. Long curved knives were used with great care so as not to damage the hide.

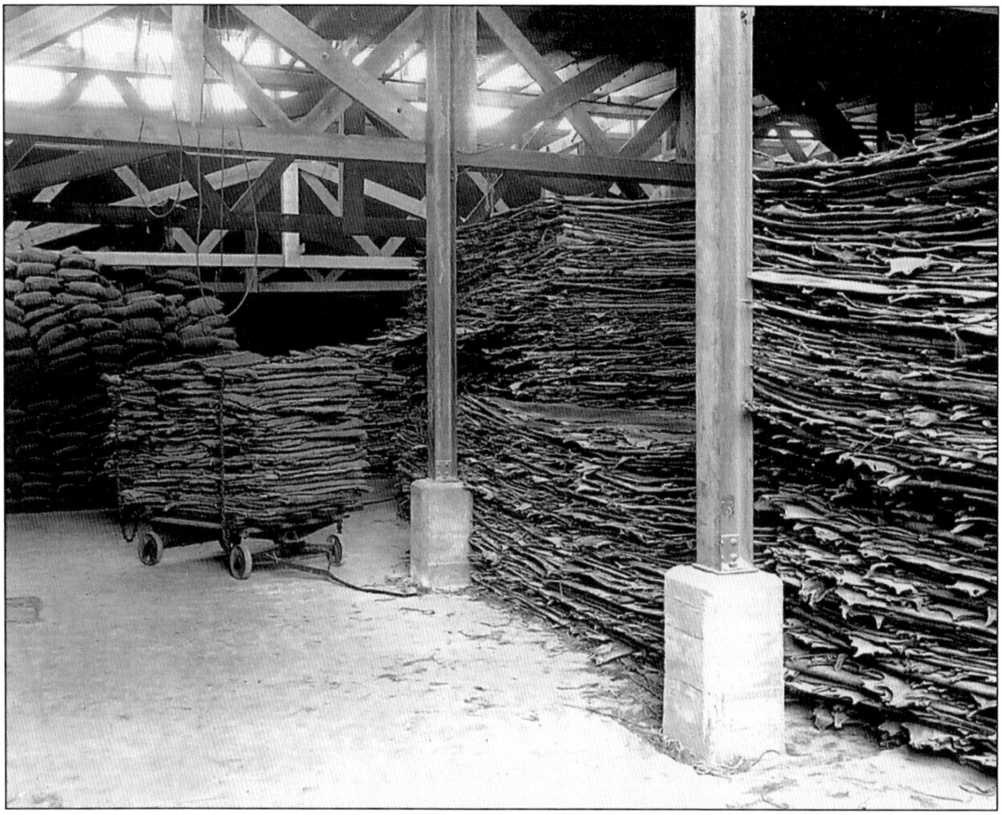

During the 1930s, the average stock of hides in storage at Endicott-Johnson was 350,000. About 80,000 hides were used each week. Labeled "Hide Store House," the *c.* 1920 photographs show the huge mounds of hides and bags of lime used in the tanning process and the sturdy crew that tended the warehouse. At this point the hides were very stiff and dry.

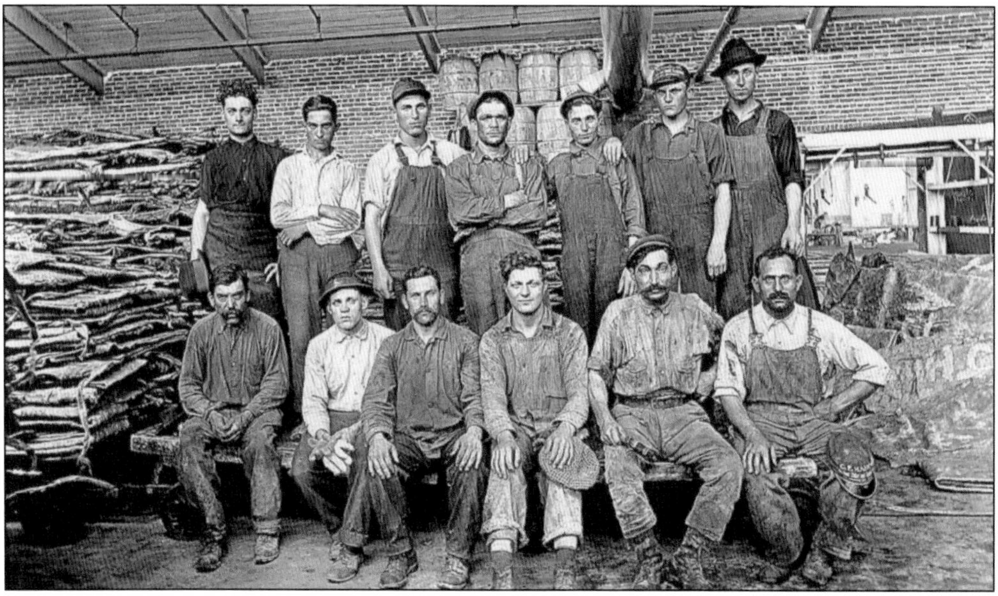

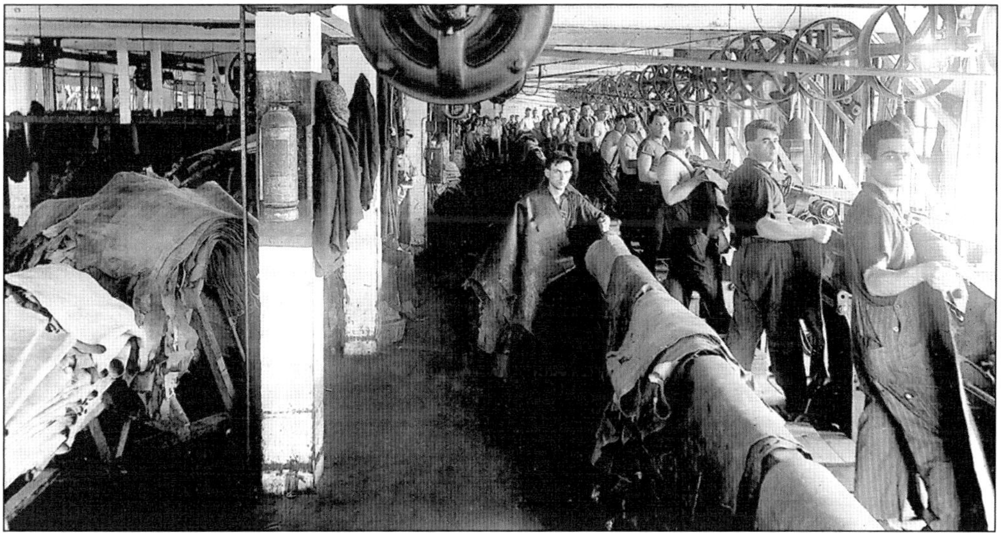

This is the buffing department in 1916. This department was where the outer, or grain, side of the leather was scoured.

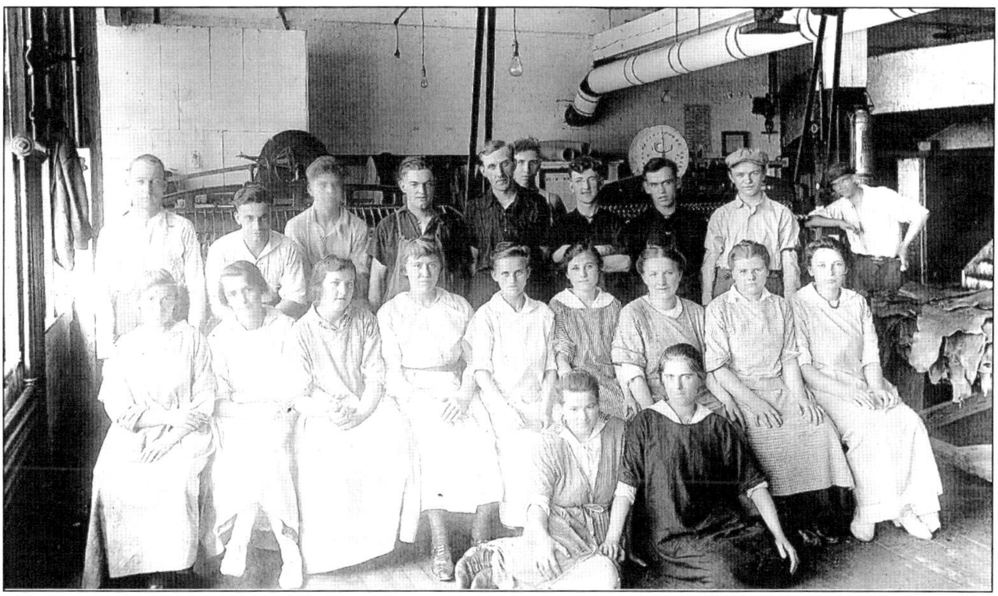

The Endicott-Johnson shipping room was the last stop in the chain of shoe-processing departments. These workers are posing among hides, boxes, and scales in the year 1919. Every day, 13 rail cars filled with shoes were shipped to all parts of the world.

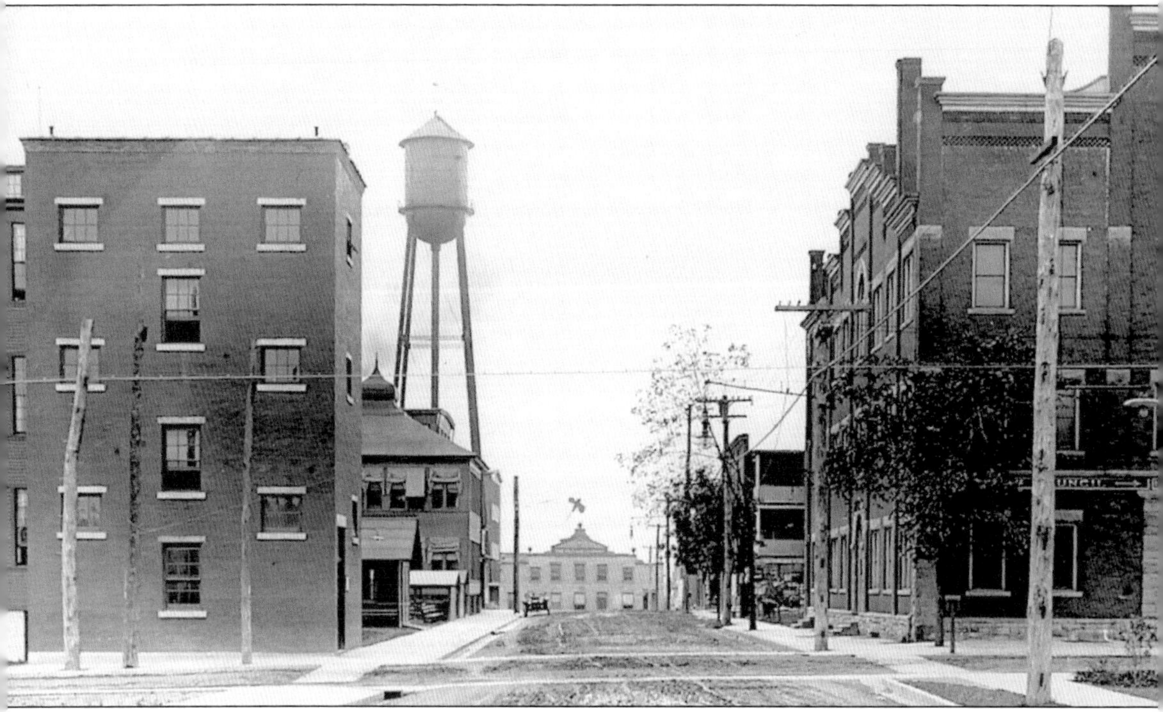

In 1931, a crook netted $10,000 in a robbery of the Endicott-Johnson payroll department in the Corlis Avenue factory in Johnson City. Eluding capture for several months, the bandit "spent lavishly, and buried a stolen cash box in his basement"—not a sophisticated plan. When the man was caught, George F. Johnson demanded prosecution, saying there was no excuse for robbery. The man was convicted and sent to jail; when released, he apologized to Johnson, who loaned him money to start over and open a gas and service station. Pictured is the burgled factory; a few years later, this same "mother of them all" factory was beginning to show its age. It was only 39 years old, but the west wall partly collapsed, causing 900 workers to be sent home. The building was constructed in 1897 and, in 1936, was the oldest of the EJ factories.

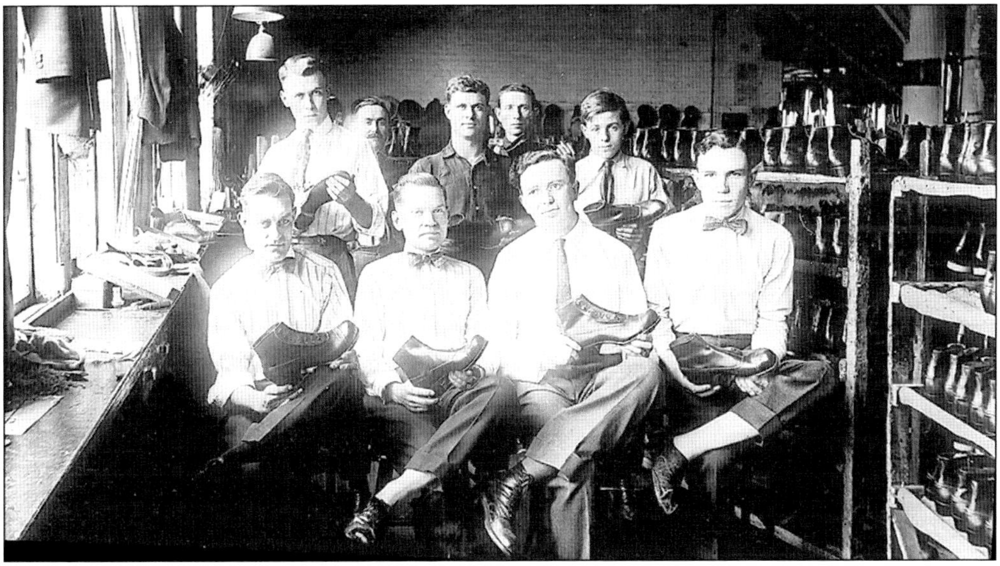

Men working in an Endicott-Johnson shoe inspection department are holding the product of their labors in 1912. The man on the far right looks as though he could use a new pair of shoes himself. The pictured shoes use buttons for closures. By 1936, an *EJ Workers Magazine* article advised the community, "Look what EJ has done for Broome County since 1900. Every man, woman and child in Broome County should wear nothing but Endicott-Johnson shoes."

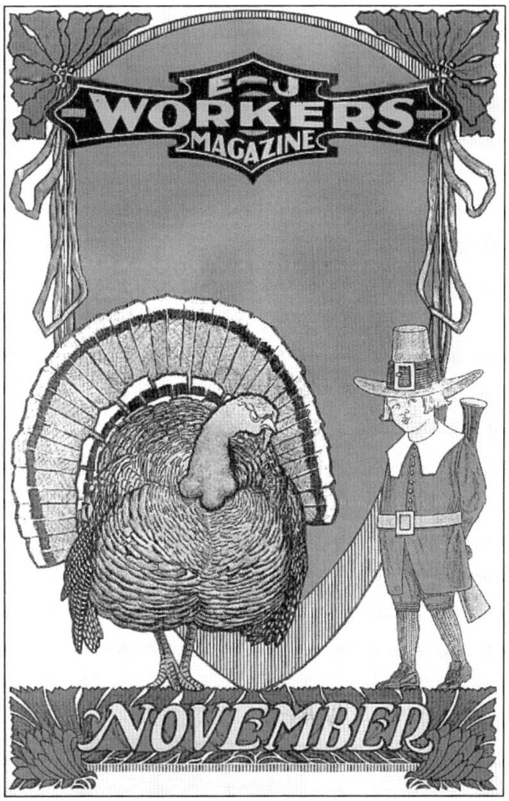

George F. Johnson instituted a magazine wherein all workers could ask questions and give their opinions without fear. It was also an opportunity for George F. to write lengthy sermonlike letters to the employees, covering a multitude of topics such as thrift, loyalty, bigotry, and who knew best. This is the cover of the 37-page booklet from November 1924. The publication was printed for several years, and upon discontinuation, a full page in the local newspaper was set aside for Endicott-Johnson news.

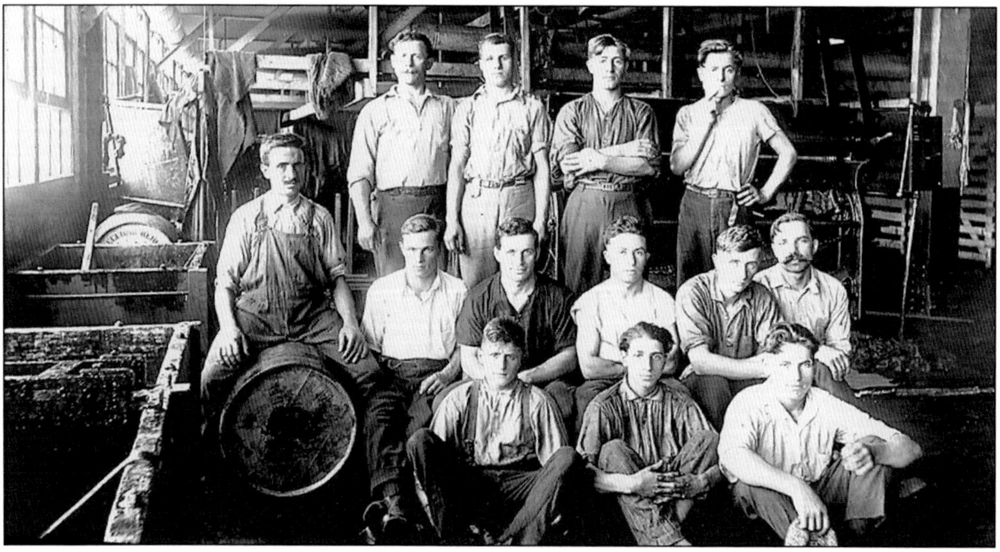

Pictured is the Endicott-Johnson Calves Skin Tannery in 1916. One 80-year-old man remembers trips to this factory when he was a small boy. The workers were always glad to see children and would often dismantle a large barrel that had contained tanning chemicals to give each boy a pair of staves for use as skis. An old automobile inner tube would be cut into strips to tie the staves to shoes.

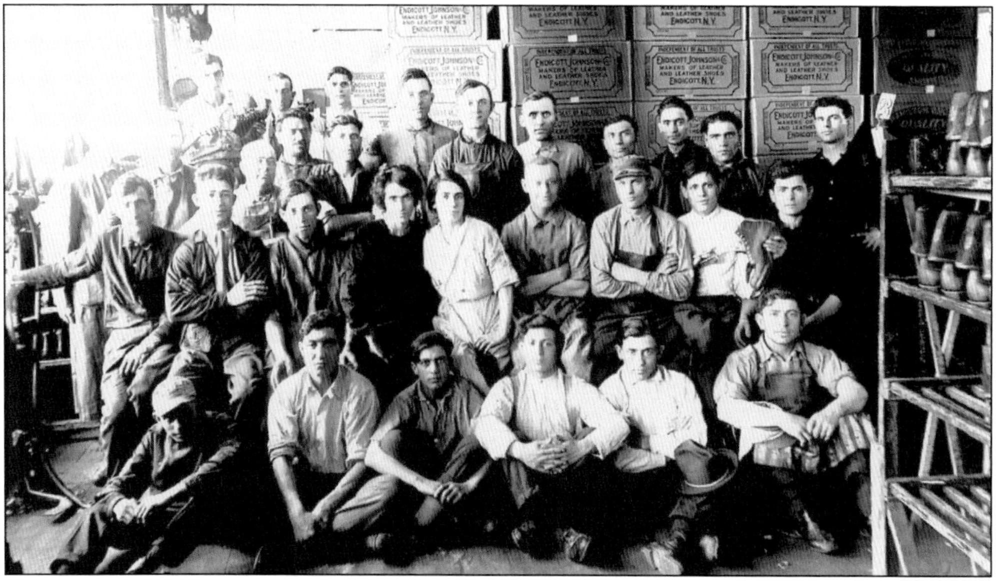

Shown is a finishing room in the welt factory in 1916. In this area, the bottoms of the outsoles were finished and the lasts were removed. At this point, the sock lining and the heel pads were inserted. Note the EJ packing crates stacked in the background.

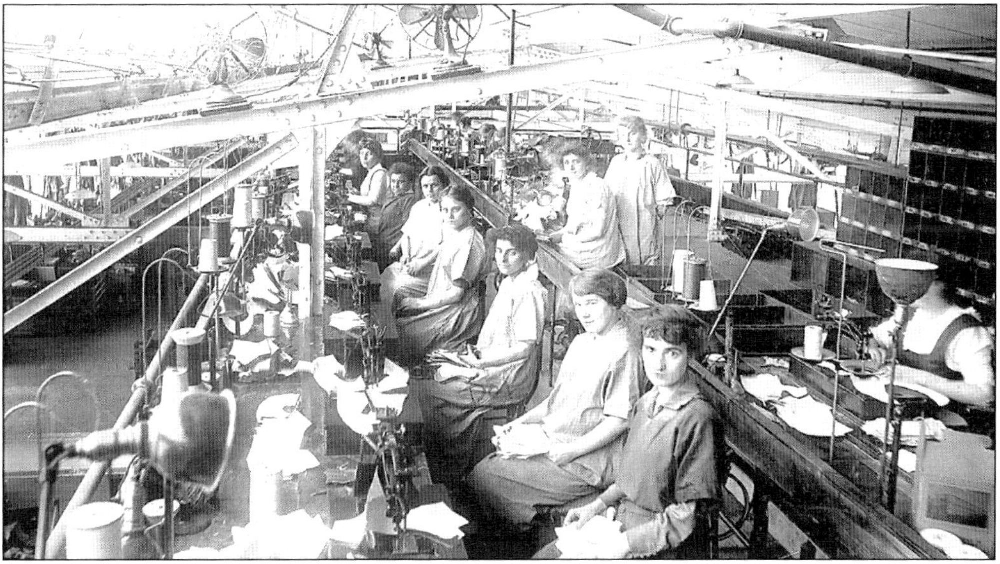

Endicott-Johnson had better-than-average factory conditions, but problems did exist. Tanneries were reported to have a high death rate from exposure to caustic chemicals. Leather dust in the cutting rooms caused lung problems. Leather "disease" was common from contact with dyes. Rashes and severe skin conditions were frequent complaints. Limbs and digits were lost in huge machinery. Noise levels were deafening in sewing rooms, such as the one pictured, and tanning odors permeated the valley—but there were few complaints.

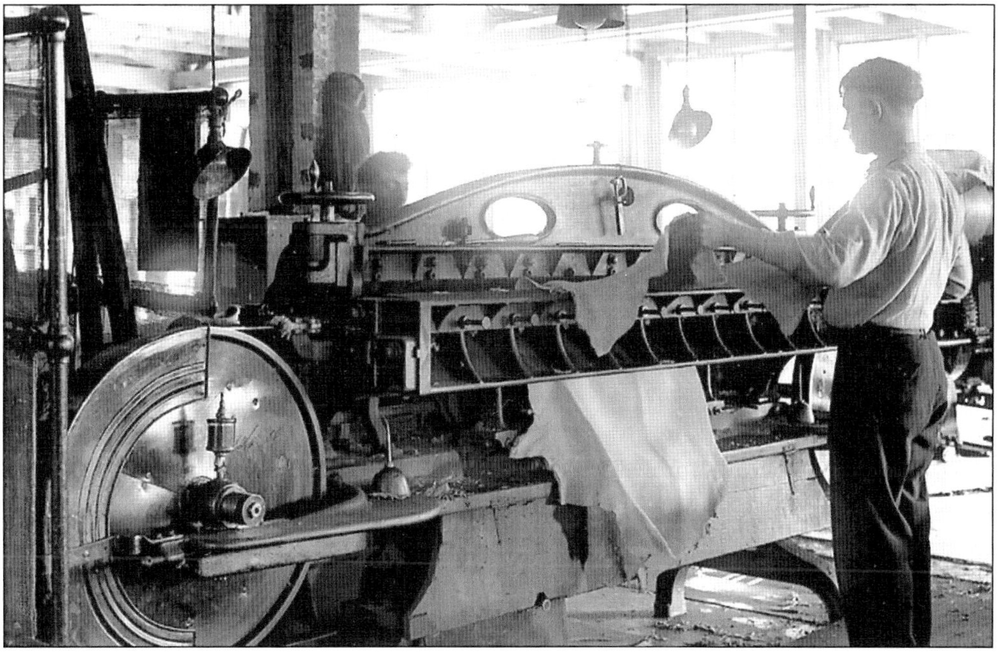

All employees were entitled to consult with company lawyers. "We have a legal department which will be most happy to advise you . . . free to all employees . . . with a staff of competent attorneys available." Workers were encouraged to consult the lawyers for financial advice and investing, as well as for legal problems. The 1916 photographs shows a worker processing leather.

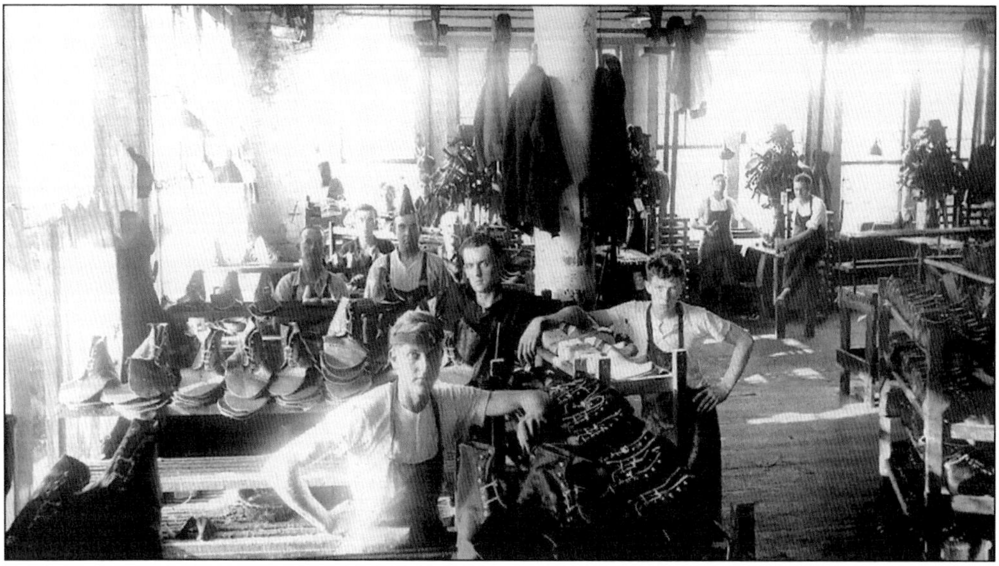

A profit-sharing plan was inaugurated in 1919. George F. Johnson told the workers, "you have a share in surplus profits . . . your own selfish interest demands that you protect this business . . . I want to see the day when you will all be special policemen to stop 'time killing' and 'dead beats' and the leaches which gather around industry." Each year, workers would be issued a check for their personal share of Endicott-Johnson profits. The photograph shows typical workers in the EJ factory on North Street in Endicott.

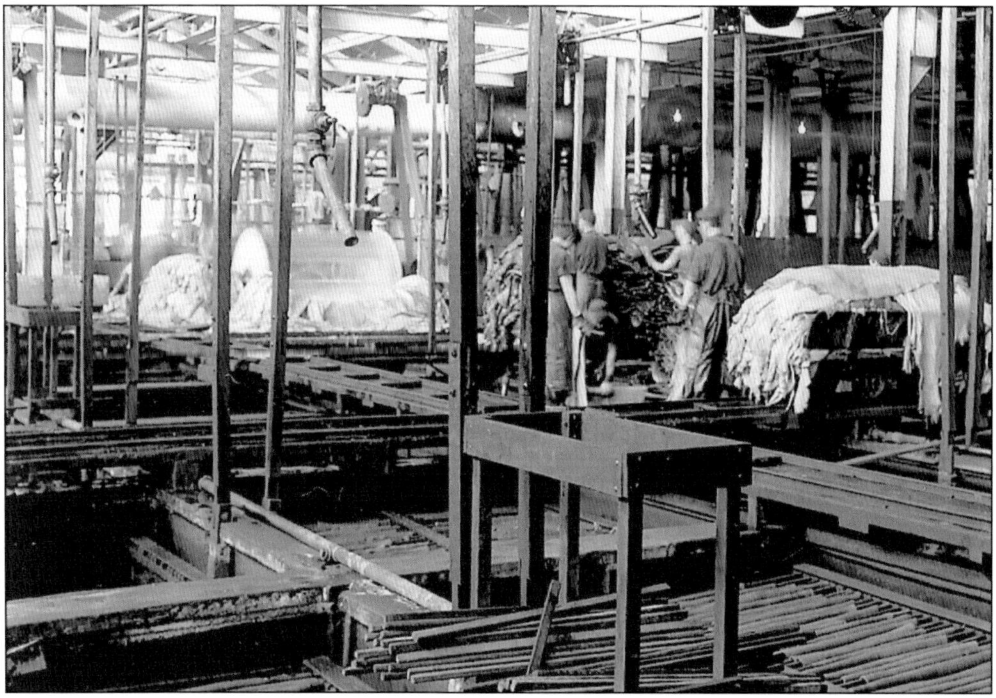

Shown is the Endicott-Johnson factory hide-drying rack area in 1919. This picture was made from a glass lantern slide. Hides tanned at EJ were also sold to other manufacturers of shoes and leather goods.

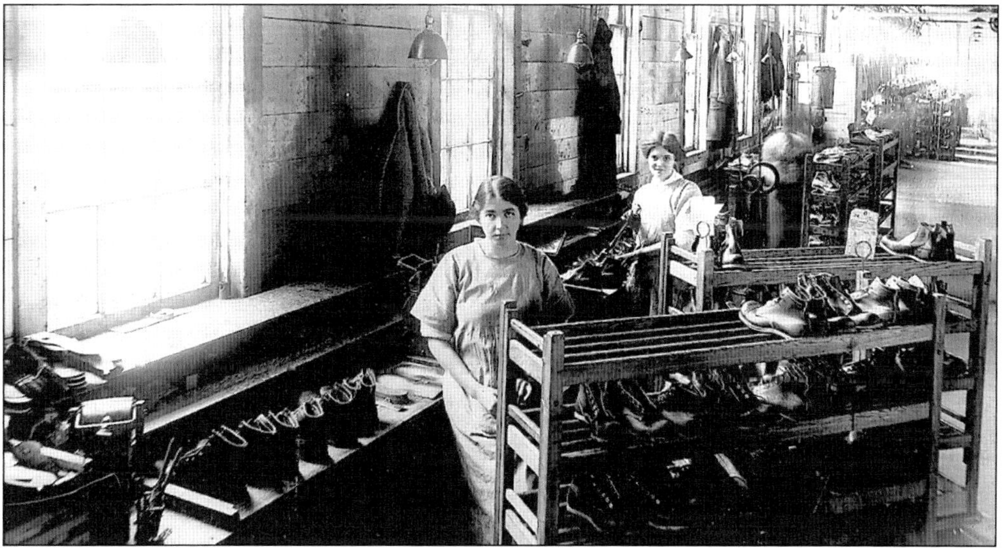

Owosso, Native American for "peaceful place," was the name of the Wagner Farm in Kattelville. It was a large old house with a garden, farm, and greenhouse. Endicott-Johnson owned the farm and used it, as was described in an early EJ medical booklet. "Women workers go here for rest and relaxation when their directors at work notice that they are below par. It is for women in run down condition . . . a place to woo jaded nerves back to normal and to purify the blood. Supervisors at EJ are always on the lookout for anyone who looks 'peeky' or is performing at less than their best . . . particularly among the women employees." Workers were closely watched for any indication of physical or mental problems that would adversely effect the production of shoes. The facility was also called Ideal Rest.

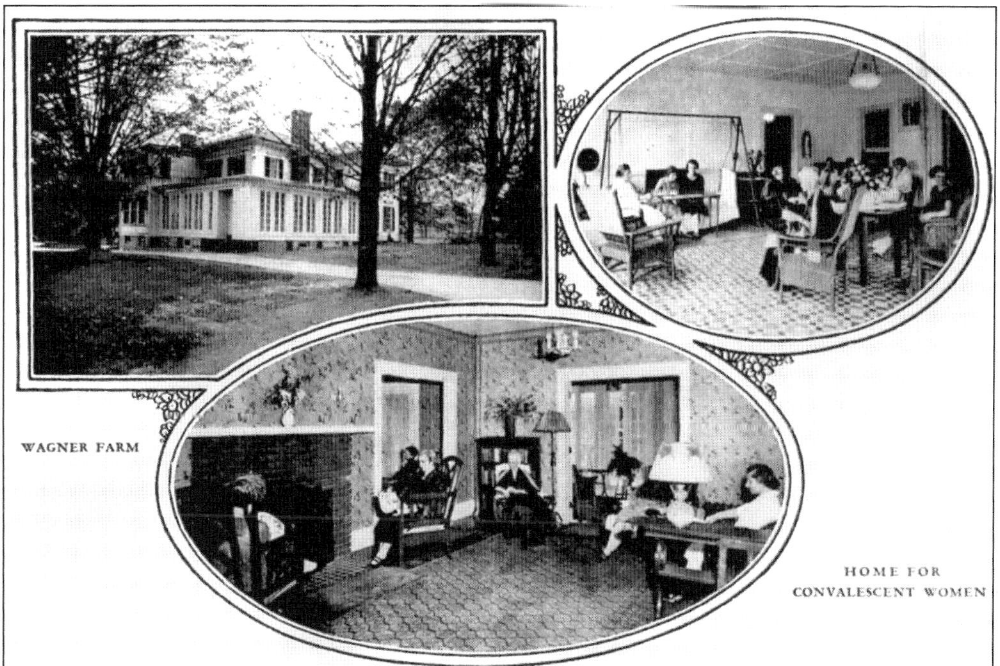

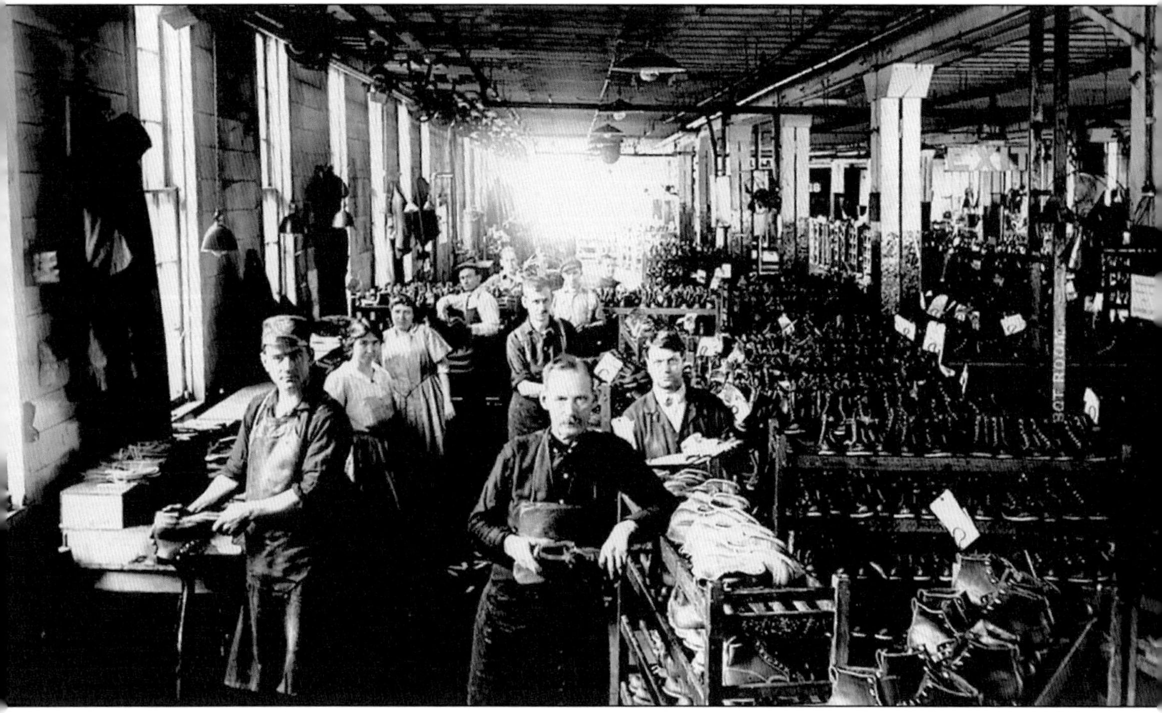

Endicott-Johnson employees were advised that "there is no better stock for you to own in the world than Endicott-Johnson. Why buy one you know nothing about . . . AVOID THIS! Worthless stock will flinch the plain people every time. I knew a man in EJ employ who actually sold his EJ stock and bought some other kind which he knew nothing about. This little sermon is offered for your consideration with love and pity and sorrow. Pity because there are so many who act so foolishly . . . in spite of all the foolishness and folly . . . I have learned to care for you . . . you have a real desire to do just what is right and fair . . . you don't know the way..."The problem with these extreme paternalistic attitudes was that employees were regarded as children. The workers allowed their "big friend" George F. absolute cradle-to-grave guidance, although most were grateful for this service.

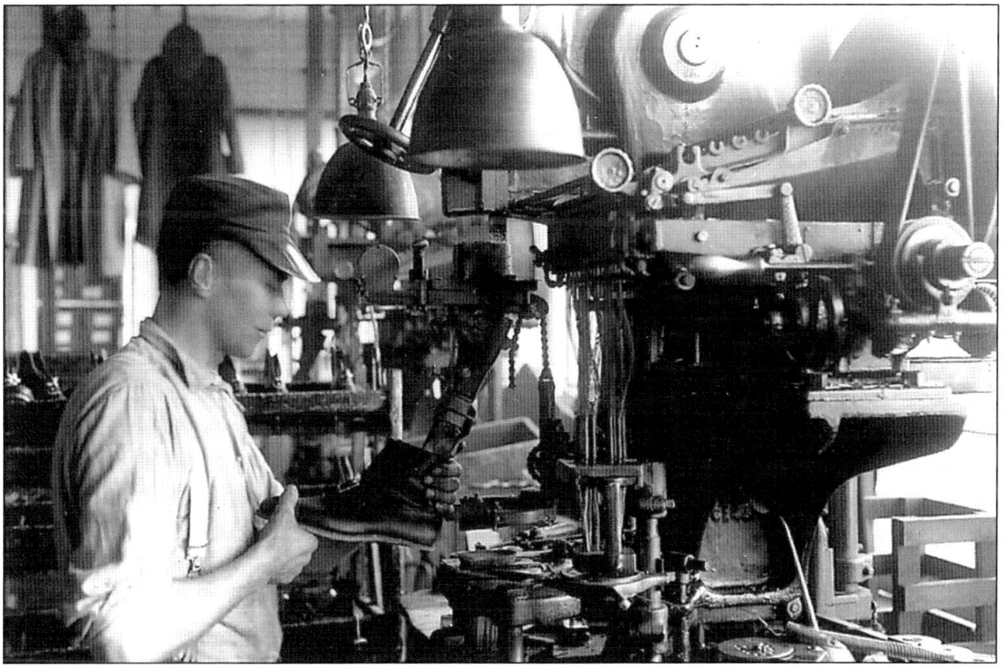

By the time it had been in business for 70 years, Endicott-Johnson was processing 31 million pairs of rubber heals and 15 million pairs of rubber soles a year out of three rubber mills. Much of the rubber used came from recycled tires in EJ's own reclaiming plant.

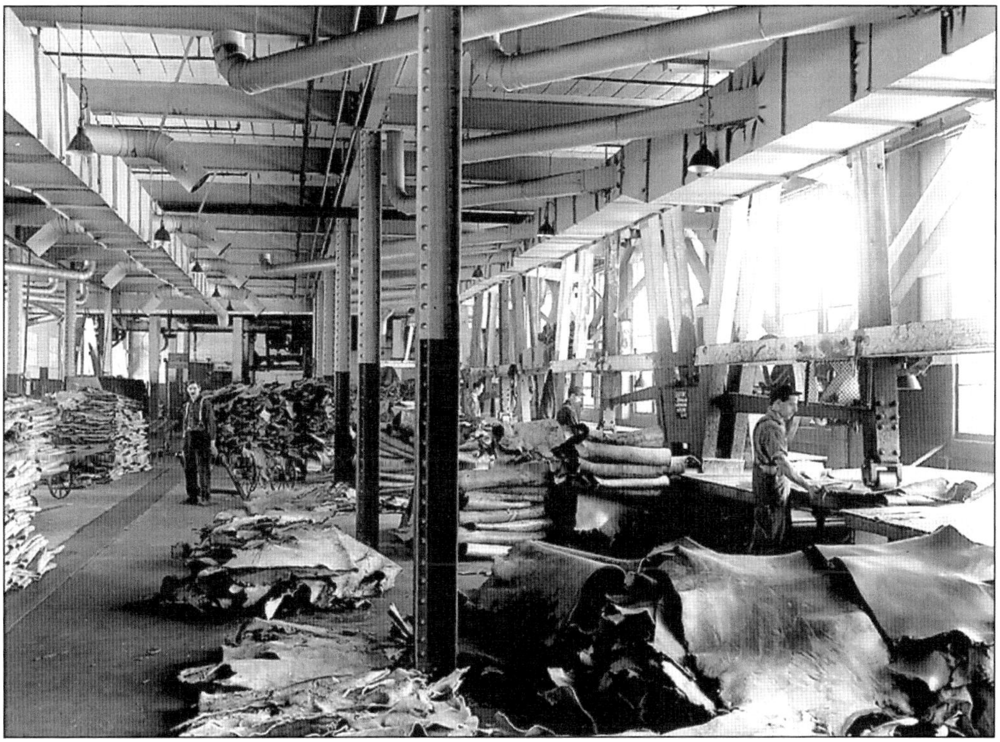

This 1919 image shows the hide-polishing machine and operator.

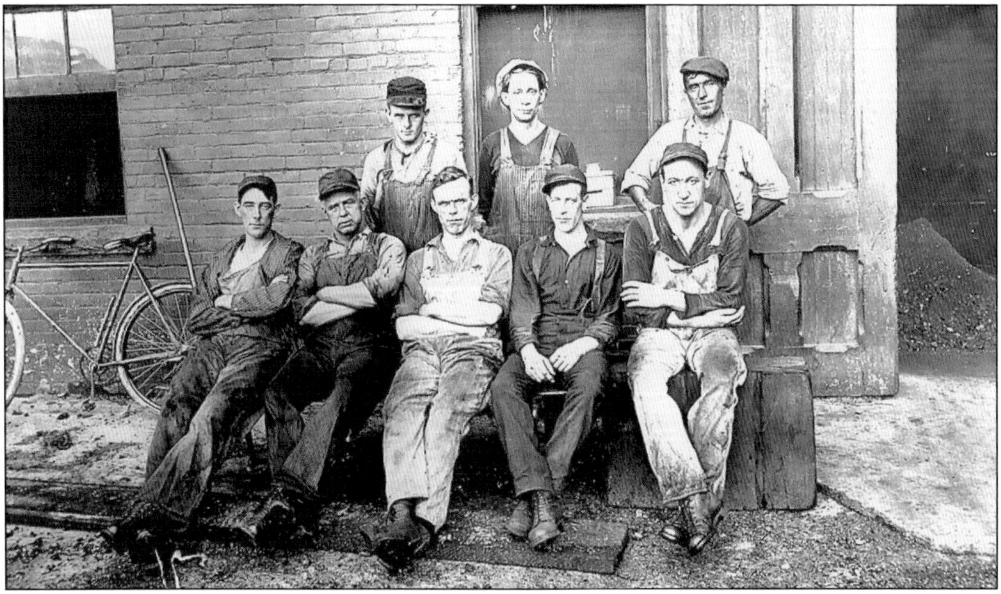

Endicott-Johnson engineers and firemen pose in front of their workplace. A tin lunch pail on the window sill and a well-used bicycle add to the atmosphere of 1913. Only four names are written on the back of the photograph: Chief #5, Alexander, Shanley, Mike.

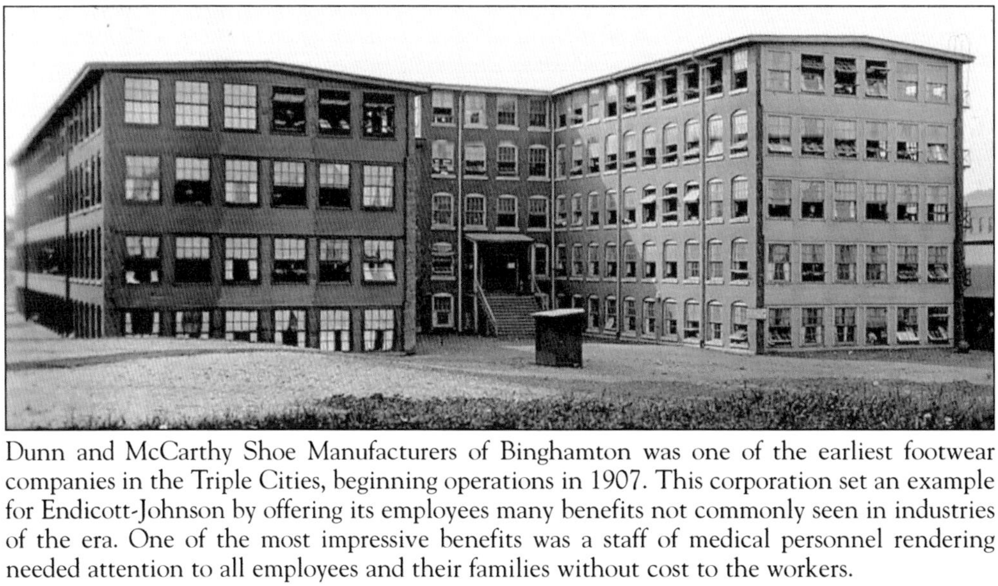

Dunn and McCarthy Shoe Manufacturers of Binghamton was one of the earliest footwear companies in the Triple Cities, beginning operations in 1907. This corporation set an example for Endicott-Johnson by offering its employees many benefits not commonly seen in industries of the era. One of the most impressive benefits was a staff of medical personnel rendering needed attention to all employees and their families without cost to the workers.

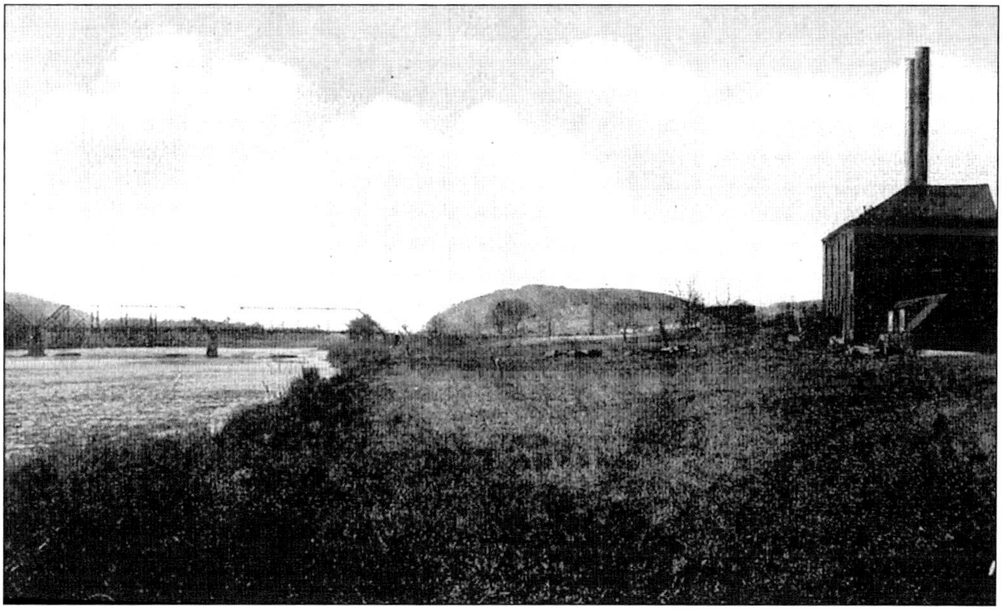

Water in Magic City was provided by a central pump station, with wells drilled by Endicott-Johnson. The basic system was constructed in the early 1900s west of Ideal Park near the Susquehanna River. In 1910, "Old Sireen," a whistle previously used in an EJ factory, was placed at the water station to be sounded in the event of fire. It was the first fire alarm in the new village. The pressure activating the alarm was so strong the distinctive siren could be heard 20 miles away.

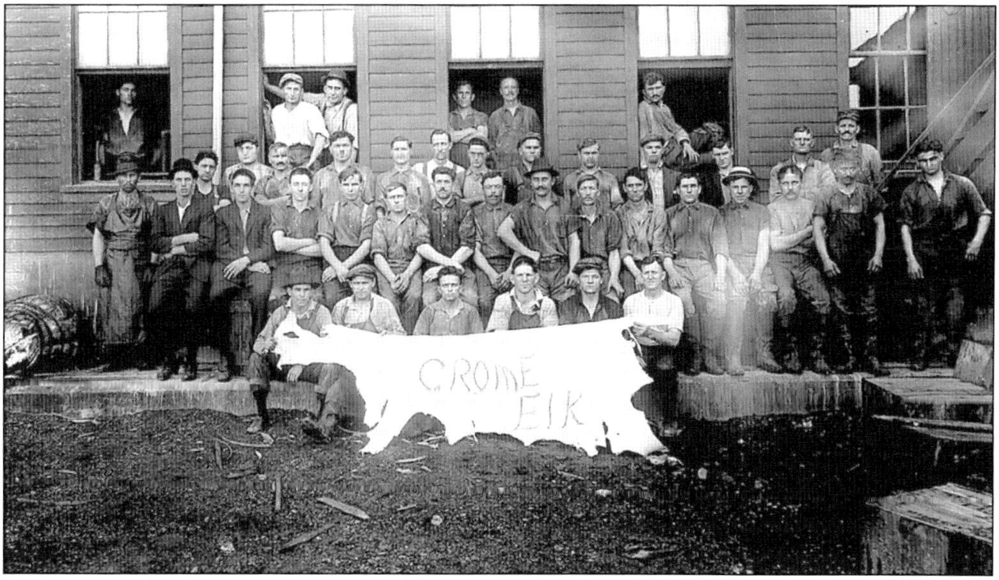

The Crome Elk tanning crew poses outside the factory in 1916. Chrome-tanned hide is accomplished using bichromate potassium, a violent poison. Elk refers to the look of this tanned leather. It is strong, tough, and resembles elk skin. The caustic chemicals used in tanning are now known to cause lung diseases, cancer, and leather diseases.

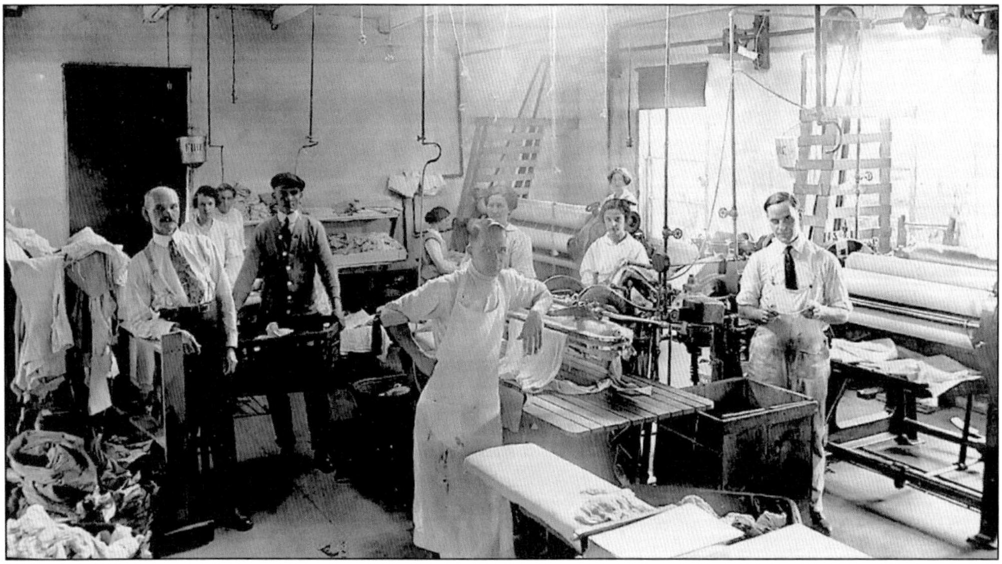

Endicott-Johnson operated its own laundry, located in the rear of the sole leather tannery near the carpenter shop. An article in the *EJ Workers' Review* in 1920 gave a report on the department. The laundry processed 22,600 pieces per week, including 1,000 colored overalls. Employees here were recognized as some of the hardest workers in the EJ family. The supervisor of the department was known as the "washee washee man." This photograph is *c.* 1916.

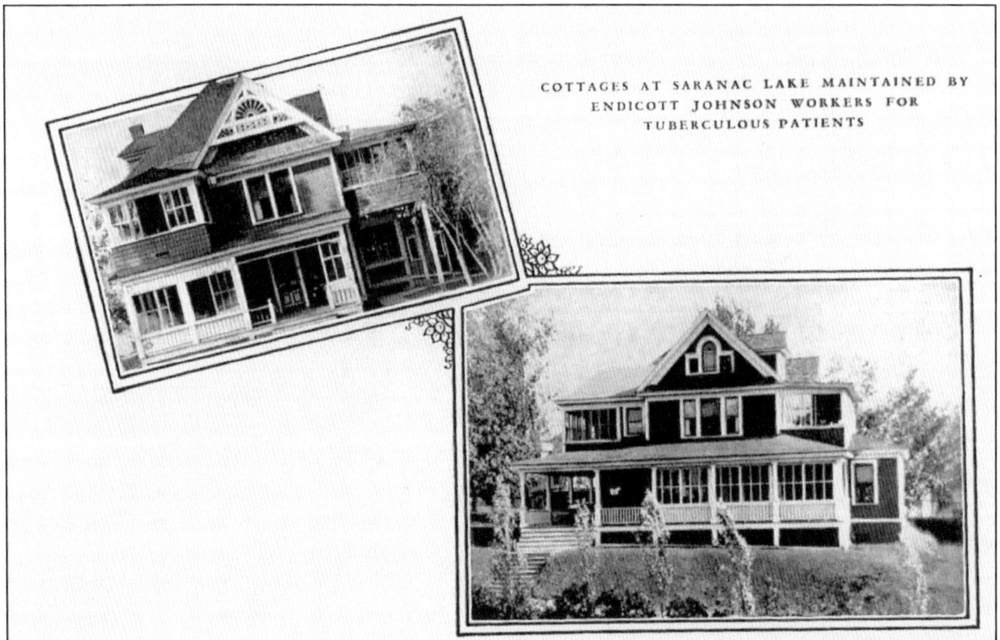

Endicott-Johnson operated tuberculosis cottages at Saranac Lake. The sanitariums were for the care and cure of the tuberculosis. In 1927, there were 29 patients, and in 1934, 56 workers were being treated free of charge. Payments were issued to families while the patient was under care.

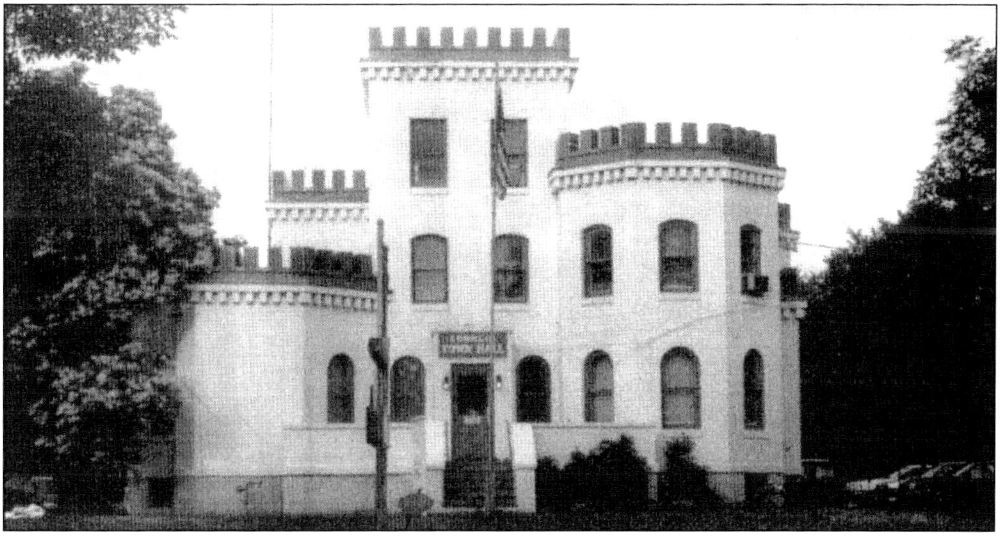

In 1930, George F. Johnson purchased an unusual building in Conklin known as the castle. It was put to use as part of the Broome County Humane Society and Relief Association. Children whose health was devastated by the economic depression came from near and far to spend the summer months enjoying fresh food and clean air. In 1944, Johnson donated the castle to the town of Conklin for use as a community center, specifying that no alcoholic beverages were ever to be served on the premises.

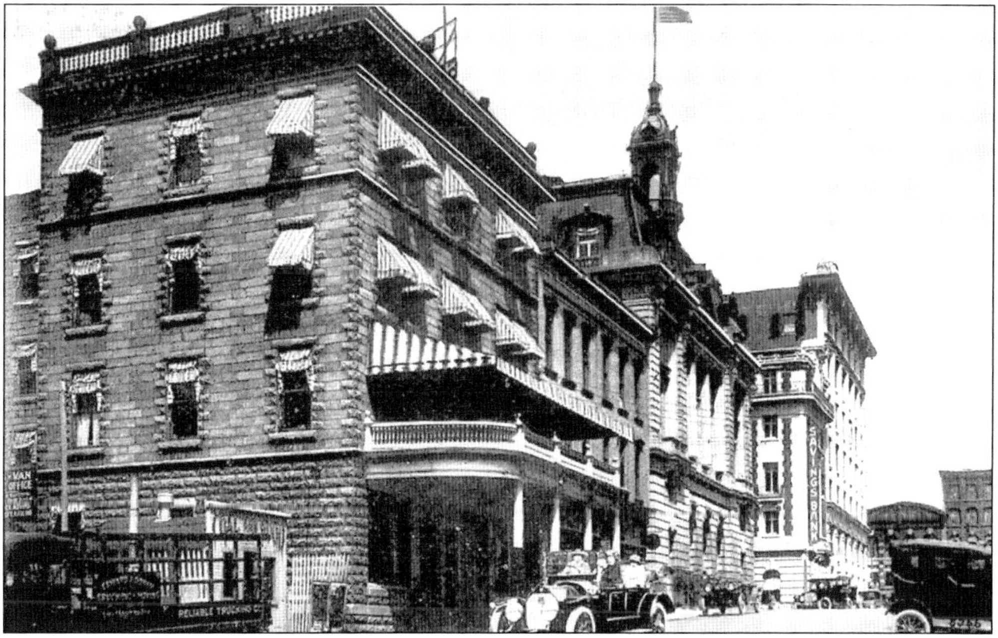

George F. Johnson gave support to the Community Service House in Binghamton. His philosophy was, "get hold of children and give them wholesome recreation and Americanize them before the poison of Bolshevism gets into their veins." Statistics indicated that after the project started, juvenile delinquency in the community decreased by 75 percent. However, Johnson did not approve of a community chest program, saying, "it is too professional and unkind and unchristian to the worker to have to give . . . that makes it just like taxes."

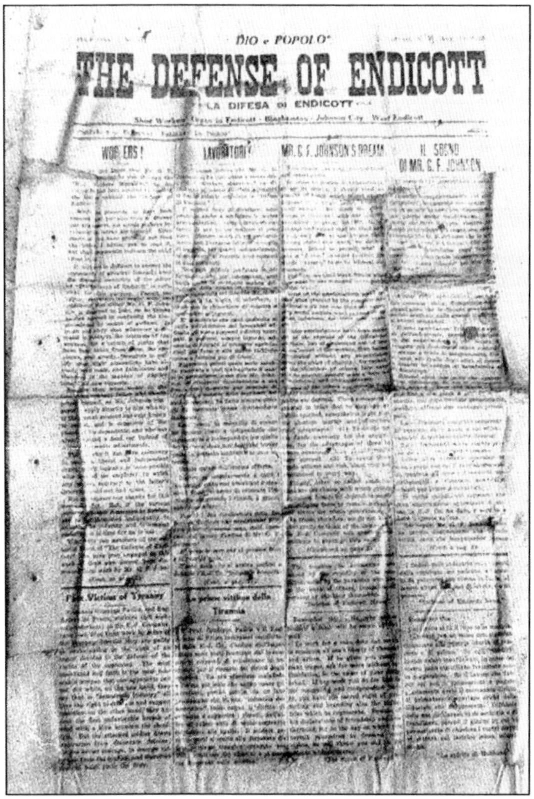

DIO e POPOLO

THE DEFENSE OF ENDICOTT

LA DIFESA DI ENDICOTT

WORKERS! | LAVORATORI! | MR. G. F. JOHNSON'S DREAM | IL SOGNO DI MR. G. F. JOHNSON

A small newspaper named the *Defense of Endicott* was published in both Italian and English editions. Very few copies of this publication remain. Most of its articles expressed dissatisfaction with Endicott-Johnson management. In 1925, George F. Johnson responded: "You are lying! Wages at EJ are good . . . yes there are odors near the tanneries but I do not find this offensive—we play fair! You quote the Bible saying 'The wealthy will have a difficult time entering the kingdom of Heaven,' but a shroud has no pockets for the rich or the less rich!"

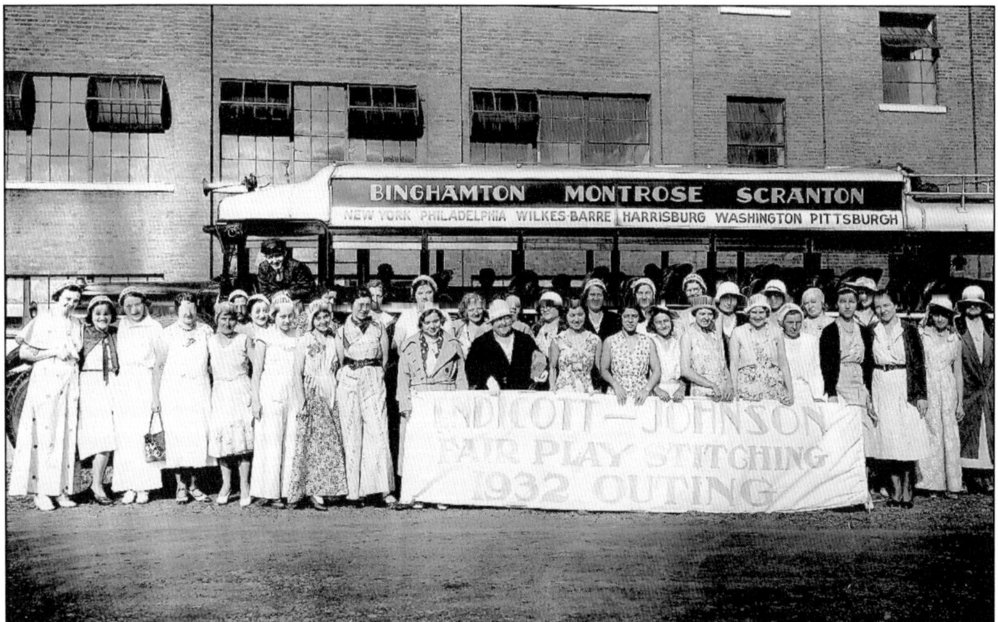

Employees of Endicott-Johnson were encouraged to consider each other part of the corporate family. Special outings, trips, and parties were organized for after hours. In 1932, the people of the stitching department in the Fair Play Factory were photographed in front of their tour bus.

There is still discussion about the Millionaire Tilt story. Is it a hoax or fact? According to several 1906 newspaper accounts, both local and in Chicago, a Joseph Tilt left his Chicago mansion to help establish the new village of Endicott by accepting a job as plant foreman. After a few months, he left Endicott-Johnson and returned to his former life, leaving little behind but questions and rumors of disagreements with the Johnson clan.

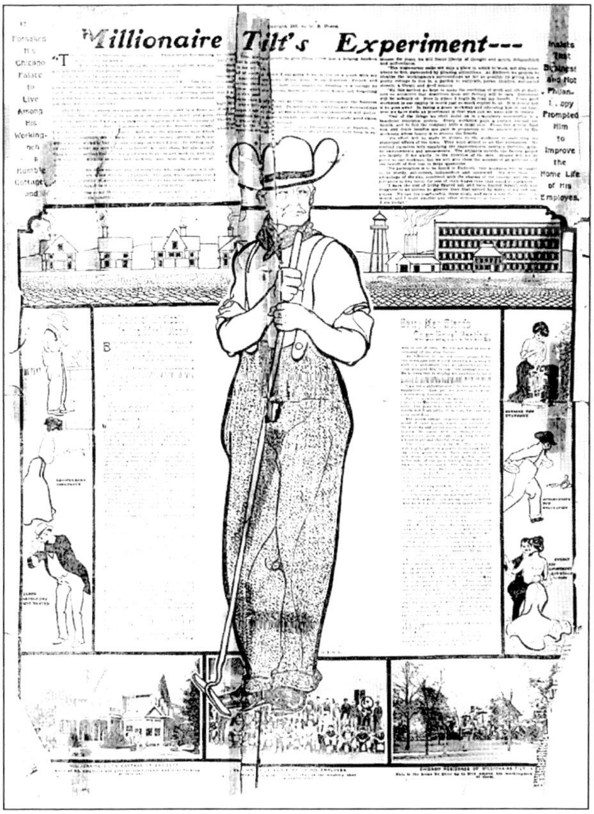

Millionaire Tilt's Experiment---

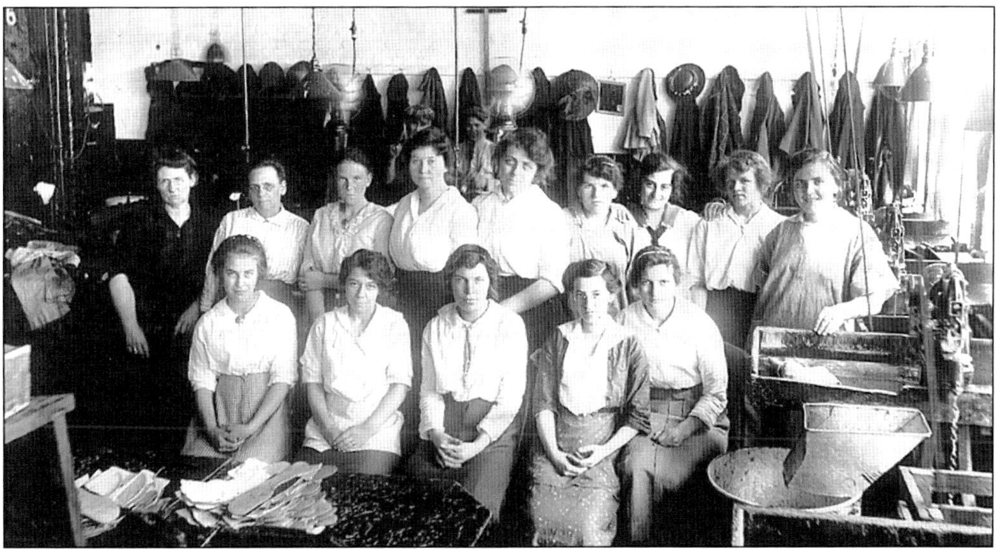

The insole room of the Endicott-Johnson fine welt factory is pictured in the year 1916. As part of the company policy to prevent fires, the area was swept often to remove scraps from the floors and tables. This photograph was made from a rare glass negative. (Ed Aswad collection.)

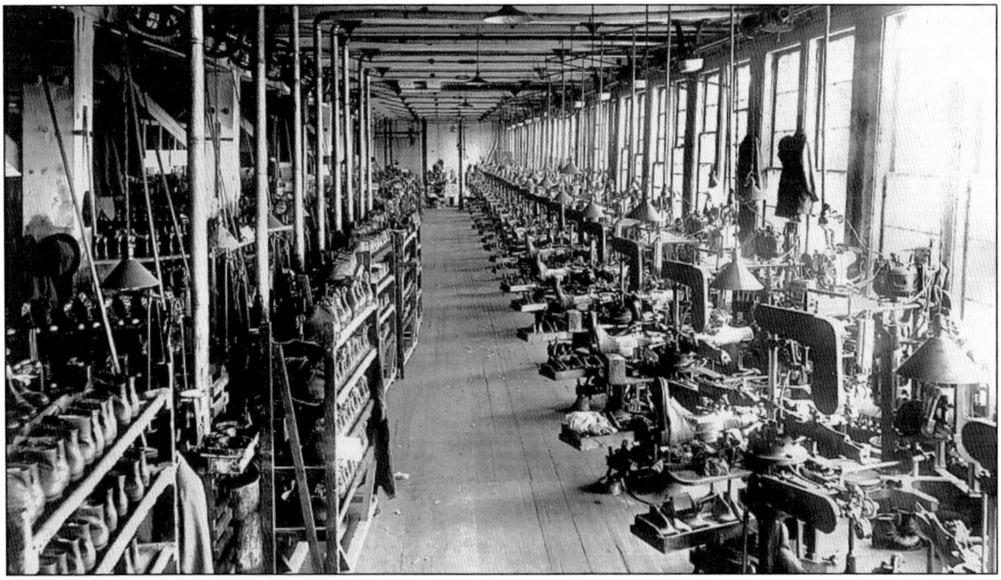

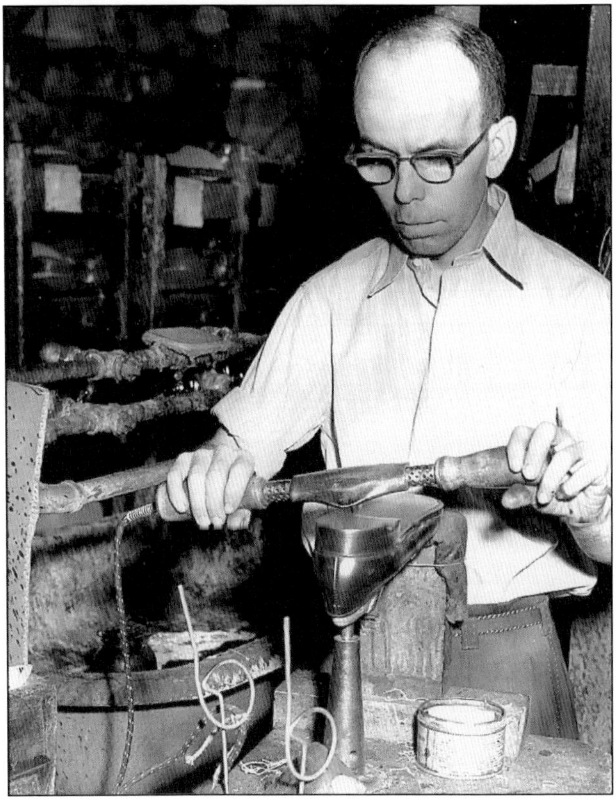

The treeing room of the factory was one of the last stops before the shoe was finished. The process "dresses" the shoe and makes it as attractive as possible. The photograph above was taken in 1916 and the one below in the late 1940s. George F. Johnson began his career in the Lester Brothers Shoe Company doing this job.

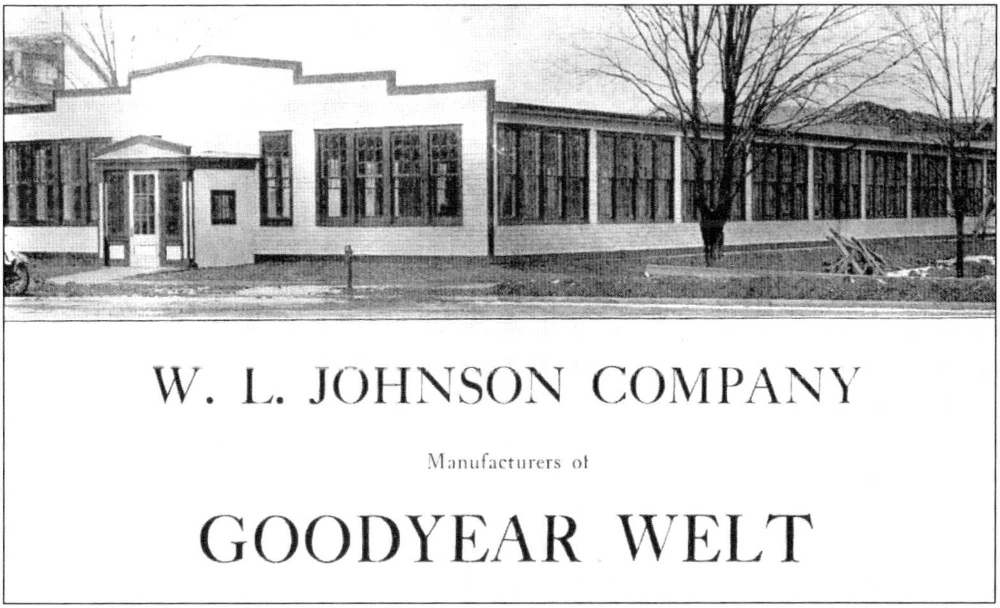

The forgotten son of George F. Johnson, Walter L. Johnson, owned the W.L. Johnson Company, manufacturers of Goodyear Welt, on North Street in Endicott. He lived in Vestal and raised championship cattle at his Ideal Farms. His business was purchased by Endicott-Johnson as a subsidiary in 1954. He lived until 1959, dying at age 82 in relative obscurity, just the way he had lived—in the shadow of his famous relatives.

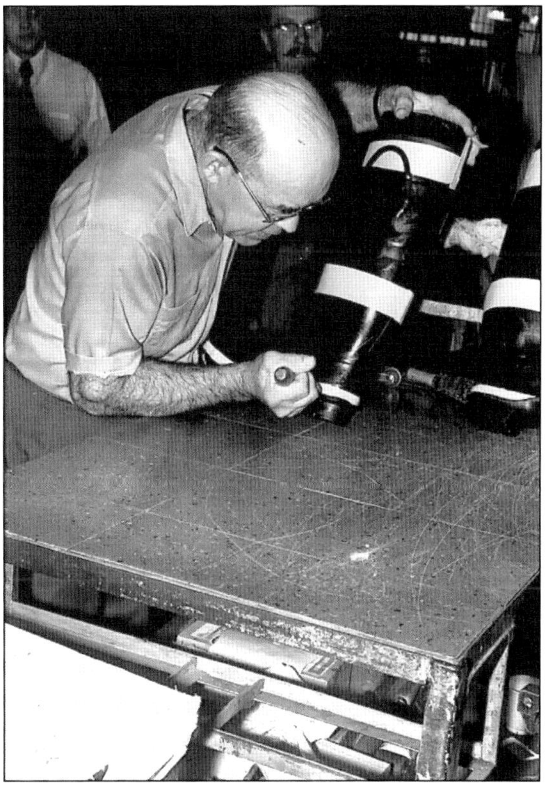

All kinds of boots and rubbers were produced by Endicott-Johnson,using recycled rubber. Policemen and firefighters were given free shoes and boots each year. This photograph shows one of the finishing procedures for firemen boots.

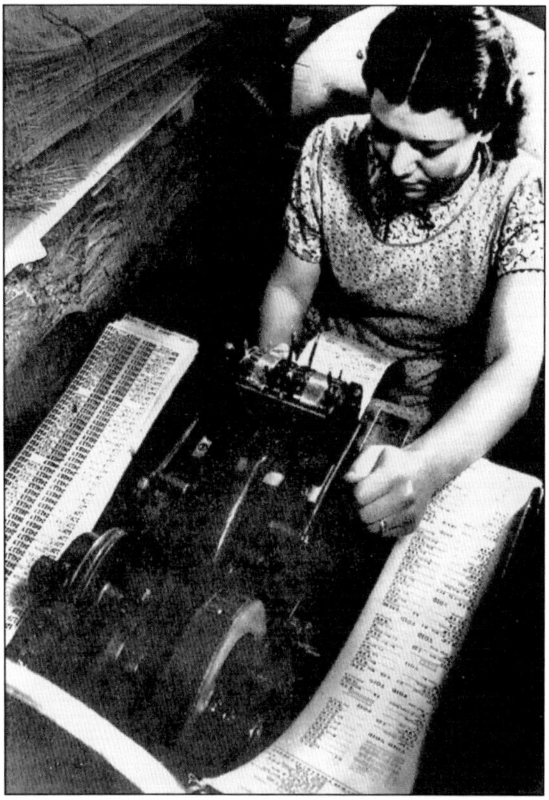

Paychecks of many EJ employees were based on the piece wage system. When an assigned process in shoe manufacturing was completed, the worker would snip and save the attached coupon, each worth a few cents in pay, to be turned in at the end of the week. A worker had to be fast, but not so fast that he earned the resentment of fellow workers or that the supervisor would up the quota due to earn the coupon. The photograph shows a machine producing the coupons.

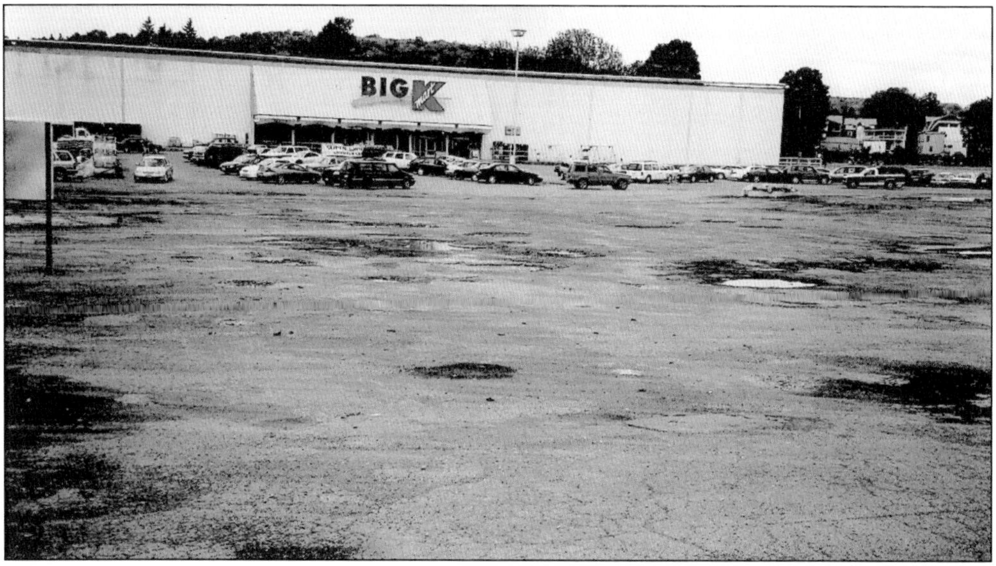

The Endicott Plaza exists on land that was originally a 30-foot-deep swamp. The municipality, Endicott-Johnson, and many corporations dumped garbage and barrels of industrial acids into the murky depths. When the swamp was filled, it was reused for a schoolyard and a shopping plaza. But the swamp is getting its revenge. The refuse churns and bubbles. As anyone who has seen the rather lumpy parking lot can attest, filling the swamp with trash was a very unsettling thing to do.

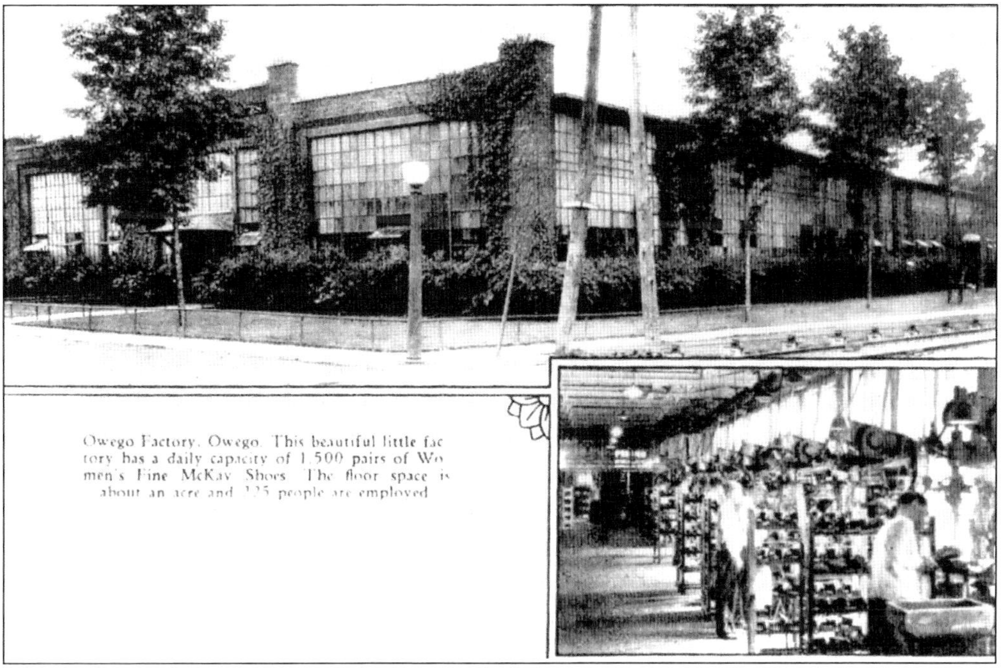

The Endicott Johnson company expanded into Owego. In 1927, that plant had 225 workers and produced 875 dozen pairs of shoes each week. Plans to build more factories in that area did not materialize.

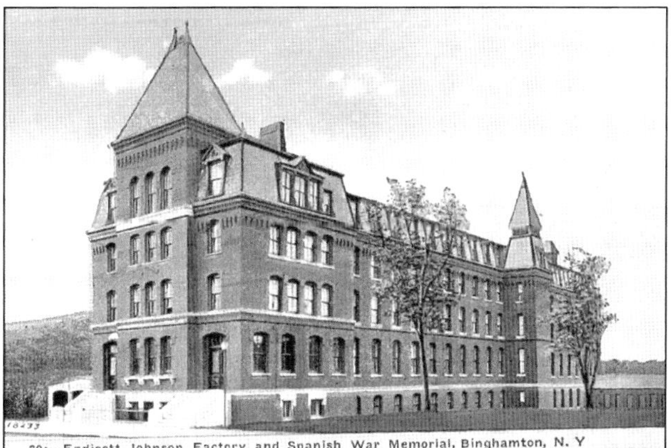

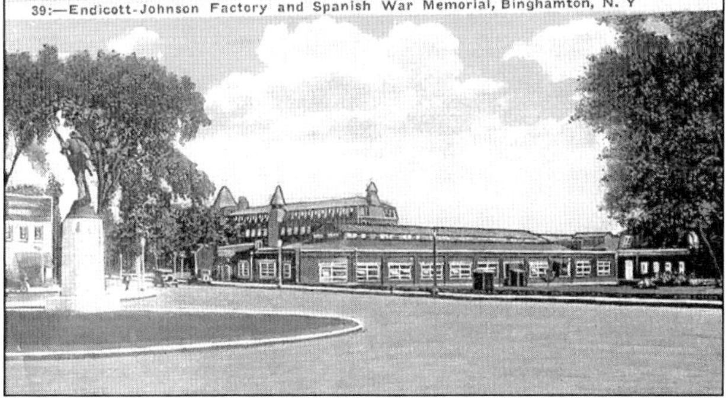

During Endicott-Johnson's great expansion era of the 1920s, the corporation opened factories in Binghamton. The old Weed Tannery became the BBB factory, located near the GFJ Tabernacle Factory in the center of Binghamton. Both pictures are c. 1930.

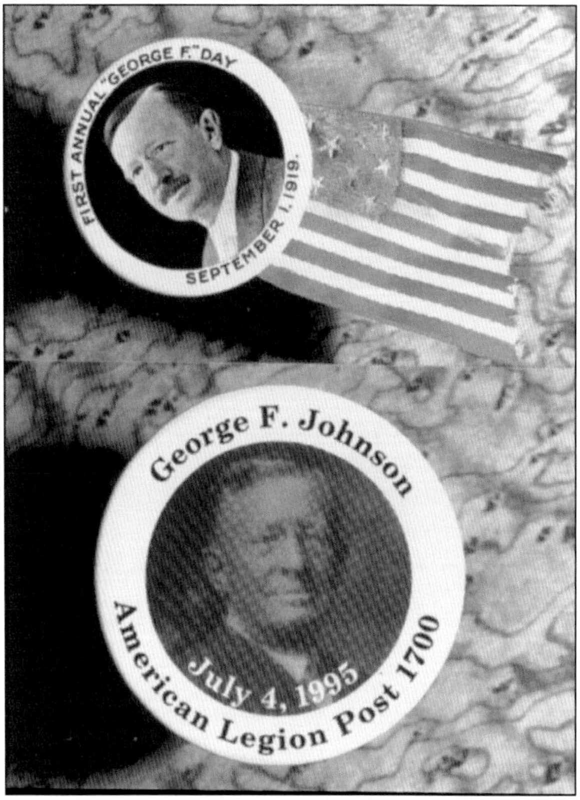

Many years separate the production of the pictured pin buttons. One was made for the first "George F." Day in 1919, and the tradition continues with memories imprinted on items today. George F. Johnson died more than a half-century ago and the factories are gone, but odes and songs are still being composed to the Endicott-Johnson era, and schools are still named in honor of a great industrialist and benefactor.

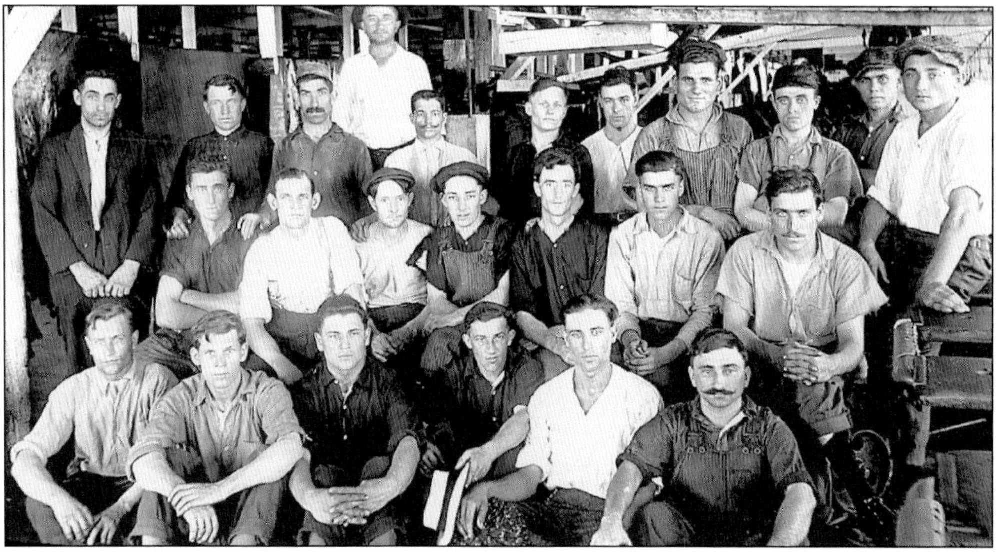

A group of workers from the stacking room in the upper leather factory pose in 1916. Their modern work facility was supplied with all necessary facilities—including spittoons. One spittoon for each workspace was provided in hopes that the numerous tobacco weed chewers would use the kettle instead of corners and knotholes in the floor, as had often occurred.

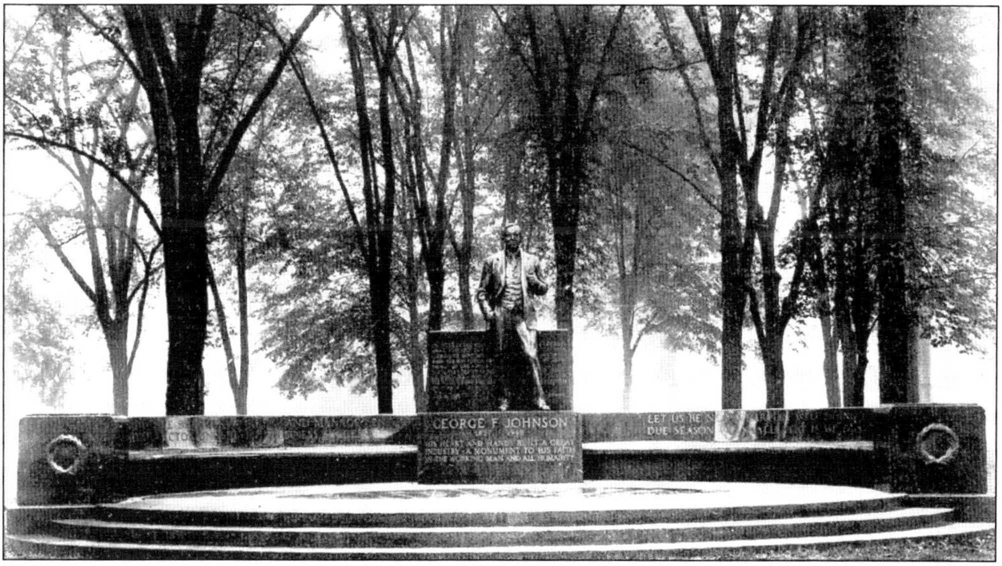

A statue of George F. Johnson was erected in 1951 in what at the time was Enjoie Park in Endicott, near the EJ recreation center. The full-size likeness of Johnson was executed by artist Charles E. Keck. The base of the monument contains a bronze urn with the microfilmed names of 100,800 contributors to the memorial fund. The sculpture is now on property owned by the Union Endicott High School, on Main Street in Endicott.

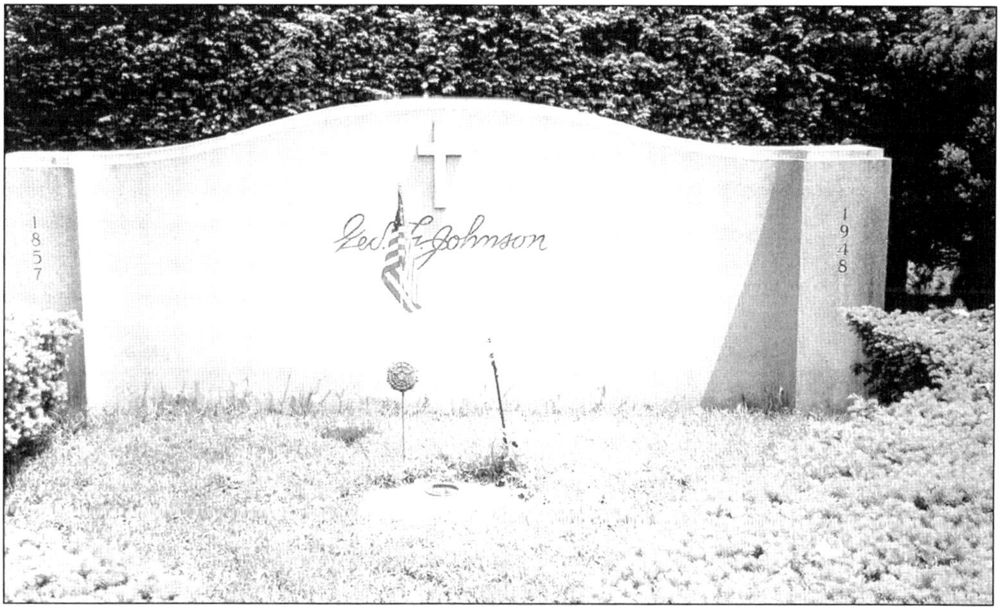

George F. Johnson had opinions on death and tombstones: "To die wealthy is to die disgraced. A man should share his wealth with those who have helped him acquire it. The wealthy have large funerals and huge monuments to show off wealth even unto death. It is a pity to express wealth in a funeral service. And a pity we can not overcome desire to inform our fellow citizens that living or dead we have wealth . . . this is vulgar and unpleasant." George F. Johnson's tombstone at Riverside Cemetery in Endwell is simple, but large and elegant. Our memory is preserved not by one's own hand but by those who remember . . .

Bibliography

Binghamton Chamber of Commerce. *The Valley of Opportunity*. Binghamton, New York: Charles W. Baldwin, 1920.

Binghamton Illustrated. Binghamton, New York: H.R. Page and Company, 1890.

Binghamton Past and Present: Its Commerce, Trade and Industries. Binghamton, New York: The Evening Herald Company, 1894.

Bothwell, Lawrence. *Broome County Heritage: An Illustrated History*. Woodland Hills, California: Windsor Publications, 1983.

Broome County Historical Society collections at the history center in the Broome County Public Library, Binghamton, New York.

Combination Atlas Map of Broome County New York. Philadelphia: Everts, Ensign and Everts, 1876.

EJ Workers' Review. Broome County Historical Society bulletins.

Endicott Johnson Corporation. Books, pamphlets, and letters produced by the Endicott Johnson Corporation in private collections.

Endicott Johnson Corporation. *Partners All: A Pictorial Narrative of an Industrial Democracy*. Photographs by R.C. Aikins. New York: Huntington Corporation, 1938.

Fiori, James V. *A History of Endicott*. Endicott, New York: published by author, 1982.

Inglis, William. *George F. Johnson and His Industrial Democracy*. New York: Charles Scribner and Sons, 1964.

Lawler, William S., ed. *Binghamton, Its Settlement, Growth and Development*. Century Memorial Publishing Company, 1900.

The New York State Archives Collections. Albany, New York.

Putnam, Dr. Frederick, comp. *A Documentary History of Broome County*. Manuscript collection of the Broome County Public Library history center.

Seward, William Foote, ed. *Binghamton and Broome County, New York: A History*. New York: Lewis Historical Publishing Company, 1924.

Smith, Gerald R. *The Valley of Opportunity*. The Donning Company Publishers and the Broome County Historical Society, 1988.

Smith, H.P., ed. *History of Broome County*. Syracuse, New York: D. Mason and Company, 1885.

The Valley of Fair Play, pamphlet. Johnson City, New York: JC Publishing Company, 1920.